"We stand upon the precipice of change.
The world fears the inevitable plummet into the
abyss. Watch for that moment... and when it comes,
do not hesitate to leap. It is only when you fall that
you learn whether you can fly."

— DRAGON AGE II

LEVEL UP!

UNLOCK BONUS CONTENT AND OTHER DIGITAL GIFTS WITH YOUR BOOK'S NFT (NON-FUNGIBLE TOKEN)

CLICK OR SCAN THE QR CODE TO ACCESS ALL THE BONUS CONTENT!

 Exclusive access to Metarena's future events

 Special discounts on amazing video games

 $1K Jumpstart Esports Masterclass, from MetArena

 $5K Esports Viewer Dossier, powered by Midia Research

 Priceless insights about the future of gaming & esports by Marcus

 Behind the scenes content of the book being produced and printed

The INNOVATE® Gaming & Esports Team would like to give a special thanks to all the participants and the following companies for their support and assistance in making this project a reality and supporting education in gaming via the Scholar Gamers Program.

  Meet the people that are building a better **GAMING & ESPORTS** for tomorrow

INNOVATE® GAMING & ESPORTS: A MULTIMEDIA EXPERIENCE AND MORE.

SVEN BOERMEESTER, FOUNDER/CEO, INTERNATIONAL GROUP PUBLISHER

Sven Boermeester, Founder/CEO, International Group Publisher with **Callie Van Graan,** Global Village COO

The world of gaming and esports has certainly come a long way from its humble beginnings in corner stores and first-generation gaming systems. With the gaming industry permeating every facet of life as we know it and gamification fast becoming a norm from marketing to education, Global Village is enormously proud to be publishing *INNOVATE®* Gaming & Esports, the most comprehensive overview of one of the fastest-growing industries in the world.

INNOVATE® Gaming & Esports is a showcase of the leaders and innovators shaping the future of gaming, identifying the key players and mapping out the gaming ecosystem. Embedded in its pages, you will find scannable game demos and augmented reality videos accompanying certain features. By using the free GLOBAL VILLAGE augmented reality app, the world of the future will open up on the pages of this legacy publication.

But *INNOVATE®* Gaming & Esports is far more than a tech-enabled publication: it is a multimedia experience centered around a deluxe hardcover coffee-table book, which includes AR videos, an online web platform, and multilevel social media networking. It is also available as an NFT – one of the first in the publishing world! The book is also available as an eBook and will be viewed in the millions through the **InnovationsoftheWorld.com** library.

This publication aims to celebrate those involved in the gaming and esports ecosystem, but it is also meant for all business leaders, educators and decision-makers who can affect change in the gaming industry across the world.

We publish *INNOVATE®* Gaming & Esports for the open-minded folk who want to know more about the exciting changes that have recently transpired in the gaming and esports ecosystem and who play or want to play an active role in its growth and development.

This inaugural edition of *INNOVATE®* Gaming & Esports is just part of a global series. We are currently launching volumes in our *INNOVATE®* series in cities throughout the world, as well as shining a spotlight on the topical Blockchain, Cryptocurrency and NFT industries.

By experiencing *INNOVATE®* Gaming & Esports, you are part of our Global Village network and we are happy to have you. I trust you will join us as we continue the journey of the *INNOVATE®* series.

Sven Boermeester
Founder/CEO
International Group Publisher

| **Marcus Howard** | **Sue Rooney** | **Anita Govender** | **Ravi Handve** | **Evan Rothman** | **Justin Jones** |
| Publishing Partner | Operations | Production | Art & Design | Copywriter | Marketing |

CONTENTS

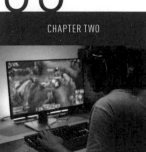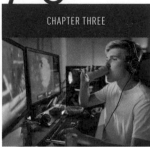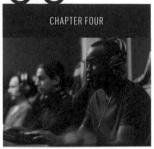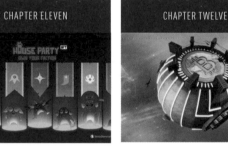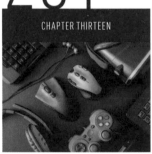

INNOVATE®
InnovationsoftheWorld.com

GLOBAL VILLAGE.WORLD
CONNECTING MINDS · BUILDING COMMUNITIES

Global Village CEO
Sven Boermeester

Global Village COO
Callie Van Graan

Publishing Partner
Marcus Howard

Art Direction & Design
Ravi Handve

Production Manager
Sue Rooney
Anita Govender

Operations Manager
Sue Rooney

info@globalvillage.world
www.InnovationsoftheWorld.com

info@globalvillage.world
www.InnovationsoftheWorld.com

www.GlobalVillage.world

© Global Village Ventures LLC
ISBN: 978-1-949677-25-6

IT'S A KIND OF MAGIC...

Look for the Global Village Play Logo

Scan and watch images come alive

DOWNLOAD THE GLOBAL VILLAGE AR APP
TO ENJOY THE AUGMENTED REALITY VIDEOS IN THIS BOOK!

To experience the future of print, download the Global Village AR App from the IOS or Android App stores. Open the App and hold it about 30cm above any page that contains an image with the "play" Icon.

Download on the **App Store**

ANDROID APP ON **Google play**

Make sure your back camera is pointing at the page. Click the Play button that appears onscreen and immerse yourself in the latest updated content with reference to that page.

> ❝ **HAVING CHILDREN INTRINSICALLY MOTIVATED ME TO BE PART OF THEIR SCHOOL'S ESPORTS EXPERIENCE, THE CONVERSATION NOW BEGINS TO SHIFT TOWARDS THINGS TYPICALLY NOT ASSOCIATED WITH VIDEO GAMES – POSITIVE MENTAL AND PHYSICAL HEALTH. ❞**
> JAMES O'HAGAN, FOUNDER & CEO, THE ACADEMY OF ESPORTS

Would you be so quick to shut off your child's video game system if you knew that it could be a portal to a scholarship at an international university or a career in a billion-dollar industry? What about if it led to a reduction in your child's anxiety, better connections with his/her peers, or an interest in developing better sleep and nutritional habits?

Thanks to the exciting evolution of esports and media attention to events like 16-year-old Kyle "Bugha" Giersdorf $3 million purse win at the Epic Games Fortnite World Cup in New York, these are the types of questions both parents and educators are asking themselves in environments where esports is done right: holistically considered and responsibly deployed.

But first, a pause for those quizzically cocking their heads to the side. Esports? What's that?

Esports is organized, competitive, multiplayer video gaming. Much like how when we talk about traditional "sports" it encompasses basketball, football, and swimming, there are a lot of games that fall into the realm of esports. Titles such as "League of Legends," "Overwatch," "Super Smash Bros. Ultimate," "Rocket League," and, of course, "Fortnite" are among the most popular. Dedicating hours to playing these games does not, on its own, make someone an esports athlete- just as tossing a ball around the yard with friends can be considered "playing football" while it takes organization, dedication, discipline and training to be "a football player." The difference is similar between casual gaming and esports.

In schools across the United States, we are always looking to engage children in new and dynamic ways. Of paramount importance is meeting children where they are: what do kids naturally love to do and how can we add value to that space without negatively impacting the joy they find there? Pew Research shows 97% of boys and 83% of girls ages 13-17 in the U.S. identify as being a gamer of some kind. Those demographics cut across race and socio-economics. To responsibly guide the evolution of esports in education and harness its potential, we must tap into the intrinsic motivation- or behaviors based on inherent enjoyment- of gamers and embrace the opportunities for connection offered on the gaming field.

Being respectful in our messaging is one of the first steps to take. Would we tell kids that they draw too much? Dance too much? Play an instrument too much? Hopefully not. Yet too often, video games are

dismissed as "just a waste of time" by adults who have not researched the profoundly positive impact they can have when implemented responsibly. The modern space in which the majority of children are choosing to engage in some way is in video games. Let's meet them there and understand why instead of negating their passion for play.

Which brings us to this question: Why embrace esports? There are five core reasons and they should be at the heart of any program your child joins or your school implements:

1. Redefine Athletic Culture
2. Diversify Opportunities for Student Participation
3. Promote Good Mental and Physical Health
4. Create Career and Collegiate Scholarship Pathways
5. Honor the Importance of Play

Esports redefines athletic culture by encouraging children of all races, abilities and genders to compete in a space where their passion for play is the most prominent part of their identity as an athlete. Esports is an opportunity for everyone to come together in a shared space around a love of gaming.

In bringing children together across demographics, you diversify opportunities for their participation in extracurricular activities. Research shows that students engaged in extracurricular activities have higher grade point averages, better attendance and increased graduation rates. So many children who do not fit traditional athletic ideals are often left on the margins. Esports participation draws them into a community in which they belong.

Having children intrinsically motivated to be part of their school's esports experience, the conversation now begins to shift towards things typically not associated with video games - positive mental and physical health. The importance of good sleep habits, proper nutrition and a dedicated exercise regimen are critical aspects of a responsible esports program. Kids are far more likely to pass over energy drinks in favor of water when they learn how their gaming performance is negatively impacted after the sugar crash or to choose snacks that increase their focus during tournaments and exercises (like yoga and weights) that help regulate their

heart rate and add stamina during matches. As part of this ecosystem, we employ aspects of traditional sports training: weight training helps develop complex reasoning skills and aerobic training promotes problem-solving skills. Additionally, research indicates that two of the best ways to promote good mental health are with positive adult interactions and through play. The key is meeting kids in the space they love to deliver the message.

Colleges and universities in the United States have also begun to take note of esports and are attracting students with scholarships of varying sizes. In 2023, there will be an estimated $100m (roughly 90.6 million Euros) in scholarship money available related to esports. The opportunity to access these scholarships is greatly enhanced when primary and secondary schools formally embrace esports. Higher learning institutions recognize that esports is a billion-dollar industry in which playing games is just one element. Marketing, sports nutrition, broadcasting, psychology, esports law, business management, digital art, storytelling, computer science... these are just some of the career paths through this new ecosystem.

Probably the most important aspect of esports to be considered is that, at its heart, this is all about play. By providing these environments for children to play, we are helping to defray the issue of online toxicity and helping them navigate their world as we would on a traditional playground.

As adults, most of us are standing on the edge of a virtual world that our children have already entered. Esports provides a realm to master their passions and develop tangible opportunities. Let's pick up a controller and join them there.

The Academy of Esports
+1 (262) 676-2244
The Academy of Esports
taoesports
jamesohagan

taoesports.com

> ## "SINCE THERE ARE MORE THAN 100 STEAM CAREER PATHS IN THE GAMING INDUSTRY, THERE'S AN EXCELLENT CHANCE THAT YOU CAN BUILD A REWARDING CAREER IN VIDEO GAMES, REGARDLESS OF YOUR PROFESSION.
> — MARCUS HOWARD, PUBLISHING PARTNER, INNOVATE® GAMING & ESPORTS

Miles Morales : When will I know I'm ready?
Peter B. Parker : You won't. It's a leap of faith. That's all it is, Miles. A leap of faith.

If you didn't catch the reference above, put down this book (just for a couple of hours lol), and go watch "Spider-Man: Into the Spider-Verse." Like Miles' journey to becoming Spider-Man, this entire book is a leap of faith for me. As I type this introduction, I'm less than a week away from

publishing my book, while frantically finalizing the last pieces of content, and hustling to cover the book's production costs. Keeping it real, there were times that I almost quit because it felt too ambitious to finish. If you're reading this, then I've managed to do the seemingly impossible.

I was inspired to create this book after partnering with the Global Village team on one of their previous books, and reflecting on my lifelong hobby of video games and the rewarding STEAM career that I've built in the gaming industry over the last decade. My parents bought Super Mario Bros 3 and the Nintendo Entertainment System (NES) for Christmas when I was six, and I've been playing video games ever since. In the fifth grade, my teacher asked everyone in our class "What do you want to be when you grow up?" I answered "Video Games," almost immediately.

Video Games inspired my identical twin Malcolm and me to learn coding in the 9th grade so we could build a "Zelda" game on our TI-83+ graphing calculators. Though, it wasn't until after I graduated college that I understood there was an entire ecosystem and supply chain for my video game hobby. In hindsight, I didn't get into the gaming industry earlier because the people with the greatest influence on my life (parents, teachers, mentors, etc.) and I weren't properly educated about it. I also recognize that my efforts to grow local ecosystems over the years might have been more effective if local investors, business executives, community leaders and elected officials better understood the gaming industry, too.

Globally, the $180B* video game industry is larger than the film and music industries combined. More than 3B* people worldwide play video games, which means that gamers make up nearly half of the world's population. Just in the United States, the video game industry employs nearly 300,000* people. Since there are more than 100 STEAM career paths in the gaming industry, there's an excellent chance that you can build a rewarding career in video games, regardless of your profession. With blockchain gaming, AR/VR gaming, and the metaverse on the horizon, the career and wealth opportunities here are endless.

Today, video games are practically a universal language transcending age, race, gender and geography. The $1B* global esports market is just half a percent of the global gaming industry, but it's quickly becoming a household name. The global esports audience is expected to reach 474M* this year. Several esports teams/orgs/startups are even publicly traded on stock exchanges. In the future, gaming and esports will be more transformative to our personal lives and businesses, than social media has been over the last two decades. Given that 97%* of kids (in the US) between the ages of 12 and 17 play video games, 82%* of Gen Z skips ads, and more than half* of Gen Z block ads, the gaming industry may well become the future of brand engagement. I created this book to help prepare you, your family, your business, and your community for that future.

Thank you to the amazing people and companies who collaborated with me on this book. It's packed with over 300 pages of awesome content that will inspire, educate, and entertain you. The first chapter of the book, titled "Thought Leader" has unapologetically bold perspectives from some of the most forward-thinking professionals in the industry. In addition to the

stellar thought leaders, I've curated exceptional companies from around the world (all of the continents except Antarctica) who constantly push the envelope to create a sustainable and accessible future in the industry. I also partnered with some amazing indie dev teams to include demos of exciting games in this book (just like the gaming magazines used to do back in the day). Last, but certainly not least, I'm providing you with an NFT (non-fungible token) regardless of whether you purchased a digital or physical copy of my book, which unlocks some exclusive additional content for you. You'll learn more about that later in the book.

My goal for this book is to help start meaningful conversations about the video game industry, for gamers, students, parents, teachers, and business/community leaders. If you're intrigued by this interactive experience, and it helps create a significant impact for you, your family, your business and/or your community, then I've accomplished that goal. If you have any questions about the industry after you finish the book, or want introductions to any of the people/companies featured in it, connect with me on LinkedIn/Facebook (Marcus "Esports" Howard), Twitter (ThereAreTwoOfMe), or send me an email (marcus@metarena.gg). If I can't answer your questions, I can certainly point you in the right direction. I'm thrilled to share that I'll be partnering with the Global Villages team to donate 20% of the book's net profits to support youth STEAM education. Thank you for supporting my book, and the next generation of innovators!

*(All stats are as of the time of this book's publication, November 2021)

marcus@metarena.gg
Social Media 🔗 📷

metarena.gg

"It's a funny thing, ambition.
It can take one to sublime heights or
harrowing depths. And sometimes
they are one and the same."
— DISHONORED

CHAPTER 1

THOUGHT LEADERS

IT IS EASIER THAN EVER TO BE AN "INNOVATOR" BECAUSE THERE IS SO MUCH LEFT TO DO IN THIS SPACE."

KATHRYN DE SHIELDS-MOON, CO-FOUNDER, DIVERTEGA

TRUE INNOVATION TAKES COLLABORATION, AND GAMING IS THE PERFECT PLACE FOR THIS

My ideal future for this industry is one rich in diversity and equality, from developing games and the content within them to more comprehensive professional representation in gaming and esports for minorities and gender minorities. It will take all of us working together to make this reality, and there is plenty of room at the table of opportunity for everyone. Let me tell you why:

The exciting thing about working in an emerging industry is that there are boundless opportunities for innovation, connection, and rapid evolution. In many ways, gaming and esports are just now becoming mainstream in the US. Whether it's the way gaming is being associated with STEAM careers or how the esports industry is creating policies and practices to reflect the diversity of this nation's gamers, the capacity for discoveries, alliances, and new perspectives is the perfect environment for innovation. The Star Wars fan in me calls this "Lightspeed Advancement," meaning new businesses, services, nonprofits, and organizations are all bootstrapping, developing, iterating, learning, and pivoting at a breakneck pace simultaneously. All of this action leads to companies solving existing problems, discovering new ones, identifying niches, and developing the industry at an equally exciting and terrifying pace. If there was ever a case of known knowns, known unknowns, and unknown unknowns, there are plenty of all of the above in this ecosystem.

It is easier than ever to be an "innovator" because there is so much left to do in this space. However, with everyone and anyone inherently being able to "innovate," as pioneers in an evolving industry, how does one truly stand apart as an innovator? The answer is counter-intuitive. The answer is strategic collaboration, and the gaming and esports industry is the perfect place for it.

Border-crossing collaborations will be the driving force behind the next phase of growth. Esports teams working with non-endemic companies, gaming-focused nonprofits partnering with school systems to create curricula, indie game studios making esports-ready titles that appeal to a broader audience. The intersectionality of markets and causes will exponentially grow the ecosystem and pave the way for the next generation of innovators.

There isn't a mapped-out hiking trail that leads to innovation already cleared of brush and branches, but there are a few things we can do to guarantee we're going in the right direction:
- Be willing to work with people who don't look like you or share your background.
- Make an effort to listen to perspectives that differ from your own.
- Make it a point to challenge your assumptions and biases.

It is difficult, personal work, to be sure, but it is an integral part of stoking the fire of meaningful innovation within you and growing the industry at large. In my experience, introspection and creativity will always be the root causes of fantastic advancement and change. Inclusivity will always be the seed to re-ignite and revolutionize an industry.

Never forget that gaming and esports got their start with the community -- be it couch co-op games or rallying around a favorite esports team with other fans. Gamers used to be the outcasts, and many of my colleagues in the industry (myself included) were told this hobby was a complete waste of time. Now that this sentiment is changing on a global scale, we should always strive to capture that same spirit of community that made us fall in love with gaming and extend a hand to those who believe in the future of gaming and esports.

After nine years of work as a newspaper reporter and in various marketing roles, Kat landed her first job in the gaming industry as a games journalist and communications manager for GameSkinny & Launch Media Network. Since then, her career has taken her all over the gaming industry, including full-service marketing for indie games with Novy Unlimited, esports community management with Hi-Rez Studios, and esports partnerships at Skillshot Media. Currently, she is the PR manager for Schell Games, a studio specializing in VR experiences, co-founder of Divertega, and the host of season two of the Women in Esports Podcast produced by the Pittsburgh Knights and PNC Bank.

Divertega
kathryn@divertega.co
culturynlife 🐦
Divertega_co 🐦
Divertega 💼
DivertegaCo 📘

divertega EST.2020

divertega.co

"RATHER THAN DISCUSSING THE REACH OF ESPORTS AS COMPARED TO OTHER LIVE SPORTS, WE NEED TO TALK ABOUT THE DEPTH OF FANDOM WITHIN ESPORTS VIEWERS."
PHIL RANTA, CEO, WORMHOLE LABS

WORMHOLE

ESPORTS ISN'T A SPORT, IT'S THE IDEA OF SPORTS

Since the birth of video games, we've played to win. It began with high scores and simple 1v1 games, progressed through games with an objective of story completion and now, finally, an online free-for-all where a kid in Japan and an adult in Mumbai can duke it out in a battle royale without ever meeting.

Video games were bound to eventually become competitions made to be consumed publicly on a global scale.

In 2021, the Free Fire World Series had 5.4 million concurrent viewers. Not concurrent players. Concurrent viewers.

So why don't we have esports on primetime network television?

I pose that we need to stop talking about esports as a sport. Esports isn't a sport. It's thousands of sports.

A diehard Fortnite fan may not find a StarCraft II tournament compelling, whose fans in turn may not care for Forza or Rocket League.

As of 2020, there were 2.8 billion gamers on planet Earth. But there exists no world where all 2.8 billion watch one esports tournament. 3.6 billion people watched the World Cup, and that was just one sport.

So does that mean esports is screwed? Are there not enough fans of each individual game on a competitive level to make it work?

Absolutely not. But we need to talk about it in the right way.

Rather than discussing the reach of esports as compared to other live sports, we need to talk about the depth of fandom within esports viewers. Its specificity is its greatest attribute. Many people like baseball, but don't spend hours per day playing baseball. For Fortnite, many fans are playing for hours per day.

Esports markets a monetizable and specific game that viewers can enjoy without much additional expense (assuming fans already own a computer). Data capture is strong for these fans as all require a login, so remarketing is easy. The second-screen experience is the actual game.

The market will thrive if and only if the specific esport is able to tell this story properly.

Phil Ranta is a digital media veteran building creator networks at Facebook, Mobcrush, Studio71, and Fullscreen. He is also a lifelong gamer who grew up with NES / SNES RPGs and tries his best to fit gaming into his life as the CEO of Wormhole Labs, a husband, and a father to two amazing babies.

Wormhole Labs
philranta in 🐦 📷

wormholelabs.com

"INNOVATION IS A LABEL APPLIED AFTER THERE'S BEEN A CREATIVE SUCCESS.
KWAMÉ BABB, PRINCIPAL VFX ARTIST & MANAGER

Each morning from my desk at Schell Games (pre-pandemic, obviously), I can look through the Station Square windows at the Monongahela River and the skyline of the city of Pittsburgh, which if you've never visited is probably one of the most beautiful in America that not everyone knows about. On occasion over the past 14 years, I've been visited by the same fleeting thought.

This was never the plan.

I'm not saying that with regret, but with a sense of wonderment at this journey I started in 1997. I was an artist-turned-game designer polishing resumes, fine-tuning a not-yet-finished portfolio, and preparing myself to head to gaming hubs like California, New York, or Texas, where the majority of large game development studios were based.

But then, one of my professors at the Art Institute of Pittsburgh told me about this young company based in the city and run by a former Disney executive who also taught at Carnegie Mellon. Before I knew it, I think I was the 13th employee at Schell Games, a studio with no HR or marketing department to speak of that was doing contract work for big-name companies but living in anonymity under airtight NDAs. Gradually that veil lifted as we began producing original IP. Today, I might find myself working on a VR fighting or mystery game or an award-winning educational game.

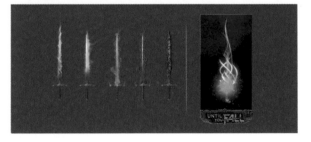

I started as a 2D and 3D texture artist, even though I had a portfolio brimming with lighting work, modeling, level design, and countless art disciplines. Looking back, I wonder if I might not have felt trapped if I had stuck to "the plan" and joined a AAA studio. Before long at Schell Games, texture art gave way to lighting and then to world-building and then VFX, where things really took off.

My ability to explore was buoyed by an emerging company culture that encouraged employees to find their creative truth without constantly worrying about being "innovative." I feel chasing innovation can be quite misleading. For me, innovation is a label applied after there's been a creative success. So to "innovate" actually means being unapologetic with your creativity until it creates significant energy that forces people to focus on it and recognize its uniqueness.

The future is bright in this industry. I'm excited to see more and more games that are blacker, and queerer, and more ethnic, games that present more underrepresented perspectives. I'm proud to already be on the right side of that conversation, all from this

underappreciated hub of technology and art here in Pittsburgh. And yet, I can't help but wonder if I could say the same things if I made a different decision 14 years ago. Maybe I wouldn't have lasted 14 months!

There are two truths I would pass on to someone aspiring to be a game developer or VFX artist. First, don't think you can't do it. Second, study like crazy. So much of the art we create is inspired by the elements. Wind blowing through a tree. The way water splashes as it lands in a fountain base. Movement, ambiance, and the energy that moves it is everywhere. Always be taking in the world around you and creating with what you've learned. And then, if you can find somewhere that lets you experiment and try different things, even if you fail, you should weigh those factors against the charted courses.

Don't worry about chasing innovation or being outside the box. Build the box. And don't worry if you don't have a plan. Inspiration rarely does.

Kwamé Babb
Schell Games
akimbab@gmail.com
kwame@schellgames.com
kwamebabb [in]
kwamebabb
Akimba

SCHELL GAMES   schellgames.com

"BUILDING A SUCCESSFUL ESPORTS PROGRAM REQUIRES A COMPREHENSIVE, 360 PLAN TO FULLY SUPPORT ALL ASPECTS OF THE INDUSTRY. "

SARI KITELYN, DIRECTOR OF ESPORTS AND PROJECT DEVELOPMENT, FULL SAIL UNIVERSITY

FULL SAIL
UNIVERSITY®

According to a study done by the Anti-Defamation League, in 2020, over 80% of Americans ages 18 – 45 experienced harassment while gaming online. Alarmingly, 53% of online multiplayer gamers who experienced harassment reported that they were targeted because of their race/ethnicity, religion, ability status, gender, or sexual orientation. As harmful as these reports are, only a small amount of those targeted are reporting their harassment. While publishers and platforms are developing initiatives to help combat these problems, we know that this industry started at the community level, and real change needs to start at the community level.

Those of us leading in the esports and gaming space have an obligation to make inclusivity a priority, by not only instituting a zero-tolerance policy for toxic behavior, but also by developing active initiatives and strategies to combat toxicity. As more non-endemic leaders enter the space, they can bring education and knowledge to improve the health of these communities. The success of the future of the esports industry relies on endemic gaming community leaders and non-endemic business and strategic leaders coming together for both growth and evolution.

With over 15 years in this space, I am proud to be a small part of the road to inclusivity. People considering developing a career in this space, remember to listen to the community, regularly reinvest your commitment to this space, and lead with a growth and evolution mindset. Together, we can make sure success and positive impact go hand in hand.

For the past 15 years, Sari Kitelyn has been responsible for developing brand initiatives for Full Sail, with a focus on building their esports ecosystem. Under Sari's leadership, Full Sail has been recognized as a top performing program and has been applauded for their efforts in diversity and inclusivity. Sari earned her bachelor's degree in law and her MBA from UCF, and she holds her Project Management Professional Certification (PMP).

Building a successful esports program requires a comprehensive, 360 plan to fully support all aspects of the industry. Most importantly and often overlooked – community. The gaming and esports community is the foundation of this explosive industry. Each game genre has unique community identities, and you'll find both variations and similarities among streamers, players, fans, and teams. Trying to build a program without a full understanding of the community foundation will significantly limit audience development opportunities, and charging forward without a developed plan for community support will lead to program failure.

For those wanting to enter the esports space, it's important to remember that this field is not new. With a history of over 30 years, the grassroots foundation of esports is a strong part of what has made this industry such a viable and enticing opportunity, but it needs to evolve in order to grow. Breaking down long standing toxicity, creating a truly inclusive space, and elevating underrepresented voices are key in the continued success of the esports industry.

Full Sail University
FullSailUniversity
fullsail

fullsail.edu

"OPEN-SOURCE TOOLS ARE GAINING TRACTION TOWARDS BECOMING STANDARDS IN THE GAMING INDUSTRY."

MALCOLM HOWARD, CO-FOUNDER & CTO, METARENA

By day, I build distributed systems as a backend engineer, but in my spare time, I learn and teach about game development using open-source technology. Generally speaking, open-source software is computer software released with a license that allows users to freely use, modify, and distribute it.

My career in software development was heavily inspired by video games. The more I played, the more curious I became about how games were made. I remember writing my first program. It was an impossible attempt by my brother and me to create a first-person Zelda clone on a TI-83+ graphing calculator. We had no clue what we were doing. However, when the simple text displayed as a title screen, and the basic, pixelated sword moved across the screen, I felt the magic of creativity.

10 years later, after gaining a little more programming experience, I attempted game development again as part of a college game development course. The course was designed around Microsoft's XNA Game Studio. Microsoft provided a free version of its game development framework. However, XNA could not help us create our games' visual assets. Many of us could not afford some of the proprietary tools like 3DS Max on a college student's budget, so we sought out open-source tools like GIMP for sprite editing and Blender for creating 3D models. In addition to learning how to make a video game, I learned how expensive it can be to access the tools needed to make video games.

I didn't pursue a career in game development, but I still dabble from time to time as a hobbyist game maker and game dev camp instructor. When I teach after-school and summer camps, I intentionally select open-source game development tools, so that students can freely access the technology if they want to continue their game development journey. With every new aspiring game maker, I hope to add a new voice to an increasingly diverse and innovative gaming industry.

It is no secret that diversity is a catalyst for innovation. In fact, some research suggests that diverse teams are nearly twice as likely to innovate than non-diverse teams: "Diversity yields superior outcomes over homogeneity because progress and innovation depend less on lone thinkers with high intelligence than on diverse groups working together and capitalizing on their individuality." If diversity drives innovation, then open-source software will be one of the main vehicles for the gaming industry.

Open-source technology contributes to gaming industry innovation in many ways, including:

- Lowering upfront costs to game development, reducing barriers of entry for small teams and underrepresented groups
- Allowing anyone, regardless of their background, to contribute to public projects and gain valuable experience in the process
- Iterating software more quickly to develop features needed by the community, which increases the speed of innovation

Open-source tools are gaining traction towards becoming standards in the gaming industry. In the past 2 years, Godot, an open-source game development engine, has grown to be the 3rd most popular game engine for the Global Game Jam. Last year, it accounted for more Global Game Jam submissions than the combined submissions from the proprietary Construct and Gamemaker game development engines. This market growth is not limited to game jams and other game prototypes. Of all PC games published to the Steam Store, open-source game engines represent 4 of the top 10 most popular engines.

As more STEM programs incorporate game development into their curriculums, they will naturally seek out the most affordable technologies that can run on the greatest variety of hardware. Free, and often lightweight, game development tools that can run in the browser or on budget-friendly computers will be the most practical choice. Over time, as these new creators enter the gaming industry, they will bring their open-source experience and diverse perspectives with them. Wherever open-source leads, innovation will soon follow.

MetArena
MetArenaGG
metarena.gg

❝ LOOKING FORWARD, ESPORTS AND OTHER FORMS OF COMPETITIVE PLAY WILL BE THE LIFEBLOOD OF A CONTINUED HEALTHY GAMES INDUSTRY.

ERIK REYNOLDS – GAMES INDUSTRY EXECUTIVE, UNIVERSITY LECTURER, CONSULTANT

Erik Reynolds is a communications and brand executive focused on esports, entertainment and games culture. In his 20-year career, Reynolds has launched more than 50 games and worked for or collaborated with some of the most culturally impactful companies, brands and personalities of all time spanning multiple industries, including Microsoft, Sony, Activision Blizzard, The CW, Paramount, Bioware, The Sims Studio, Katy Perry, 50 Cent, Nintendo, Riot Games, Yahoo! and Universal.

I know what you're thinking...what can a textbook teach me about esports when the sector changes so rapidly? The lessons of esports adoption, growth and mainstream success have yet to be written so to commemorate them in a book may seem like a fool's errand. The truth be told, despite the fact that we are living the history of esports as I write this and as you read this text, the lessons that will impact your careers and aspirations have already been written by countless persons, myself included who have helped contribute to the growth of esports by building a strong foundation for the games industry itself. Without a healthy games industry, there are no esports and the trend that we are witnessing today is that the inverse is now also true - without esports the games industry may lose the energy that has fueled its meteoric growth since 1990.

So what is esports innovation?

There are many camps within esports that want to establish that the esports movement was an unrespected tribe of raconteurs who despite all odds being against them rose up and created competitive play.

In some cases that's very true. There are certain people who from the very beginning saw the potential of live events and competitive play. The folks behind Quakecon, Dreamhack, ESL, Riot Games,Blizzard, and MLG to name a few, truly zigged when others were very happy zagging down the same retail-focused paths within the industry. These innovators looked at an industry which was largely investing in platforms/tech (VR, AR, Mobile, Online Multiplayer) and in genres that were most popular (MMO, RPG and single-player shooter) and decided to place a very risky bet that people want to celebrate gaming the same way they want to celebrate sports - they want icons, they want bragging rights, they want a home-field advantage and they want spectacle.

They were right. But for some were about 15 years too early.

Innovation is ugly. It's hard and its most recognizable byproduct is failure. Here enters the unsung heroes of the esports revolution - the marketers and publicists (check my bio - I am bias).

Bridging the gap between the now and the then was this ugly middle-ground where tournaments and esports were largely the stomping grounds of the folks whose job it is to promote and ensure continued engagement in a game. These folks with marketing money to burn poured millions into community-focused events like Dreamhack and Quakecon and helped evolve them into the juggernauts that they are today by focusing on the organized play aspects of those shows, 1 v 1 tournaments, Squad v Squad and other promotional activities lead to some incredible talent emerging from the pack like Fatal1ty and Thresh.

It was promotional dollars that invested in these scenes first before the publishers, developers and brands realized the value.

Looking forward, esports and other forms of competitive play will be the lifeblood of a continued healthy games industry. As we see every strata of competitive play find its community and support (Kindergarten to College to Pro) like we see in traditional sports, games will continue to evolve into a multigenerational culture of creativity, competition and technology.

And that is innovation, because when you create a culture, you can create a legacy that can last hundreds of years. We know this because we know soccer, we know this because we know baseball and we know this because we know esports.

Aggregated Media | buzzspinner 🐦 | **aggregatedmedia.com**

> ## "WHEN YOU'RE MET WITH A DIFFERING OR CHALLENGING PERCEPTION, IT PROVIDES AN OPPORTUNITY TO LEARN."
> ### KEISHA HOWARD, FOUNDER, SUGAR GAMERS

MEET THE **NEW** FACE OF GEEK CULTURE

Pursuing your dreams

The gaming industry faces a stumbling block. Playing (and making) games isn't the only goal of the industry. The gaming industry is Big Business with entrenched systems, processes, and structures. Today's gaming space inspires and connects people in more ways than ever before and has the power to promote even greater levels of diversity and inclusivity. The bridge to this is innovation. An environment of innovation. The gaming industry lacks that; it needs to re-align itself.

This is undoubtedly one of the most competitive job markets and industries in the world. To get ahead means to innovate. Pursuing your dreams as an entrepreneur muscling into the gaming industry working for a large company means compromising your value system.

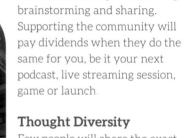

Independent thinking and autonomous decision-making are the foundations of innovation. In a traditional corporate environment (such as the large game developers and publishers), it simply isn't possible to create unorthodox solutions. As a programmer or otherwise, you're hired to fulfil a role, to be a cog in a machine. Deviating from that takes away from the company's resources and efficiencies; it destroys its structure. What this does for the individual is it inhibits innovation and change to create a state of cognitive dissonance. For innovation to take place in the gaming industry, companies need to embrace the entrepreneurial spirit. Entrepreneurs buck the status quo.

The Power of Risk

Advancing the gaming industry requires risk and innovation. When more people question the status quo the system will adapt and change. Entrepreneurs are simply less risk-averse. Harnessing this spirit and unbridling creativity will lead to innovation. This won't only make better games and technologies, but it will lead to greater inclusivity and create greater sustainability within the industry.

Community Support

The gaming industry – and eSports in particular – needs to adopt a different approach to generate innovation. Therein lies the need for risk.

The business of games is sales numbers. Gamers connect with emotions in a shared global experience and create a community. The gaming industry needs to foster its community. It means risking its structured position. To be vulnerable is human; it forms the building blocks of community.

These voices and messages from authoritative positions must be authentic. These have the power to unite, drive change, shape and influence communities. The fundamentals of any relationship are give and take: listening and learning; brainstorming and sharing. Supporting the community will pay dividends when they do the same for you, be it your next podcast, live streaming session, game or launch.

Thought Diversity

Few people will share the exact perspective and opinion you do. When you're met with a differing or challenging perception, it provides an opportunity to learn. Check yourself. Step back to discern from where those emotions stem, how people make their emotional connections. You'll grow from the power of being supported by the people who disagree/ differ with you.

Subject Matter Expertise Versus Talent

One of the fundamental aspects of breeding innovation is prioritizing subject matter expertise over talent. It is, basically put, the difference between being a doctor and playing one on TV. What this means for the gaming industry is that experts in each realm of the gaming community possess more authority on a subject than a person with talent. It broadens the opportunities for innovation and learning. Gaming is fun, fluid, and subjective. Removing obstacles only enhances the experience and rewards all in the community.

Sugar Gamers
sugargamers

sugargamers.com

"THE FUTURE GROWTH OF ESPORTS IS MORE ABOUT ENTERTAINMENT, LESS ABOUT GAMING."

KAROL SEVERIN, SENIOR ANALYST AND CO-FOUNDER AT MIDIA RESEARCH

Written on : 12/8/2020

For an activity (like playing video games) to turn into a publicly-observed competition (like esports), first there needs to be a demand to know who is best. Then, for the competition to grow a mainstream appeal and audiences to expand beyond the initial enthusiasts, it needs to have entertainment value.

Esports is currently beginning the journey from step one to step two.

STEP ONE: The informative value - i.e. who is the best at this?

Interest in this information is key for any public passion or activity to become competitively organised and publicly observed. This question is typically first raised by those most involved in the activity itself; these are the pioneers.

In a competition's early stages, the pioneers typically do not need to think too much about the public entertainment value of their activity – they are already entertained by taking part. The early audiences of any growing competition are thus formed from those who are (passionately) involved in the said activity.

Esports have done the first part right by growing an audience as a subsegment of gamers. In Q2 2020, 6% of consumers watch esports. This rises to 15% among console gamers and 11% among PC gamers. The growth of esports today is still largely driven by passionate gamers. While there is room for growth among passionate gamers, having enough partakers is not always sufficient for a proposition to blow up in terms of consumer culture.

More people ride a bicycle than play American football, but the media audience and commercial media value around the latter is much larger because it managed to grow beyond its initial partaker base and provide entertainment value beyond the competitive activity itself.

STEP TWO: The entertainment value - i.e. why is it fun to watch or experience?

While information value is what sparks a competitive movement, it is the entertainment value which helps competitions grow mainstream. While esports can and will continue to grow within gamers, it needs to attract the attention of more casual players and non-gamers.

To achieve this, esports needs to define its entertainment hook(s) – something the audience will keep coming back for, besides the games competition itself. For cinemas, this ended up being popcorn; for music, festivals; for baseball, its family atmosphere (for the most part), stadium food and singing 'Take me out to the ball game' in the 7th.

How can esports find its entertainment hook(s)? It is vital to pay attention to entertainment behaviours of esports audiences across entertainment, well beyond just gaming. Identifying and taking mutually shared entertainment behaviours and preferences of esports viewers and non-gamers will be key to open up the bridge to mainstream audiences.

Bringing non-gaming aspects from across entertainment into esports events, content and communities will also enable current esports advocates to spread the word more easily. That is because the "I don't play games" argument currently ends the discussion. But, what if there was something worth watching or experiencing besides the joy of playing games itself?

This is perhaps the most important moment for esports so far, as it finds itself at a crossroads. If it succeeds to reach and entertain audiences beyond gamers, it has the potential to become the next basketball or American football in the coming decades. If not, it will end up more like cycling.

MIDiA Research

midiaresearch.com

"A SELFIE OF YOURSELF. A MOVIE. A PIECE OF ART. A WEAPON OR SKIN IN A VIDEO GAME. YOUR BRAIN DOWNLOADED AND TURNED INTO AI. LITERALLY ANYTHING."

CLAIRE CAWTHORN, CHIEF MARKETING OFFICER, HELICONNFT

NFTS AND GAMING: THE PERFECT MATCH?

Hello, I'm Claire Cawthorn, Chief Marketing Officer of HeliconNFT, a play-to-earn NFT ecosystem that gives gamers the power to monetize their in-game assets by tokenizing them into NFTs and allowing them to play with these NFTs in amazing blockchain games on our platform.

Throughout my whole career in the tech space, I've had the real pleasure of seeing how the power dynamic between businesses and their consumers has slowly shifted. It's argued that every product is now a service, and every service is now an experience that is completely defined by the consumers themselves. The power is in the customer's hands. Just look at Uber, AirBnB and Amazon. Now let's add blockchain technology into the mix, and we really have something exciting and game-changing.

Speaking of blockchain technology, I'm sure you've all heard of NFTs recently, even if you're not quite sure what they are. Perhaps you've seen a meme about a CryptoPunk selling for $7.58m, or a post on your Instagram feed about Snoop Dog's whopping $17m NFT collection. What the hell are these NFTs? How are some of them worth so much? And what's all the fuss about? Whatever they are (and we'll get to that), the hysteria is real and undeniable - they are completely revolutionising everything as we know it, from gaming to social media, to film and art. NFTs allow people to do the unthinkable and the previously impossible.

NFTs (non-fungible tokens) are simply digital assets that cannot be replicated. They are completely unique. I'm sure you didn't know that you can NFT anything. A selfie of yourself. A movie. A piece of art. A weapon or skin in a video game. Your brain downloaded and turned into AI. Literally anything.

Unlike sought-after pieces of art, NFTs can't be faked. If you were to buy a physical piece of art, for example, it would have to go through a rigorous authentication process, and even then, its genuineness might

well be disputed. This is not the situation with NFTs. There are no ifs or buts - the uniqueness of the NFT is an indisputable fact (thanks to blockchain technology). This creates an incredibly transparent and fair landscape when it comes to buying and selling your digital assets. It can also make your NFTs extremely valuable.

When it comes to gaming, it's a similar story. Up until now, gamers don't actually own their in-game assets. If the game shut down tomorrow, all those fancy weapons and skins they have worked very hard for would be lost forever. Not only that, but they also can't monetize these assets, making them essentially worthless (despite their possible rarity within the game).

NFTs completely change the power dynamic here and are completely revolutionising the gaming landscape. If a gamer tokenizes their in-game assets and turns them into an NFT, not only is their ownership undeniable, they also have full control to buy and sell them as they please, on any platform, between any game. Much like Uber, AirBnB and Amazon, this is a complete power shift away from the business and toward the consumer. The fact there are nearly 3 billion gamers in the world, and with a growing base of users showing an affinity to both virtual gaming and decentralized assets, we have the perfect catalyst for the mainstream adoption of NFT gaming.

So is it fair to say, blockchain and NFTs are changing the game?

HeliconNFT
971-521673826
marketing@heliconnft.com

heliconnft.com

"I AM A UNIQUE STORY. HOWEVER, MY STORY IS NOT UNIQUE. IT'S OK. TAKE THE TIME TO READ THAT AGAIN".

SEBASTIAN "CHOSEN1" BURTON, DIGITAL ADVERTISING & ESPORTS THOUGHT LEADER ACTIVATING BRANDS WITH CONSUMERS VIA ESPORTS & GAMING, GOLD STANDARD GAMING

The way I see it is that the gaming/esports ecosystem is an interesting experience that reflects the games we all play. Need an example? God of War, Uncharted and The Last Of Us are all blockbuster titles that are classified as action-adventure games. However, if we start digging deeper we'll find unique traits in each that make them special. That's what makes gaming such a special pastime for all of us.

Now- I started my gaming journey out as a fan, just a kid who was in love with the colors and sounds of my uncle's Super Nintendo and my SEGA entertainment system. (Ironically, years later my nickname in high school was SEGA). By then, I was a full-blown gaming enthusiast, waiting for the new Game-Informer magazine to hit my front door so I could peruse the pages and learn about the newest titles and technologies in my favorite industry in the world.

By 15 years old I was traveling the country playing games semi-professionally. My game of choice was a fighting game called "Dead Or Alive." It was my first competitive title. I spent hours mastering my craft to become the best and while I was able to climb to the top of the mountain and compete against some of the best players in the world, the best gift DOA gave me was travel.

See, travel is a cure for ignorance. Ignorance is something that has been around since the beginning of time and it lives within all of us. No matter how you do it, it is your personal responsibility to educate yourself so that you can become a better person. Gaming unlocked those doors for me. Learning about different cultures and different lifestyles of people across the world opened up my eyes to the opportunities that were available to me in my life. Coming from a poverty environment, it was an ABSOLUTE game changer. I have no doubt that playing video games competitively changed my trajectory in life 100%.

By 2010 I was able to start working with multiple companies as a Brand Ambassador and attend events like E3, PAX, SXSW and more. Starting as a Brand Ambassador was a HUGE part of building my career in Esports. These opportunities allowed me to find a passion in marketing and I started working with Tecmo-Koei America on their marketing campaign for a game called "Dead Or Alive 5". Full circle right?

By 2017, I had worked with various companies and agencies in the space. I had been freelance consulting for multiple companies and I knew I had a knack for entrepreneurship. (Another skillset learned from gaming) So with a heart full of passion and a mind full of ideas, I started Gold Standard Gaming. An experiential marketing agency centered around esports and gaming activations. 4 years later we are one of the most premier agencies in the esports and gaming space. We've worked with various publishers, developers, celebrities, influencers and creators to bring esports fans of all genres, events, tournaments and activations that are truly one of a kind.

If I had one piece of advice for my younger self or anyone trying to get into the gaming space (Or any career they are passionate about). Never quit, perseverance is the ONE thing you can CONTROL that will affect the outcome of your ENTIRE life. Just like when you are running out of lives in your favorite game, you have to learn from all the times you've failed and you MUST be willing to go forward confidently and accept the challenges that come with it. No magic. Just perseverance. Lastly, if you ARE reading this because you want to make your mark in the gaming industry, I leave you with this. No matter what you do, remember this.

ANY GAME. ANY GENRE. GO FOR GOLD.

Gold Standard Gaming
434-284-0515
Sburton203@gmail.com
ochosen1o
sebastianburtonthechosen1

gsgagency.com

"THIS IS WHAT THE FUTURE OF INNOVATION LIES ON—HAVING A DIVERSE GROUP OF PEOPLE WITH A VARIETY OF DIFFERENT BACKGROUNDS".

SARAH DETOMA, DIRECTOR OF GROWTH, AQUATIK

Just over a year ago, I started my journey in the esports industry as an intern. Fast forward to today, and I am the director of an esports/media company while also leading our newest endeavor – Aquatik Studios. Interestingly, Aquatik is my first job post-college. I made sure to take every opportunity available to me while I was in school. Internships, club participation, and founding a sales club were all steps in my pursuit of opportunity. If there was one thing I learned during school, it was that a network rich in both size and diversity is the key to successful growth as a professional.

This key is what unlocks the doors to the future of innovation in our industry. A team of diverse individuals bringing the knowledge pool from a myriad of backgrounds will find new ways to tackle issues. As the thoughts collected in a team evolves, so too will the industry they seek to impact.

If diversity is the key to the future of innovation, then inclusivity is the lock which holds the door in place. If a team can cultivate an environment of inclusivity and allow all members of the team to feel needed and welcome, their voices will bring forth new ideas and new methods of expression that ultimately benefit the industry at large.

Gaming and esports have been viewed as a single-demographic activity by many in the past. To progress toward the future, we must acknowledge that both gaming and esports are for everyone. A key lesson I learned when helping to start Aquatik in 2020 was that the potential of this unique industry is limitless. The opportunity to revolutionize and evolve the human social experience through experiential media is ripe for the taking by those willing to pursue it.

In my role as the lead of Aquatik Studios, which is pioneering the way that development studios of all shapes and sizes launch their latest games via turnkey content solutions, we provide unrivaled access to modern production studios and state-of-the-art technologies. Whether it be content creation, administrative support, or a team of industry experts, Aquatik Studios is disrupting the status quo of game marketing and game release strategy at its most fundamental level.

Every day I am grateful for having the opportunity to work with the Aquatik team. Their years of experience and diverse backgrounds has not only allowed me to grow in my position and as a person; these opportunities enable me to positively impact the gaming industry for the next generation of professionals.

Aquatik
hello@aquatikesports.com
855-255-8641
neptjungaming ⓘ
aquatikesports ⓘ
Aquatik Esports ▶

aquatikesports
neptjun
NeptjunGaming
aquatikesports

aquatikstudios.com

I DON'T CARE WHAT YOU DO, GET INVOLVED IN GAMING AND ESPORTS!"
TOMMY KNAPP, PRESIDENT ESPORTS DIVISION, OPTIMA SPORTS GROUP

After making the plunge into the ecosystem myself, in 2017, I found myself telling people this everywhere I went. Whether it was at an industry breakout conference at DreamHack, as a panelist on a YouTuber Zoom discussion, on a college campus speaking to Sports Management students or just in daily conversations with colleagues, I believe ANYONE can and should join the movement.

In an industry that innovates and evolves at exponential speeds, opportunity is everywhere. And if you don't see the opportunity today, rest well and wake up the next day to digest the headlines. Opportunity will be there!

Gaming is pushing us into world's exciting and unknown. Proof? A decade ago the NFT didn't exist, the metaverse was just science fiction and ray tracing, cloud gaming, 4G and Oculus were just babies entering the universe of video games. Today all of these innovations have created vast, unique, exciting opportunities.

This was all news to me as I entered the space four years ago.

Similar to endemic sponsors, those whose services and products directly relate to gaming, such as HyperX headsets or Alienware keyboards, there are jobs, opportunities and careers that are obvious (and very good paying), such as software developers, game designers, audio engineers, computer programmers and testers or quality assurance specialists. This made sense to me, and it still does.

However, what often goes overlooked are the many traditional professions that are now crossing over into gaming and esports due to the sheer volume of business and success of the industry. These professions are critical to the continued evolution and development of the space.

I have often said, "if you are an attorney get involved in gaming and esports! If you are an accountant, a financial advisor or wealth manager, get involved in gaming and esports! If you are in the medical field get involved in gaming and esports!"

In the legal field the need for representation, advice and counsel takes many forms. From intellectual property to licensing agreements, player contracts to mergers & acquisitions and fantasy esports regulation to broadcast agreements, lawyers are understanding a veritable tidal wave of work across the industry.

When it comes to finance, the same issues that have faced traditional sports athletes and entertainers for decades are now prevalent in esports, streaming and content creation. Young, talented people are making a lot of money and, often, they do not know how to manage it. If you gave a 16 year-old $3 million would they, or their parents, know how to handle that. Well, that was Kyle Giersdorf, "Bugha," after winning the Fortnite World Cup in 2019.

And, regarding the medical field, both preventative and reactive care, as well as physical therapy, mental health and nutrition are all major factors in the overall fitness of the individual athlete and the industry as a whole. It's a massive segment in an industry that shows no signs of slowing down.

I only offer three examples above because they provide a very clear path to opportunity. However, as the industry continues to evolve and money pours into companies on the cutting edge of innovation, these and many more professions will continue to crossover into esports and gaming. Fields like executive search and recruitment are exploding due to the need for experience, talent and leadership from higher education, as well as other industries. Real estate, construction, data and analytics, transportation, event management, sales, marketing, human resources, operations, teaching, coaching, food and beverage, insurance, retail...

I don't care what you do, get involved in gaming and esports! Make a difference in the most exciting and dynamic industry on the planet!

Tknapp@TheSportsBoardroom.com
tommyknapp in
Optima Sports Group
optimaanalytics.com

"WE UNDERSTAND THAT THE UNDERREPRESENTATION OF FEMALES IN THE GAMING INDUSTRY WAS MAN MADE."

JESSICA MEDEIROS– FOUNDER AND SUZANNE DUNCAN, CO-FOUNDER, FEMME GAMING

As women representing a mosaic of cultural diversity in the esports and the traditional sport industry, both Jessica Medeiros & Suzanne Duncan are no strangers to the heavy lifts asked of female leadership at executive tables in the gaming space.

As the founders of Femme Gaming, we are both passionate gamers and accomplished businesswomen. These two things shouldn't be mutually exclusive but at times in the present esport ecosystem, certainly feels like they are. Being afforded the appropriate respect, credibility and compensation is a constant challenge. Regardless, we are in it to win it.

As empirical thought leaders and entrepreneurs in this space, we understand that the construct of this industry regardless of how "innovative" it purports to be is designed by the same architects and lenses that constructed most of our institutions – men. Going even further (in the western hemisphere) - Caucasian men. Encompassed in the one billion dollar plus industry of esports and the 100 billion dollar plus gaming industry are 46 percent of all gamers - females. Taking those figures into account from a business lens alone, it can be assumed that women represent a large percentage of those consumer dollars, so what gives? Looking at it even further the respective global fan base of female gamers is less than one quarter of that differing from country to country. A few obvious aesthetic factors aside that could count out some of the female fan base, lies the biggest, most obvious one. The esports and the gaming ecosystem doesn't value or know how to talk to the female gamer.

Why doesn't our economic contribution add up enough to support an "inclusive" image of players on the screens, or in all the greatest esport publications or even as a shadow image on the box of the latest Monopoly Game of Esports? Which by the way was heralded as the example that Esports was finally being recognized as "mainstream". Let's not even go into the multitude of female-absent stock photos or industry content in the esports ecosystem? Well we hardly see this "mainstream" as cause for celebration because once again, we are literally being left out of the picture.

French for the word "Woman", Femme Gaming is a team of like-minded, multi-culturally diverse, talented women who love video gaming and are working hard to champion the skills of women in esports and gaming. We live the experience of underrepresentation and often mistreatment of women in this industry in business and within the games themselves. With an idea to drive strategic change, we started Femme Gaming as a safe space specifically tailored for women, by women to make meaningful connections and showcase their skills as gamers. We are more than a brand, we are a global community fulfilling a promise of amplifying the recognition and prowess of women in the esports industry, worldwide.

Shouldn't be as rad as it sounds but Femme Gaming thrives in the disruption of the complex matrix of the esport ecosystem and games development that continues to taut itself as the cutting edge, authentic,

#JessOfAllTrades

#MaverickMaestro

Jessica Medeiros, Founder   *Suzanne Duncan, Co-Founder*

unstoppable, sport take-over of the future. The irony that men continue to purchase the skins of diverse, bad-ass female characters to slay and win, while we women turn our mics off to try and win....tells the whole story.

Organizations are quick to share they are "working on it". But their own internal snapshot tells a different story. How does a "culture shift" if everyone in your organization looks like you?

How can you share with any authenticity the conviction to change if your own organization doesn't represent that at face value? Females are not going to believe you and many of us will stop making an economic investment in the game unless this is corrected. The world of esports is failing to live up to the mantra of the one "real level playing field" in sports in multiple ways, much less the way brands engage in this space. We are putting it on "blast" with the #FemmeEffect, the push for mixed gender teams as a standard and tournaments owners and game developers to close the gap. We are showcasing organizations that are partnering with us to make it their business imperative to be the change and invite women fully into this space. We aren't going anywhere, you're on notice. #TheFutureIsFemme.

Femme Gaming
info@femmegaming.gg
femmegaming ⓘ
femmegamingGG 🐦
femmegamingGG ⓣ
femmegaming ⓕ

FEMME GAMING   **femmegaming.gg**

"AS A PODCASTER WITH OVER 15 YEARS OF EXPERIENCE, I CAN TELL YOU THAT IT IS NOT EASY AND IS NOT A GET-RICH-QUICK ENDEAVOR".

RICHARD BUTLER, FOUNDER, RAGE WORKS

When it comes to content creation and having a voice in the space, I am in a unique place as I have my toes in different sandboxes, but the one driver has and always will be podcasting. Over the last fifteen years, I have been an on-air talent, producer, and mentor in the podcasting space. The one constant I strive for is motivating, inspiring, and introducing more creators to the podcasting space, especially those within underrepresented groups in the podcasting space. While the new podcasts debut daily, with 2020 alone having 700,000 podcasts, many underrepresented groups need creators to plant their flag in the space decisively, and I hope to be someone who changes that either through sharing my own experiences or teaching others how to get started!

So why take advice from some random dude on the internet? The thing is, you shouldn't! At least not all of my advice, and that is because everyone's journey and circumstances are truly different and like Bruce Lee once said, "Absorb what is useful, Discard what is not, Add what is uniquely your own." What I ask is that you find parallels in my story to help you plot your course. With that said, allow me to share a bit about myself. I am a lifelong New Yorker and an 80s baby born in the Bronx. Growing up, I had no aspirations of being an entertainer, teacher, or content creator.

On the contrary, I had a passion for cooking and working with animals which I pursued. Sadly, that pursuit was only relegated to high school. My mom felt the law was my calling, but unbeknownst to her, I was learning about criminal science and law enforcement with very little interest in being a suit and tie lawyer. All of that came to a screeching halt when my mother's cancer returned after being in remission, and she passed away in 2000, leaving me at 19 overseeing the care of my special needs siblings and running a home, and dealing with all the responsibilities that come with it.

At the time, I was directionless and in survival mode, helping to keep my home running and with no aspirations on what to do with my life, but on a fateful day in 2006, I learned about podcasts and their debut on iTunes. I was blown away by the sheer volume of podcasts covering all kinds of things, and I gravitated to podcasts covering gaming and entertainment as those were my past times, with Video Game News Radio being the one that got me truly hooked. After listening to the show and being active in their community, I was invited to do guest spots a few times. Eventually, I was told to give podcasting a try both by fellow listeners and even the hosts. So I started my podcast with a Logitech headset and recorded nonstop for three hours covering wrestling, mixed martial arts, gaming, and entertainment, and just like that, My Take Radio was born. I had zero idea about what I was doing, but people seemed to like it, and I enjoyed doing it but got burned out because I genuinely had no idea what I was doing. This is something that creators and entrepreneurs will experience, and one should not shy away from it as sometimes a step back is crucial to moving forward. Things like depression and imposter syndrome

sometimes derail even the best creators, but you have to dig deep and claw your way out of that mindset because it will hamper your journey.

I shelved the show for a bit, but in 2009 I resurrected it as a call-in podcast on Blog Talk Radio and started taking things seriously with a complete website for the podcast that doubled to create additional content based on the show's topics. I covered numerous events and conventions and interviewed various actors, fighters, and personalities in the gaming space. The show also allowed me to bring on a fantastic stable of writers who were slowly getting into podcasting after being on My Take Radio a few times as guests and contributors, much like I did with VGN back in 2006. Our content offerings grew well beyond My Take Radio, and I decided to rebrand the site as RAGE Works and start the RAGE Works Podcast Network with My Take Radio as the flagship show. Those writers who got the podcasting bug launched podcasts of their own on the RAGE Works Podcast Network with many still hosting shows with us today. The fact that these fantastic individuals believed in me and what I was trying to do made it easy for me to retire the My Take Radio podcast at 400 episodes and over 100K downloads at the time. While I did retire the podcast, my work with RAGE Works and the RAGE Works podcast network continues.

I hope that my story and the hardships I shared fire you up to start that podcast, YouTube channel, Twitch stream, or other creative endeavors. It may not only change your life, but it may make a considerable difference to those that are either just like you or in similar circumstances. While you may think that you'll get lost in a sea of similar creators, make it a point to be yourself and use that as the foundation for any creative endeavor!

So stay hungry, stay humble and be of service, and always aspire to leave a room better than when you entered it!

646-880-9155
richbutler6 [in]
rageworks [o]

officialrageworks [f]
rageworks [t]
rageworks.net

"I SEE A BRIGHT FUTURE FOR THE CARIBBEAN IN TERMS OF INNOVATION, SPECIFICALLY HERE IN ANTIGUA WHERE I CALL "HOME".

JASON CASSIDY – CHIEF EXECUTIVE OFFICER, GAME CREDITS

GAME CREDITS

Living inside of the cryptocurrency sector for eight years gives one a unique perspective on innovation. Things move so quickly with blockchain technology that innovation tends to happen right in front of our very eyes. I grew up in the Caribbean when I was younger and there was virtually no technological footprint to speak of in the 80's and 90's Returning back down here over twenty years later, it was like stepping into a new World.

Smart phones were in the hands of all the locals and tourists and the islands were becoming digitally connected. Since my focus is on blockchain technology, I have made it a goal of helping to raise the collective awareness of this transformative technology in the Caribbean. There are some real lessons to be learnt here with regards to innovation and a lot of that stems from a thirst for knowledge, embracing curiosity and always looking towards the future.

Blockchain enables so many different areas and games are probably the most obvious and fun application. One in three people globally play some type of game, it is ingrained into virtually every culture. Gaming on the blockchain can be a real winner as it allows gamers, the target audience, to take ownership of their in-game items. This also allows gamers to have full assurity that no cheating is happening when results for games are recorded on a public ledger.

Once a technologies time has come it is often difficult if not impossible to stop that evolution, and innovation is the key ingredient in achieving this all, We are now witnessing this taking place as NFT (non-fungible tokens) replace in-game items and digital wallets replace the need for numerous username and passwords. Even esports is getting a shot in the arm from blockchain as it allows players, teams and leagues to monetize their brands in numerous new ways previously not possible.

The Caribbean has a rich history with football, cricket and several other sports including the Olympics and now there is a new generation of youngsters who are competing on the virtual pitch. Embracing blockchain gaming will allow entrepreneurs and the youth of the region an new outlet, one that comes with near limitless potential.

The geography of the region also lends itself well to being a venue for esports tournaments and festivities, and could serve the same purpose for blockchain-based games that begin to find their way into the traditional esports realm. The future is very bright when it comes to the Caribbean and for a change, it's not solely due to the sunny weather.

I look forward to helping continue the narrative of innovation in the Caribbean.

Game Credits
GAMECredits in 🐦 f ⊙
info@gamecredits.org

gamecredits.org

"EACH OF US HAS SO MANY TALENTS, ASSETS, WISDOM, AND POWER TO MAKE THINGS HAPPEN WHEN WE CAN COME TOGETHER TO CHANGE, BEING ANNOYED AT THE OBVIOUS."

TAMIKA MOULTRIE, FOUNDER, GEEK GAME TYTE

Holding a Master System controller at three turned into REDinFamy The Master Geektress. My passion for wanting to discover more people that look like me in this space by changing the narrative. My journey to fulfill that goal began when I started my career in media, delivering news and interviews in the gaming industry, tech, and esports ten years ago.

Interviewing legends from Walter Day, Sundance, Sespo, Developers, Execs, Pro athletes, and Trailblazers with various well-known media outlets. When I discovered the FGC (Fighting Games Community), what I call the heart of Esports, Black and Brown professionals surrounded me in the industry that I yearned to have.

I had the honor to meet and befriend Esports legend Triforce Johnson on the issue of lack of representation in the industry. It was disheartening to learn that his team, Empire Arcadia, the Guinness World Record holder for the most wins as a team owned by a Black man, was never on the newswire as much nor talked about, even by Black news outlets at least. There are many Black-owned organizations and companies within esports, so why does someone like Drake or Kevin Durant not know of them to invest?

Through my experience in this industry, I learned that there are Black and Brown creators, but our voices are either silenced or hidden. How is it that the Godfather of Console Gaming, Jerry Lawson, a Black Engineer, is now receiving his recognition in this space? Not enough exposure to what my people have contributed to in the STEAM and Geek culture industry inspired me to create **GEEK GAME TYTE** in 2015, a media company showcasing Black, Hispanic and Native people in the Gaming, Tech, Geek, and Sciences. We contributed to the foundation of it all, and are the breathing culture, yet not the face.

So instead of basking in the words of the ancestor, Fannie Lou, "tired of being sick and tired," I wanted to change the narrative and create a room full of tables to sit at. A media push for my people to shine, get exposure and educate every one of our existence, not a pledge for acceptance. When you see someone who looks like you, it gives hope, but it ignites

that person that they can achieve it at a higher rate.

During the lockdown of the pandemic, I was inspired to create two shows, Hidden Code, a talk show interviewing Black, Hispanic, Native developers, and Innovators in the Gaming and Tech Industries due to the lack of media presence.

Uncovering Black Women in Esports was the next venture that became precious to me because it was my truth, along with so many in this industry, that constantly gets overlooked.

A thread conversation inspired the show on Twitter by the award-winning Champion Pro Tekken Player, Jeannail "Cuddle_Core" Carter, who discussed her disappointment and annoyance of not seeing Black Women spoken of nor showcased in Esports as much as their White and Asian counterparts. When I witnessed this from a fellow Black woman in the industry, I had to do something because I have always felt that same way for a decade. Uncovering Black Women in Esports debuted at **PAX Online** and continued as an ongoing series to do the job that the industry purposely lacked to provide.

Each of us has so many talents, assets, wisdom, and power to make things happen when we can come together to change, being annoyed at the obvious. To form the platforms needed to educate more. For allies, it is beyond a click, and alike, it is boots on the ground to disrupt for change.

As we move more into the digital age, aka "Metaverse," we as Black and Brown have a stake in STEM, blockchain, crypto, and more, but sharing resources to build together should always be the goal for countless generational wealth and power.

redinfamy@geekgametyte.com

geekgametyte.com

"GAMING & ADVERTISING — MAKING THE TRANSITION TO THE MAINSTREAM REQUIRES A MUTUAL UNDERSTANDING OF AUDIENCES".

CLEMENT TSANG, MANAGING DIRECTOR, AUSTRALIA

annalect

As of the writing of this article in October 2021, the Twitch Influencer payment hack was making its way through the metaverse, enabling a comparison between the compensation that influencers and broadcast anchors enjoy, and the relative engagement they have with their audiences and the business models that underpin their ecosystems – broadcast versus social.

As a mature-aged gamer, the significant difference in advertising spend between these 2 audiences – TV broadcast and gaming is an area of frustration given that I have been engaged in gaming for more than 20 years, and also work in advertising and feel that my identity in, and the engagement channel of 'gaming' has less understanding and priority.

The behaviour change needed with advertisers, their buyers and their strategists, is a translation to their language, the identity and the profile of audiences and participants in the gaming ecosystem. By using the same language, technology and frameworks that they are familiar with, the gaming eco-system will allow for scaling of revenues.

To start off with, Advertisers tend to rely on 'personas' to develop their communications plans when 1-to-1 audience profiling and targeting is not as easily accessible.

What would be of further interest to advertisers and what makes gamers different to many other affinity groups (like music or fashion) is that their involvement tends to follow life stages that inherently assume differences in access to gaming - from technology (devices) to connectivity (5g vs fixed), and which might follow these types of character and player development that are dependent on their free time to invest in their characters:

1. Free-to-play players – more experienced mobile/console players who are limited in their ability or interest to invest in the loot to upgrade their characters, and whom
2. Glitterati – the new player that loves tinkering with the in-game virtual look, movement & accessories, doing so either with the free skins or paying a little to unlock new looks
3. Tick the Boxer – the freemium unboxer who follows the daily routines in order to slowly accumulate the credits needed over years to possibly unlock an asset
4. The completionist – the semi-veteran that is now going deep into titles, unlocking every single reward program and campaign achievement, because they can, and love to
5. Performance optimizer (future Esports) – the 'veteran' of gaming that has been through the previous 4 stages, and has ample time to invest in hardware and loot, and is now trying to reach the next level of their amateur efforts
6. Whales – time-poor but resource-rich players whom want that exhilarating respect, and have moments of brilliance

What each of these life stages can inform an advertiser, is a glimpse into that gamer's life as a consumer of real-world products and services. By creating a common framework between how advertisers and the gaming ecosystem identify participants – starting with personas, but eventually connecting identity systems, both sides of the communications equation can more efficiently address their needs.

For advertisers – this means targeting the audiences that matter to them, by going deeper than the generic 'gamer' profile, and seeing participants as everyday consumers.

For the gaming eco-system – this means gaining an understanding of players outside of the boundaries of in-game economics, by connecting systems to broader media systems that can illustrate their profiles through 3rd party data, and powering deeper segmentation, and thus value to all stakeholders.

As gaming enters the mainstream, the ecosystem needs to empower advertisers with the ability to understand participants in the same language that they are used to. Partner with Annalect and Omnicom Media Group to evolve our practices to accelerate to that future.

Annalect
clementt [in]
annalect_global [o]

annalectgroup [f]
ClementDTsang1 [y]

annalect.com

MY GOAL IS TO SHOW THE WORLD THAT GAMING IS GOING TO BE ONE OF THE MAJOR MEDIUMS FOR EXCHANGES OF VALUE, IDEAS, EDUCATION AND MORE".

GIANNI MAIORANO, CONSULTANT—ONLINE BRAND PROTECTION & DOMAIN NAME SECURITY

Gaming to this point has been a profoundly positive experience that has helped shape my life and who I am today. Providing me community, challenges, identity, entertainment and more, I can safely say I would not be the person I am today without gaming and its continued evolution. Currently, I work with some of the largest video game companies in the world, offer consulting to top brands for securing and protecting their online presence and work with kids that need assistance in mathematics for school. As a father of two budding gamer daughters, I truly see the value gaming can bring to the next generation as it did for me as well. This is why I have taken an advisory role with MetArena, and assist with business development strategy and more to enable young people to further connect through gaming and eSports. It all began with my Nintendo that I received just before my 3rd birthday...

My parents definitely thought that gaming would be a passing phase which would teach perseverance, hand-eye coordination and more. What they didn't know is that gaming would teach me leadership, coordination, problem solving, interpersonal communication skills, tactical and strategic thinking to name a few more. It is because of this that I sought to further apply my experience in gaming to a professional atmosphere. How could I make a career out of this? My options at the time were, become a developer, or move to South Korea and be a pro gamer! Both were not for me, so I stayed tangential to the business and enjoyed its outputs.

Over the years, I got into sales and eventually consulting, won numerous awards for new business development, including top new business globally, and many industry connections. Through my referral network, I've been given the opportunity to have gaming companies reach out to me! DREAM COME TRUE! Gaming companies need to be protected online now more than ever, and I love helping the companies I grew up with solve some of their biggest problems. In that time, I fully developed a referral-based tutoring business for high school math. I found that I was able to use gaming to relate to the younger generation in many circumstances, and it shortened the perceived age gap between my students and me. It was here where I saw a glaring need to have gaming be effectively deployed for education on a larger scale.

Why gaming companies love to work with me is because of a phrase I have heard in many meetings. "You get it, Gianni. You just...get it." I grew up a gamer, and this comes across in all my conversations because I absolutely care about the company, the integrity of the industry and the security of the experience from millions of people world-wide. In doing this, I continue to be a professional that people can turn to for perspective, understanding and experience. The gaming world is where I belong, and I will continue to push for a better experience and engage with the community and businesses for a safe and better world for as long as I am able.

Gaming and eSports is already one of the largest industries in the world for entertainment, and I still find that it is in its infancy as far as being universally adopted as a force for good. My goal is to show the world that gaming is going to be one of the major mediums for exchanges of value, ideas, education and more. That when gaming is done well and for good, it will have a profound impact on people's lives across the globe, and connecting in ways that we still have not yet realized. MetArena will be the next step for companies, colleges and universities to augment the human experience by adding a community and casually competitive environment to foster many skills and relationships.

Gianni Maiorano [in]

cscglobal.com

"I WILL CONTINUE TO EDUCATE MYSELF AND BECOME A BETTER ADVOCATE FOR ESPORTS/GAMING OPPORTUNITIES WITHIN INDUSTRY, EDUCATION, AND COMMUNITY.

JOHN CASH, FOUNDER, EXECUTIVE DIRECTOR AND PROFESSOR
JCSU ESPORTS INITIATIVE

Service

At its essence is selflessly giving / providing necessities to others with no intent to benefit.

Wow, this is how it resonated with me prior to my commissioning as a United States Air Force (USAF) Officer the Friday before a Mother's Day graduation at Howard University. "I will support and defend the Constitution of the United States against all enemies, foreign AND domestic" (that is for another time). Growing up as a young black man in the DMV, formerly known as D.C. Metro, well, not much difference than growing up a young black man practically anywhere in these United States now. Usually looked upon warily, as a suspect, not be trusted, unpredictable, blah, blah, blah.......But now, now as a graduate and an officer I had come to the realization that I am and always have been empowered by the tenants of perspective (Col 3:2), perception (Isaiah 43:18-19) and priorities (Matt 6:33). The grounding and foundation of my family, my community and most importantly my faith instilled in me a great sense of service, even for a country that did not serve me.

What the heck does that have to do with innovation? It has everything to do with it because our lives and experiences are the origins of true change, true innovation and this varies in meaning and definition from person to person. Whether it is cultivated and leveraged for greatness is another thing. Innovation is realized as, "history is rarely historic when you are in the middle of it". I have realized that although I was a great officer and accomplished executive, I could do more that would truly benefit others in a selfless manner. I am now more cognizant of my legacy, my "footprints". I want my footprints to be so deep it will take many series of ocean waves to wash them away. Thankfully, my upbringing and career have made me focus on great innovations or opportunities that will benefit others and hopefully their children and their children's children.

The convergence of sports, entertainment, and society to drive social justice and equality. I am now realizing this through esports/gaming for underserved k-12 and college students. In all industries in the country minorities, especially Black Americans, are under and misrepresented. My goal is to think and fight like hell for that not to continue in esports/gaming, presently a $150 billion-dollar international industry. Last year I researched, and observed a tremendous five-year growth rate of esports/gaming. From zero to over two hundred Predominantly White Institutions (PWIs) and ZERO among Historically Black Colleges and Universities (HBCU). So, I decided to do something about it. I researched, developed and launched the esports "Trifecta" at Johnson C. Smith University, Charlotte, N.C. during the 2020 Spring Semester. We presented an esports curriculum/minor program, developed an esports club and presently completing a 12 – person competitive esports lab, in less than 10 months. We will expose our students to tremendous industry career opportunities, secure internships and sponsorships across the esports ecosystem and ensure they become industry leaders and influencers. This specific esports/gaming industry phase is approximately twelve years old. Although the "train has left the station", I will help track it down. I will continue to educate myself and become a better advocate for esports/gaming opportunities within industry, education, and community.

Innovation + Empowerment = Opportunity

I would hope the actions we have begun at Johnson C. Smith University would be observed and serve as a catalyst for future program / curriculum growth at other HBCUs and this one education and industry movement manifests itself across other new technology opportunities in initial stages of development. Only through inclusiveness and true "Allyship" can we impact and innovate the most important aspect of life, mutually, and respected acceptance from all for all. Yea, that is where true innovation will truly manifest itself. Not what was really on my head but in my heart.
Now go and do great things!

jcash@jcsu.edu

Charlotte, N.C.

The Narmer Group, LLC

jcsu.edu

"LET'S EMPOWER OUR COMMUNITIES TO NOT ONLY BE CONSUMERS OF THIS MARKET, BUT TO BE DEVELOPERS, DESIGNERS, STREAMERS, CREATORS, AND LEADERS IN THIS INDUSTRY. FINALLY, THEN WE CAN INFLUENCE AND IMPACT THE FUTURE OF VIDEO GAMING FROM THE INSIDE OUT". TRINIDAD HERMIDA, FOUNDER, HERMIDA COMPANY.

Parents and guardians, hear me! You play an essential role in developing and guiding our youth/young adults of this generation and the generations to come. I know this is not rocket science or new information, but I wanted to be as blatant as possible with my intentions for the next five minutes of your time. You are the gateway to understanding; you are the gateway of opportunity; you are the gateway of impact in our current times.

So why am I harping on your influence? I am harping on your influence because you can empower our youth to thrive in the current infrastructure of our current world, or you can kill their dreams all in one swoop. Our ever-changing world's current state has evolved quickly in recent years - faster than ever before. You could be left behind if you don't know about Web3, NFT's, Crypto, Blockchain, E-Sports, Video, and Mobile Game Development.

For the sake of this conversation, I am going to focus on Video Games. An industry that I hold near and dear to my heart. This industry is composed of creators, innovators, and developers, some of whom I call my closest friends. Let me start by giving you some data. Video games are a billion-dollar business and have been for many years. In 2020, the worldwide PC gaming market revenue was estimated at almost 37 billion U.S. dollars, while the mobile gaming market generated an estimated income of over 77 billion U.S. dollars.

Parents, this is money that most of us know from the consumer side. Raise your hand if you have spent money playing games yourself, or maybe you purchased a console for a special someone in your life on a particular day. I'm guilty, and I know thousands of others are guilty too. So how do we get on the other side of the coin? We start breaking down the negative stigma within this industry bit by bit.

As they trevail through primary school, many youths and young adults get asked, what do you want to be when you grow up? Some say, A Doctor, Lawyer, An Engineer, or Teacher? But why don't we hear Technical Artist, Producer, Game Designer, or Technical Program Manager? We don't hear about these careers because our parents

THE HERMIDA
COMPANY

didn't hear about these careers. We are all subject to the communities that connect us and the information we also share within our communities. We need more parents open to their children pursuing careers in the Gaming Industry. Gone are the days when we as marginalized communities were just consumers of products. We are now the developers, owners, and creators of these products.

Now, how did this industry blow up? We have buying power; we consume these products and enjoy building community with these products. Although we have the buying power, why does it feel like we are last to the party to play? I believe because of fear. Our parents, guardians, and mentors are risk-averse, but for a good reason. What parent have you EVER met that wants their child to fail? None. One of the reasons why there are so many millionaires in silicon valley is because when the start-up boom happened, many people of privilege were able to take a RISK and join an Uber, Lyft, Airbnb, Slack, or Coinbase.

When growing up, my parents never steered me towards video gaming because they didn't see a solid future for me, and they didn't want me to take the risk. Instead, I was encouraged to pursue law, medicine, or education. We have to change the narrative. Let's empower our communities to be consumers of this market and be developers, designers, streamers, creators, and leaders in this industry. Finally, then we can influence and impact the future of video gaming from the inside out.

The Hermida Company
Info@hermidacompany.com

thehermidacompany.com

"BUT CURIOUSLY, SOME THINGS HAVE REMAINED THE SAME: THE MOUSE AND KEYBOARD".

ROB NEWPORT, RESEARCH AND DEVELOPMENT, WEBURBAN

weburban

Over two and half decades ago, I remember first picking up a mouse and keyboard to play Quake on a University lab computer for over eight hours straight. Fast forward to today, and that 3dfx Voodoo graphics card has been replaced with racks of memory laden GPU cards chained to crunch matrix calculations for machine learning algorithms.

But curiously, some things have remained the same: the mouse and keyboard. Why is it that while CPUs have evolved and changed, GPUs have grown and moved to the cloud, memory and disks have jumped from platter to solid state, the mouse and keyboard have hardly changed at all?

This point has stuck with me as my academic career has grown from being a student assistant at the Multimedia Design Center to a Master's in Software Engineering where I did my thesis with the Carnegie Mellon Robotics Institute to where it is now at Macquarie University's Computational NeuroSurgery Lab. All through these years I was excitedly waiting for a peripheral that would finally introduce neural interfaces into computing in a meaningful way. Some companies did indeed try, with my first introduction into consumer neural interfaces being around 2010 with

NeuroSky. It worked, and remained a curiosity to my software consulting clients and friends, but nobody saw where it could fit into their life.

Through much of that time, I was working at Disney as a freelance games developer, and couldn't help but think that the tool you use to write essays and crunch numbers on a spread sheet should be the same tool you use to navigate a game character through a maze. With the rise of console gaming, especially seen with the introduction of the PlayStation controller, an alternative to mouse and keyboard gaming can be had. But their persistence in competitive gaming is an indicator that when it comes to user experience, they still reign supreme. Further still, most competitive gamers use wired peripherals to reduce latency and interference when competing. With this evidence, it might be easy to conclude that in those early years of computing, we may have simply hit a home run with the design of the mouse and keyboard for gaming and it has not changed because it works so well. But this would be a lazy assumption. In other fields where precision and speed are critical, for example in robotic assisted keyhole surgery, a unique physical peripheral interface was developed to control the many robotic arms in the device. Furthermore, new research by myself and others is being developed to analyse and interpret eye gaze patterns when free viewing MRI scans to see if performance gains can be made and transferred between novice and expert doctors.

But with all this research being made into reducing and optimising latency in interfaces used in critical medical procedures, could any of that knowledge be used in gaming, and specifically in esports? The answer could be seen plainly by the lengths Formula 1 competitors take when developing new materials to reduce weight in their multimillion-dollar race cars, or the elaborate measures competitive cyclists make in their clothing and gear. Perhaps an argument can be made that esports isn't yet big enough to warrant this kind of tinkering. But this also is not true, with esports matches selling out the Los Angeles Staples Center even a decade ago. It is only a matter of time before a wiz kid who likes reading PubMed articles on eye tracking hacks together an electrooculogram interface with his mouse and keyboard to give them an edge over other esports competitors, launching a bio-peripheral latency arms race between elite esports competitors, eventually trickling down to consumers as new devices.

Macquarie University
Rob Newport, R&D Consultant
robnewport 🔗 📷

rob@weburban.com

"INNOVATION IS TO HAVE TECHNOLOGY SERVE THE ORDINARY TO BECOME EXTRAORDINARY."

MARIANA MUNTEAN, FOUNDER, CINEVVA

I see millions of artists, animators, and creatives more burned out than ever before, not being able to make a living or pay bills with their talents and skill sets because of a high learning curve of tech tools.

Very often, corporations use our content on our behalf, without us knowing exactly how it's being used. This centralized approach doesn't work for the 80% of independent developers and artists building their own games or interactive content. The ideal future in this industry is when a creator has complete control back into their hands and knows where their content is distributed and how, being able to monetize it and grow it, finding rewards for their talents and skills. It takes a community to come together both to create this alternative, as well as to empower it. We are seeing creatives ignoring or avoiding mainstream platforms because of lack of trust and essentially efficient solutions. The future is in creatives' hands to support each other to rise above the outdated systems that do not serve us anymore.

As a game developer, artist, animator I have tested and learned many tools out there, Blender, Maya, Unity, Unreal, Adobe's, prototyping tools, collaboration products. Today more than ever before, content creation tools lack the fun and the joy of creating. It's in the repetitive, tedious tasks that nobody cares to simplify or automate, ultimately sucking time out of anyone's life. These tools are available in big game studios with armies of producers, engineers, and big budgets. Independent **creatives can't compete with corporations. Instead, they can create their own alternative solutions. VIO is the alternative community of rising stars to create, collaborate and empower each other with FT and NFT monetizations.**

The future belongs to us; a world that we control, not a world that controls us." — **Oleg Sidorkin, Tech Co-Founder Cinevva**

What does it really mean to live in a decentralized world and why are we pursuing it as the main direction at Cinevva? The freedom of speech and expression is at the basis of any individual's right and is superior to any politics or powers... or is it?

On one hand, we have governments around the world that control, limit, or outright ban access to information online. Recent events in the United States where massive personal databases leaked from companies like T-Mobile, Twitch, Facebook, and others reveal the levels of surveillance every individual is exposed to. They know everything about us - it's like living in "glass fortresses", a reference from "We", written by Eugene Zamyatin 100 years ago about the predictability of human nature in a surveilled world.

The world has changed; however most of us chose to either ignore it or become oblivious to it, centering around the virtual space provided by our phones, computers, consoles and TVs. 63.2% of the whole world have access to and use the internet, and just in the United States alone,

Oleg Sidorkin, CTO & Co-Founder, Cinevva

Mariana Muntean, CEO & Founder Cinevva

- *Winner of Mozilla Builders' Award 2020.*
- *Winner of 2 Minutes Drill Show broadcasted on Bloomberg TV and streamed on Amazon Prime*
- *Winner of "Meet the Drapers Season 5*

more than 3 million GB of data is shared online each minute, all which is stored and analyzed by large corporations, who sell our data to create a profit margin. Meanwhile, the creators who produce this content are underpaid, under-engaged, under-monetized and, at times, censored, thanks to outdated ad- and plugin-driven business models. Such an example can be seen in an article regarding the developer Louis Barclay*, who created a browser extension for Facebook "Unfollow Everything," was asked to take the tool down and never create another one again for the company.

No privacy, complete lack of trust and collective revolt has determined our team to build a decentralized world for independent developers, as part of the collective action pool where one always rips the benefits from. A network without tracking, without collecting personal data about you, your friends, your puppies - just you, your virtual identity and experience. We believe decentralizing access to content creation, monetization and management can solve these problems in the same way Bitcoin and cryptocurrencies are decentralizing the financial system.

We hope you can join our mission as freedom fighters for a future controlled by you.

Cinevva
mariana@cinevva.com
oleg@cinevva.com

app.vioflo.com

> ## "TODAY, OUT OF ALL DAYS, HAVING THE ABILITY TO PROBLEM-SOLVE LIKE A GAMER IS ESSENTIAL."
> ### BRETT A MCCALL, ASHEVILLE, NORTH CAROLINA, USA, PLANET EARTH

LEADING THROUGH A GAMER'S LENS

My passion for the virtual world began when I was just a boy. I grew up in the '80s, when classics such as Namco's Pac-Man and Activision's Pitfall! were just beginning to inch their way into the public sphere. These video games enraptured the young me. I was diagnosed with ADD at age 12, and gaming was one of the first outlets where I found my unquenchable zeal. Within this digital environment, my chaotic energy proved to be a feature, not a bug. Even when my often-haphazard attempts failed, I still gained new insights into the framework of the game.

This love of gaming has come to define my perspective on innovation. Whenever I'm struggling on a project, I see things through a gamer's lens. Us gamers don't fear failure; in fact, failure is how we learn. Every time we lose a level, we learn more about what does and doesn't work. Because of this, we know that our failures help us get better at the game, that we can improve the situation that we are in. Of course, the obstacles we face become proportionally more difficult as we hone our skills and increase our knowledge. However, us gamers eagerly take on these roadblocks, fully aware that the reason we're facing challenges now is because we worked hard in the past. Gamers don't run away from problems. We run towards them. When you find yourself at a stumbling block, be a gamer.

Today, out of all days, having the ability to problem-solve like a gamer is essential. In the modern era, we're faced with mammoth crises such as the pandemic, systemic discrimination, and limited resources. Most of our attempts to address these issues will fail. However, we must use those failures to grow and develop, to develop, so that we can eventually at least reduce the scope of these problems. This is why we need leaders who think like gamers--we need leaders who are willing to try to find new pathways forward in these turbulent times, even if some of those new pathways prove to be dead ends. After all, only through failure can we gain the knowledge and practice needed to get us through the herculean troubles that we face now.

Brett A McCall
sheepsknuckles 🐦
bmccall17 🐦
brettmccall 💼

bmccall17.medium.com

HPG
HIGH POINT GAMER

> **SET TIME ASIDE TO PURPOSELY CARE FOR YOUR OWN MENTAL HEALTH BECAUSE INNOVATION CAN BE TAXING ON YOU FINANCIALLY, PHYSICALLY, AND EMOTIONALLY."**

DEREK WATFORD, CO-FOUNDER, HPG

learned that due to the lack of my own personal resources, I had to forgo actual innovation. I had to suppress seeing 10 steps ahead and focus on getting others just to step 1 so that I could secure the resources to get to step 10.

I learned that innovation requires you to have the fire to pursue creating something that doesn't exist and the stamina to keep that fire even when doubt and your present day responsibilities weigh on you. In the midst of innovation there will be numerous forces calling for you to quit and settle for what is already there over working through the difficult task of creating what isn't there.

My advice for others with innovative visions would be to understand the journey will be lonely. If you start out knowing that others may not understand your vision, it will shield you from doubting yourself when they don't. Know that you will spend a lot of time on educating others. Make time to recharge yourself. Set time aside to purposely care for your own mental health because innovation can be taxing on you financially, physically and emotionally. I have seen the road to innovation be a death sentence for others because they didn't properly prioritize self care.

Evaluate how well your current location can support your innovation. I was lucky to start my innovative journey in a city like Tampa. Innovative opportunities in Tampa are everywhere right now. Tampa has seen an influx of real estate, technology and community investments. It is located in a prime area that provides access to several connected cities such as Orlando, Miami, and St Petersburg. It is a great place to build a business and have a life.

Pioneering Esports has been a journey filled with many lessons on the upside and downside of innovation. I have learned that innovation can be a lonely place for a visionary.

I established my presence in the Esports industry early on by co-founding High Point Gamer (HPG) to produce competitive video game tournaments for the youth in my community. The goal was to give teens something productive and economically beneficial to do with their gaming skills. At the time I did not know how innovative those goals were.

After several successful tournaments, I was presented with the opportunity to participate in the National Basketball Association's (NBA) inaugural 2k league, thanks to pro gamer oLarry. This opportunity gave me a behind the scenes look at how a large well established organization launched their new Esports arm. The potential of Esports immediately clicked for me and I could see all the additional areas that were ripe for innovation.

At the time, I didn't know that innovation was a form of hallucination. I was seeing something that wasn't there yet and I was trying to convince others to see it. I remember the countless meetings where I drove away doubting myself because I had failed to receive the support I wanted. I

High Point Gamer
highpointgamer 🟧 📘 🐦
high-point-gamer 💼

highpointgamer.com

NICOLAS BESOMBES
ESPORTS AND SOCIAL SCIENCES

Associate professor in Sport Sciences at the University of Paris, my work focuses on esports. From a sports sociology perspective, my research is mostly focused on (i) the socio-technical analysis of players' physical involvement and motor skills in esports, (ii) the institutionalization and sportization processes of competitive videogaming, and (iii) the esports social challenges, which include good practices, sustainability, diversity and inclusion.

Since May 2018, I also advise GAISF about the Olympic Movement's esports long term thoughts and strategy and I have been collaborating with many French National Sports Federations and Organizations (pro and am) to help them to understand the esports ecosystem and industry.

Since June 2017, I am also the vice-president of the National French Esports Association (France Esports) which (i) promote and sustainably develop esports locally, nationally and internationally, (ii) unite all esports stakeholders (players, teams, organizers, medias and publishers) within an effective collaboration platform and a federated communications channel, and (iii) act as primary representative amongst public authorities regarding regulations, standards, compensation, and the facilitation of fair competition in esports.

I cofounded in parallel the French Speaking Association for Esports Research and Studies (AREFE) in June 2018.

ESPORTS & COMPETITIVE GAMES BY GENRE

For several years now, I have been gradually working on referencing the various video games' competitive scenes. Indeed, if esports has its flagship games (e.g. League of Legends, Counter-Strike: Global Offensive, Dota 2, Fortnite Battle Royale or Overwatch), whose Internet audiences are massive and whose international finals fill stadiums (e.g. LoL Worlds Finals, IEM Katowice, The International, Fortnite World Cup, Overwatch League Playoffs), many competitive scenes exist in a relatively anonymous way and are nevertheless rich in terms of **commercial and/or societal levers.**

By soliciting different communities' experts of each genre since several years, I have been trying to map all these "esports disciplines", whether they are **very active or definitely extinct, particularly structured or totally community-based, professional or amateur, highly popular** (in terms of numbers of players, audiences and media coverage) **or destined to remain confidential.**

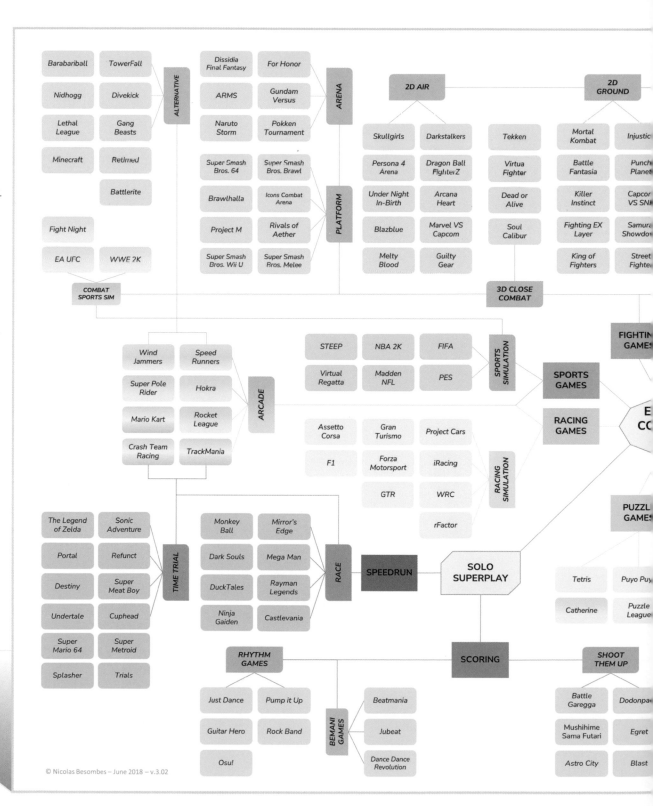

© Nicolas Besombes – June 2018 – v.3.02

Here is the result of this work, which began in 2016 and which I regularly update. The last version is from this July 2019, but I also make available the evolution of the different versions over time.

This work was facilitated by relevant inputs of:
Fighting Games: Chafik "Chaf Cancel" ARFAOUI, Olivier "Luffy" HAI, Elfrid "RZA" DE NAPATA, Mehdi "Mickadi" LADERIERE, Anthony "Shyndoa" MANALANSANG, "Viewtiful Mad".
Shooting Games: Théo "LoWkii" TÉCHENÉ, Laura "NSTY" DÉJOU, Dorian COSTANZO, Philippe "Faculty" RODIER. **Superplay:** Romain "Prospère" DESVEAUX, Chafik "Chaf Cancel" ARFAOUI.
RTS Games: Romain "FunK" ALTENBACH BERTHOD, Hadrien "Thud" NOCI. **MOBA Games:** Kévin "Shaunz" GHANBARZADEH, Léo "Lounet" MAURICE, Fabien "Chips" CULIÉ.
Collecting Card Games: Jérémie "Torlk" AMZALLAG.

ESPORTS LANDSCAPE AND ECOSYSTEM

ESPORTS ECOSYSTEM & LANDSCAPE AT A GLANCE

© Nicolas Besombes – March 2019

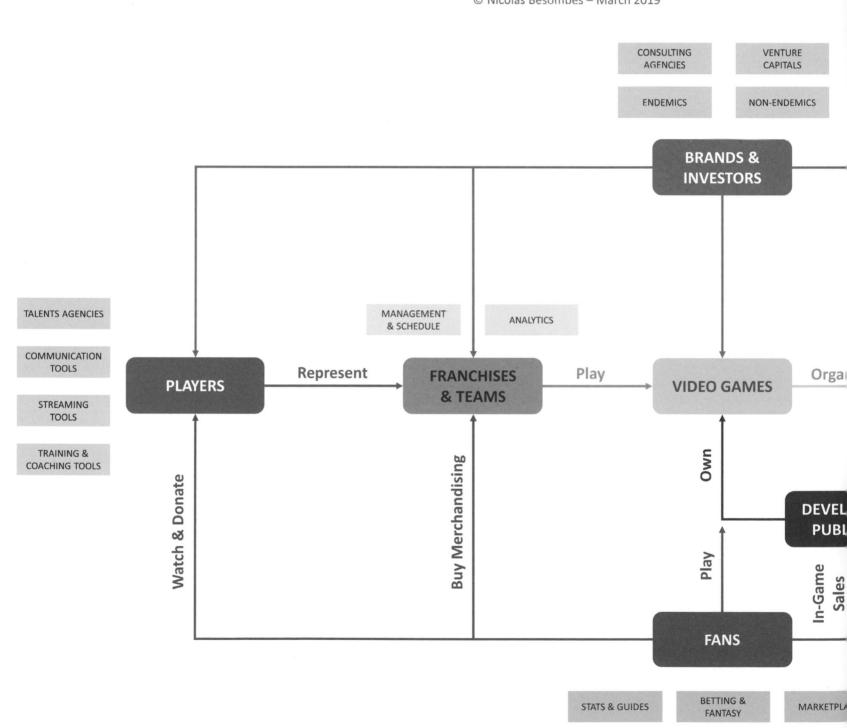

Among the consequences of the fragmentation and dispersal of the many esports stakeholders is the difficulty for people unfamiliar with it (e.g. outsiders or non endemic brands) to understand its ecosystem: Who are the stakeholders who make it up and how do they interact with each other?

Many infographics exist and try to offer the most objective and exhaustive vision of this ecosystem. However, they have never totally satisfied me because they are unfortunately either (i) too simplistic, (ii) incomplete or (iii) do not clearly represent the interactions between the different stakeholders.

That is why, after many months of using them while being dissatisfied, I tried in turn to propose a clear and faithful representation of the esports landscape. Here follows the overall result at a glance. However, there is an obvious limit: the multiplicity and diversity of competitive scenes. There are indeed almost as many models as there are games, and what is true for one is not necessarily true for the other.

One of the main difficulties in understanding the esports phenomenon is the relative complexity of its ecosystem. Indeed, the stakeholders who constitute the value chain of the sector are multiple, scattered, and sometimes have, even more and more, various and varied activities (consulting, content creation, events organization, distribution, etc.). This introduction to the esports landscape is not intended to be completely exhaustive, but should allow anyone unfamiliar with the sector to gain an overview of its main stakeholders and how they interact with each other.

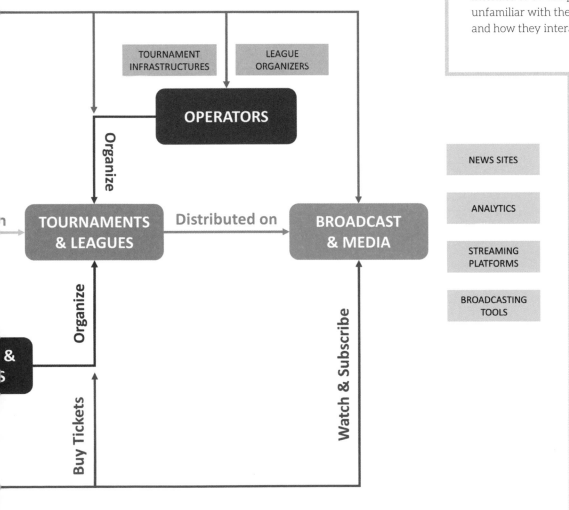

PUBLISHERS AND THEIR GAMES

At the center of the esports ecosystem are the game publishers. They are its cornerstone, as they are the intellectual property owners of the games in which competitions take place and in which players compete. Without them, there is no "virtual playground".

Historically, rights holders were little involved, if not absent, in the organization and regulation of the tournaments and competitions that took place on their games. But since the turn of the 2010s and the constant growth - economic and media - of the esports phenomenon among investors and the general public, publishers have regained "control" of their intellectual property and work in concert to varying degrees with other ecosystem stakeholders.

While a multitude of games allow confrontation between players and are likely to be played in competitions, only a few are very popular. Thus some publishers, because of the popularity of their games, are particularly renowned for their presence in esports. Let us quote for example:

- Riot Games with League of Legends, Valorant, Team Fight Tactics, Legends of Runeterra and Wild Rift games.
- Valve Corporation with Counter-Strike Global Offensive and Dota 2.
- Activision Blizzard with Starcraft II, Overwatch, Hearthstone and Call of Duty.
- Epic Games with Fortnite and Rocket League.
- Ubisoft with Rainbow Six.
- Electronic Arts with FIFA and Apex Legends.

THE PLAYERS

The players are the most visible part of the ecosystem. They are its ambassadors and stars. Performance-oriented, individual or collective, they use their physical skills (dexterity, speed of execution, visual acuity, eye-hand coordination, etc.), cognitive skills (multitasking, information processing, creativity, decision-making, etc.) spatial orientation, etc.) and social skills (communication, leadership, specialization of tasks, teamwork, etc.) to gain the upper hand over their opponents and win competitions.

Schematically, and varying with the different competitive scenes of each game, the player's typical profile is a rather young young man (aged between 16 and 25). They are, with very rare exceptions, specialists in a single game, a single license, or a single genre of game. Their careers are for the moment relatively short because of the particularly grueling nature of the game and lack of prevention of their health. At the end of their careers, some of them switch to coaches, analysts, commentators or streamers.

Finally, the players generally represent a club (an organization) which hires and pays them for their competitive activity. Sometimes, some players supplement their competitive activity with an entertainment activity (called streaming).

ESPORTS CLUBS/ORGANIZATIONS

Esports clubs are in most cases made up of several teams in different games: these are clubs that could be described as «multi-esports». For example, they can have in their ranks both a team on League of Legends, another on Counter-Strike, a third on Rocket League, as well as players on FIFA and others on Street Fighter.

In the case that the club has a team on a game whose competitive circuit is organized in a closed league format, the team sometimes becomes a specific entity which will be qualified as a franchise. Thus the North American structure Cloud 9 with teams on League of Legends or Counter-Strike, also has a franchise within the Overwatch League called London Spitfire.

The clubs are generally made up of several departments: the coaches and technical-tactical staff in charge of the performance and health of the players, but also, a marketing unit, another dedicated to communication, and other support functions such as human resources or accounting.

If the main activity of sports clubs is obviously to supervise esports athletes in order to see them perform in competition, it is not uncommon to see them diversify their activities by offering entertainment content, by hosting a channel on a platform, by creating merchandising, or sometimes by selling computer equipment. Some of the most famous clubs around the world include, for example:

- In Europe: G2, Fnatic, Vitality, SK Gaming, NiP, Navi, Virtus Pro, Astralis, Mad Lions, Rogue...
- In the US: TSM, CLG, Cloud 9, Immortals, Evil Geniuses, Optic Gaming, Team Liquid, Faze, 100 Thieves ...
- In Asia: T1, KT Rolster, Damwon, FPX, RNG, EDG, Gen G...

EVENT ORGANIZERS

The main activity of esports clubs is therefore to participate in competitions. Schematically, two models of competitive circuits coexist today in esports, depending on the choice of publishers to take charge of their organization or not.

THE INTERNALIZED/INSOURCED MODEL

In the internalized model, the game publisher itself regulates and organizes the major competitive events of its game. The entire organization of the competition is centralized by the owner of the intellectual property of the game, who is responsible for its internal regulation.

Typically, this model is league-oriented, a model borrowed from the North American sports model, such as the NBA, NFL, MLB or NHL. This is the case for the continental leagues of League of Legends (LEC, LCS, LCK, LPL, etc.) directly organized by the publisher Riot Games, or the international Overwatch (OWL) and Call of Duty Leagues (COD League), organized by the publisher Activision Blizzard. In this case, competitive seasons are often divided into segments ("splits"), after which the best teams qualify for the playoffs to determine the annual champion.

ESPORTS ECOSYSTEM & LANDSCAPE

© Nicolas Besombes – March 2019

B. INSOURCED MODEL *(League-oriented)*

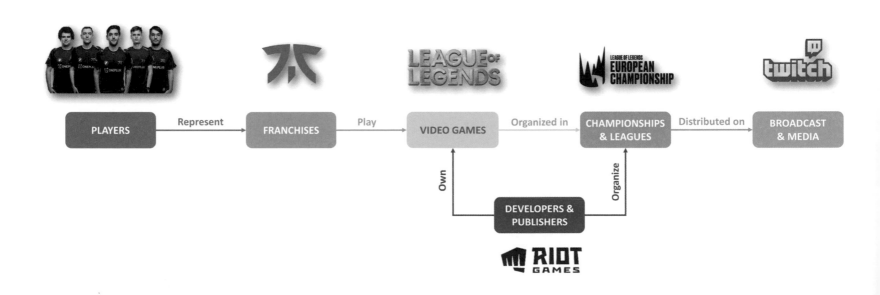

THE EXTERNALIZED/OUTSOURCED MODEL

In the outsourced model, the game publisher this time makes the choice to delegate the organization of the competitive circuits of its game to third-party organizations, while keeping the regulation of these competitions. These external operators specialized in esports events are qualified as event promoters or organizers. The organization of the competitions is therefore decentralized and the owner of the intellectual property of the game outsources their operationalization.

Generally, the game publisher opts in this case for an open competitive circuit in the form of successive (qualifying) tournaments (Minors, Majors and Premier Events) and rankings on the sports model of Tennis (ATP). This is particularly the case with the Counter-Strike: Global Offensive competitions from the publisher Valve Corporation. The publisher delegates the organization of the Majors and qualifying events by region (the "Road to") to different operators which may vary each year. These qualifying tournaments then distribute points in a ranking system, the Regional Major Ranking (RMR), with a view to qualifying for the most prestigious tournaments. However, at the same time, each organizer is free to propose his own circuits. Thus, the ESL Pro Tour includes an open

championship (the ESL Pro League) made up of events that give teams points for a ranking (the ESL World Ranking) allowing them, among other things, to qualify for Masters (the IEM or ESL One) in order to win the most important crown: the Grand Slam.

There is also in parallel the Blast Premier including a regular championship (the Premier Series) divided into two splits (spring and fall), to which are added qualifying events (Showdowns) for the seasonal finals. At the end of these two periods, the best teams find themselves in the playoffs for the Global Finals which crown the world champion. Beyond these two examples, there are a multitude of events of all levels allowing to climb the different rankings and ELO ladders.

Other games whose competitive circuits are outsourced by their publishers include Street Fighter V and the Capcom Pro Tour, or Starcraft II from Activision Blizzard and ESL Pro Tour.

There are many organizers of esports events around the world, such as ESL, Starladder, Blast, PGL, ESWC, Flashpoint, Eleague and even Face It.

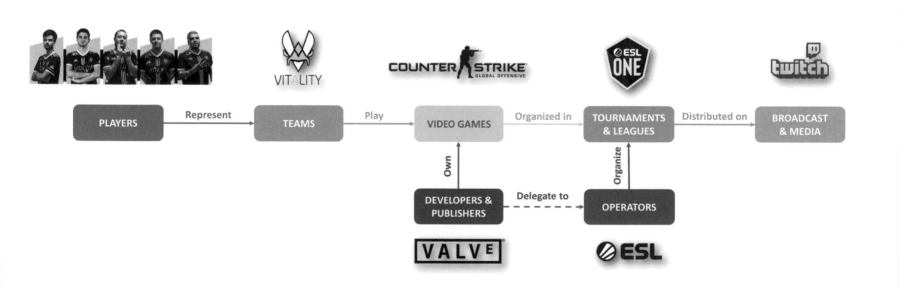

ESPORTS ECOSYSTEM & LANDSCAPE
© Nicolas Besombes – March 2019

B. OUTSOURCED MODEL (Tournament-oriented)

STREAMING PLATFORMS

This multitude of competitions taking place on the many esports games is in turn generally broadcast over the Internet through streaming platforms. They emerged at the end of the 2000s and made it possible to make esports content accessible to as many people as possible. The first ones were called Owned TV or Justin TV, but today the most important in the West are definitely Twitch TV and YouTube, while in Asia, Huya, Bili Bili, Afreeca TV or Garena Live are the most popular, respectively in China,

South Korea, Vietnam and Thailand.

While for the biggest international tournaments, it is generally the publishers and event organizers who operate the competitions audiovisual production, in the case of national competitions, the latter is sometimes delegated to local agencies who know both the cultural codes and the language of the targeted area. These local agencies include, for example, Freaks 4U Gaming, LVP or Gozulting.

BRANDS, ADVERTISERS AND INVESTORS

The esports ecosystem has always been extremely dependent on private funding (from dedicated esports Capital Ventures such as Bitkraft or Trust Esport, or brands and advertisers) which constitute the main source of incomes for the sector. However, the nature of partnerships and forms of sponsorship with the esports sector can take very different forms.

Thus, an advertiser or a brand can:
- Sponsor a player directly through an image contract (like Nike with Chinese League of Legends player Jian "Uzi" Zihao).
- Sponsor a team of a specific game within a club (like Renault with the Rocket League team of the French structure Team Vitality).
- Sponsor the whole club and therefore all the teams (like the phone builder One Plus with the European team Fnatic).
- Partner with a publisher to make their brand appear within the game's virtual universe (as the NFL did with Epic Games to allow all NFL fans to wear their team's virtual jersey favorite inside the Fortnite game).
- Sponsor a competition, league or tournament (like Louis Vuitton does with League of Legends Worlds).

- Partner with an event organizer (like what Intel does with ESL for the Intel Extreme Masters).
- Partner with a broadcast platform (like Samsung with Twitch for Twitch Rivals).

If historically it is first of all brands linked to the world of video games (Logitech for example), IT (for example Intel) or telecommunications services (like AT&T) which have invested in esport, since the takeover of Twitch by amazon in 2014, we are witnessing the gradual investments of many so-called "non-endemic" advertisers (ie outside the world of video games and esports). Their objective is therefore to promote their brand image to a population that tends to escape them (schematically, Millennials and Generation Z). The sectors of activity from which these brands come are as diverse as possible: the car industry, banking, cosmetics, beverages, fast food, aeronautics, insurance, sportswear, betting and gambling, luxury, etc.

ESPORTS ECOSYSTEM & LANDSCAPE
© Nicolas Besombes – March 2019

FANS AND SPECTATORS

Finally, the last key stakeholders in the esports ecosystem: the fans and spectators of esports competitions. As a consumer of esports content, the fan also greatly participates in the ecosystem's economic model on several levels:

- He enjoys watching his favorite players train when they are live on a streaming platform. He can subscribe to their channels and give them donations (eg. Jacob «Jake» Lyon, Overwatch League player for the Houston Outlaws),
- He can then buy merchandising from his favorite teams and players

(jerseys, caps, hoodies, mugs, key rings, etc.)

- He plays the game himself and can make purchases inside the game (for example, personalization elements or "skins" of his favorite team),
- He travels and buys tickets to the biggest international events (for example, the Overwatch League Finals),
- Finally, if he cannot make it to the competitions, he can watch the event from home and can subscribe to the channel that broadcasts the tournament on a streaming platform (for example, the official Overwatch League channel).

ESPORTS ECOSYSTEM & LANDSCAPE

© Nicolas Besombes – March 2019

FANS

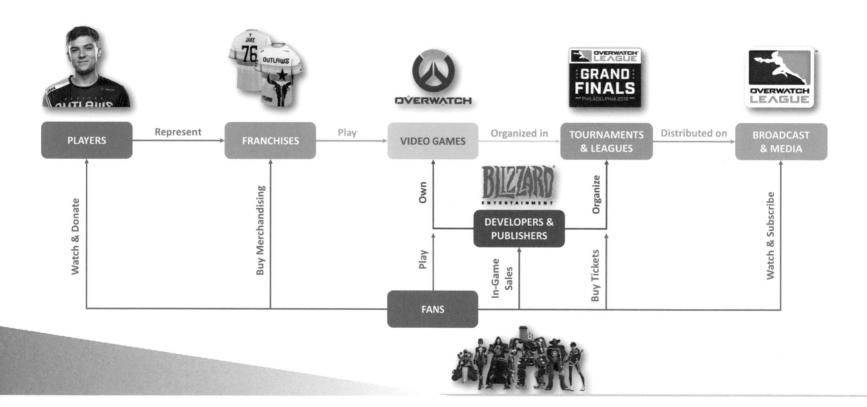

To conclude, it should be noted that around these key stakeholders in the esports ecosystem, there are others who also have an important role to play:

- Consulting agencies that are the link between investors and the ecosystem
- The investments funds that finance the various projects
- Players management agencies that support players' careers
- Providers of statistical and analytical tools that allow players and staff to do their jobs

- Tournament management platforms that facilitate the organization of competitions
- Specialized media reporting the competitions
- And many others…

It is important to keep in mind that these different stakeholders are interdependent. This is why we talk about an ecosystem. Without publishers, no games. Without players, no competitors. Without event organizers, no competitions.

ESPORTS RELATED PROFESSIONS

Since the turn of the decade, esports has been in the process of becoming more professional. The most visible side is obviously the players themselves who have the opportunity (for an immense minority of them) to live off their passion and earn a living by competing in an ever-increasing number of games. However, this professionalization is not only limited to players, but also affects all the competencies required by the various stakeholders that make up this ecosystem.

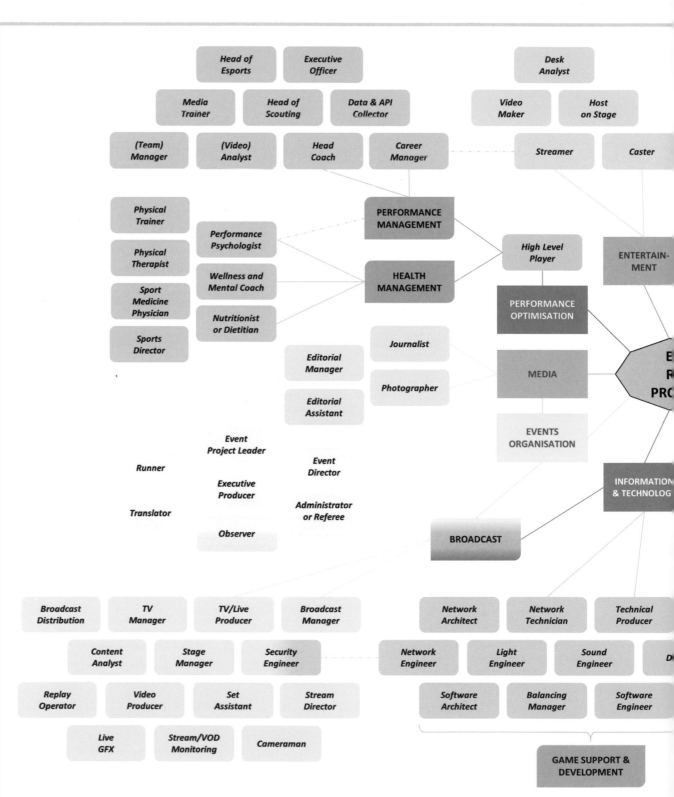

If, until recently, esports was mainly carried by self-taught multi-tasking volunteer enthusiasts, the constant growth of the phenomenon has gradually led the various stakeholders to (i) seek new skills (sometimes in other sectors of activity such as sport or media for example), to (ii) increase their human resources, and to (iii) surround themselves with increasingly qualified people.

Today, esports is the dream of many young people who would like to make this ecosystem their future professional environment. However, it is sometimes difficult to perceive what the possibilities are in terms of job opportunities, and therefore indirectly, in terms of educational pathways.

It is therefore with the objective of filling this gap that I am gradually trying to identify the numerous professions related to esports in order to (i) show the different possibilities to the youngest, to (ii) reassure worried parents that their children want to make a career in gaming/esports, and to (iii) help training organisations/schools/colleges to identify the professions they need to focus on, and thus define the appropriate educational content and relevant speakers/teachers/instructors.

PS: This work is still in progress and in constant evolution and is therefore not exhaustive.

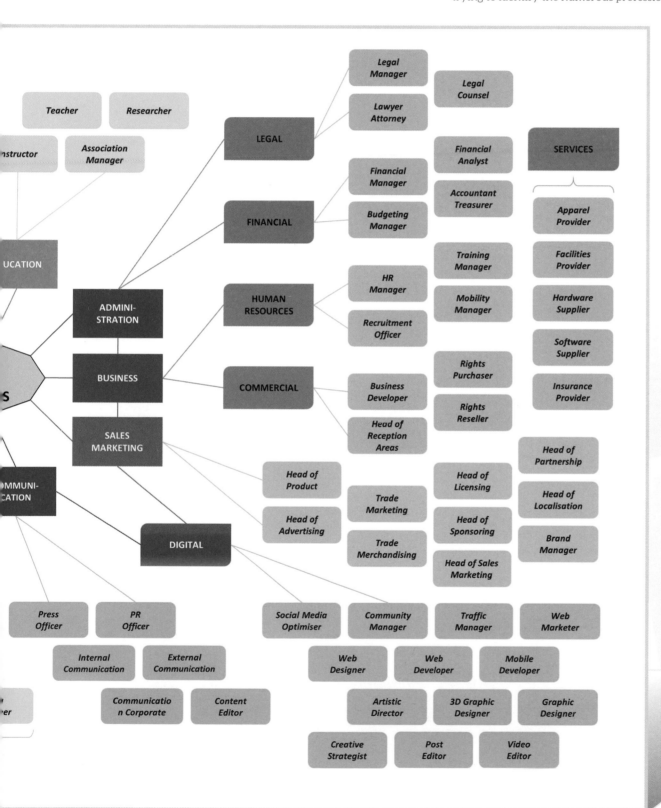

REMARKS ON THE COMPARISON BETWEEN SPORT AND ESPORTS

While the comparison between sport and esports has been the subject of regular debate since the term appeared in 1999 among the esports communities, traditional media, or public and sporting institutions, the Olympic Movement's interest for esports since late 2017 has revived discussions around the sporting dimension of esports.

Beyond the organisational, economic or political aspects of the two practices to which I will return at the end of this post, the "Achilles' heel" of this comparison (to use Emma Witkowski's expression) lies in the "physicality" given to esports practice. Whether the two practices share many characteristics that can be accepted by the general public such as regulated competitions, media coverage, task specification, regular trainings, technologised material, performance optimisation or strategic aspects, the "physical" dimension of esports still raises questions.

Whether the opinions of the persons concerned are clear-cut or more mixed, they nevertheless highlight several confusions, which are mainly rooted on the one hand in the lack of definition of the term "sport" and on the other hand in a relative lack of knowledge of the esports phenomenon.

Indeed, when it comes to comparing sport and esports, the first obstacle everyone faces is the multiplicity of representations (and therefore definitions) of what a sport is. Sport is often associated with the idea of "energy expenditure" or "physical exertion". Thus, when someone is thinking of sport, he or she thinks of an athlete running, jumping, swimming, fighting, hitting a ball, showing power, strength, or speed, and must therefore be sweating during effort.

So several problems appear: How to define a physical exertion? Would there be activities that are not "physical", i.e. that would not require energy expenditure? Don't all vital activities nevertheless generate caloric expenditure: sleeping, breathing, digesting, etc.? Are all sports energy-intensive? Is there an energy threshold below which an activity could not be recognized as a sport? The first reflex is to turn to the government institution that governs sports policy, namely the local Ministries of Sports or National Olympic Committees, but it must be said that none of them have at any time define the practice they supervise.

While some people today are trying to make comparisons with certain Olympic disciplines (highest institutional sporting recognition) that require relatively lower energy expenditure than others, such as rifle shooting, archery, curling, or golf, this was not yet obvious to many a few years ago. However, these analogies (which are judicious in my opinion) should not so much serve to demonstrate the sporting dimension of esports as to highlight the inadequacy of the necessarily "energy" criterion of sport.

This is where the sociology of sport, which has been constantly observing, describing, theorizing and defining sport since the late 1960s, can be a relevant tool for understanding this issue. After more than half a century of research on sport, the scientific community has proposed several dozen definitions. Among these, the one proposed by Pierre Parlebas (1999) seems particularly interesting to us because it makes it possible to overcome the pitfall linked to the question of physicality: according to him, what makes it possible to distinguish a sporting activity is not that much the "energy" dimension required than the "motor-skills based" nature of the activity. To put it more simply and clearly, in sport, victory depends (among other things) on the physical expertise and performance of the practitioner, whether it requires a high caloric expenditure or not. And this is where the comparison with chess (so important to many gamers) is inappropriate because it is far too simplistic: if esports requires strategic skills that can to some extent be comparable to chess, chess do not require any "motor skills based" performance. It is indeed possible to dictate to someone in real time which pieces to move on the chessboard without this affecting the result.

In esports, if not the CCG/TCG (Hearthstone or Legends of Runeterra for example), the Turn-Based Strategy Games (Dofus), and more recently the Autobattlers (TFT), all the other esports disciplines (FPS, RTS, MOBA, Fighting Games, Sports Simulations, Sim Racing, etc.) require from the players a motor skills-based expertise, certainly mainly reduced to the extremities of the upper limbs (forearms, wrists, hands, fingers), but essential/mandatory to the success of the task to be accomplished. This is ultimately what would correspond to the "technical" aspect of esports. Thus, if in basketball we learn by repetition to shoot the ball, in football to dribble or in judo to do an o-soto gari, in esports, we learn by repetition to optimize the control and movements of our units in the RTS (micro-management), to aim accurately in the FPS (skill), to make inputs with rigorous timing on the arcade stick to link combos in the Fighting Games (execution), or to effectively use all the possibilities offered by the time it takes to recover a character's characteristics in MOBAs (game mechanics). This dexterity displayed by players is at the very heart of esports practice and results in a particularly developed eye-hand coordination (visuo-haptic), high speed of execution, significant hand dissociation or developed visual acuity. Moreover, as a symptom of this technical expertise, we can notice that just as in sport some technical gestures take the name of their inventor (Fosbury in high jump, Panenka or Madjer in soccer, etc.), the same is true in esports (an inSec in LoL).

To continue, in my opinion, there is no sporting activity strictly comparable to esports. It is difficult to say that "esport is like rifle shooting" (in terms of energy expenditure, or precision for example), because it omits the fact that in esports there are two opponents (or two teams) simultaneously and they must constantly react to creativity and opposing tricks and strategies (what players call the mindgame).

In the interests of objectivity, it should rather be pointed that esports requires certain physical and cognitive skills that can be found in different sports disciplines. This seems to be the most honest and realistic way to address this topic. Thus, among the physical skills required for esports practice, the ability to control with particular accuracy the arm that handles the mouse in some FPS may be comparable to the skills required for fencing or darts; the ability to execute combos in particularly rigorous timings may be comparable to the skills required for combat sports such as boxing for reaction speed, and gymnastics or diving for the ability to respect specific timings in the sequences; the visual skills required to play FPS could be compared to those required by acrobatic pilots in aviation; among the cognitive skills, the ability to perform several tasks at the same time (multi-tasking) and the adaptive skills (cognitive flexibility) required to play RTS can be compared to those required by motor racing (F1); the information processing and environmental decoding skills required by MOBAs can be similar to those required by many sports duels: racket sports (tennis or badminton), combat sports (boxes or martial arts), team sports (football, handball, basketball...); and among the social skills, the communication and leadership skills required by all collective esports disciplines (MOBA and FPS in particular) could be compared to those required in almost all team sports (American football, volleyball, rugby....). Finally, it is rather competence by competence that I think the comparison is the most appropriate.

After having conducted a long reflection on the sporting activity that would be the most closely to esports, I have now come to the following conclusion, even if it means appearing a little provocative and not serving the cause of the recognition of esports by the sporting world: the activity that most resembles esports in my opinion is... babyfoot. Let me explain: In both activities, players compete on a symbolic field (the football table and the virtual arena on the screen); in both cases, what the players must decode is not the body of the opposing player (such as the orientation of a footballer's shoulders or feet, or the way in which the basketball player holds his ball), but the behaviours of the extension of his body (the red and blue characters on the table of table football, the avatar in esports); in both cases, the incarnated characters are controlled by the fine motor skills of the practitioners who will determine their success in the symbolic universe of the confrontation; and finally in both cases, the practitioners confront each other simultaneously, and not in turn as with darts or pool table.

It is not always obvious, however, for some esports stakeholders to understand the value of such a comparison. Indeed, sport and esports are two practices that are ultimately very similar, but quite distinct. The singularity of esports lies as much in the fact that the confrontation between players or teams is mediated by a digital tool, that it takes place in a virtual environment, that games are private property and their Intellectual Property belong to publishers who are in charge of their promotion and distribution, that its institutionalization is mainly private, that its business model is different, etc.

However, the comparison between sport and esports can be useful at several levels. First, it is a good way to introduce people who are not familiar with esports. Indeed, almost everyone is more or less familiar with sport and can relate to a discipline that they watch on television or practice themselves. Sport can then be a good mirror to understand the ins and outs of esports practice. Secondly, since the first appearance of the term "esports" in 1999, the vast majority of players have used this term rather than "video game tournament", "video game competition" or "competitive video gaming". The term has finally gradually imposed itself on the community, even in traditional media, and this choice is not insignificant since it contains the term "sport". Finally, thirdly, and perhaps

most importantly, the formal analogies between these two contemporary practices are innumerable: performance, streamlined training, coaches, analysts, championships/leagues, medals/cups, records, referees, commentators, hypertechnology of equipment, hall of fame, doping, rigged betting, media coverage, starification, transfers/mercato, sponsorship, competitive forums, specific university courses... In short, there are many examples.

The reality is that today sport is the practice of physical confrontation valued in our society: hitting someone in the street is considered a crime, but doing it in a ring allows the perpetrator to be acclaimed by the crowd. Despite all the studies that show some of the negative aspects related to sport (especially high-level sport): doping, physical injuries, eating disorders, social isolation... our society encourages the practice of sport (injunction to sporting activity by the Ministries of Sport and Health to fight obesity in particular), and promotes so-called positive "sporting" values, even though it has served the discourse of authoritarian and dictatorial political regimes (Hitlerian Nazism or Stalinist fascism used sport to control the population and justify their racist ideologies) as much as egalitarian and libertarian (capoeira is the symbol of the sporting practice of a enslaved population in search of physical and mental freedom, while the Sankt Pauli Club in Hamburg promotes antifascist, antisexist and anticapitalist football).

Finally, the comparison between sport and esports stems from a more or less conscious desire to legitimize video games and gamers, who have never ceased to be stigmatized for the three major ills they would cause: violence, addiction and social isolation.

Finally, as announced at the beginning of this post, I would like to come back to the institutional aspects of both practices. Because obviously, if sport in France is governed by a federal system recognized by the legitimate government sports body (the ministry), French esports is now recognized by the Ministry of Economy and Finance since the "Digital Republic" law of 2016. This can then be interpreted as a desire of the French government to consider esports much more as an (economic) industry than as a sport. However, it is necessary to understand that the recognition of an activity as a sport is fundamentally institutional and therefore highly cultural. Thus, although the French Ministry of Sport does not recognize esports as a sport, this is not the case in other nations of the world. In addition to the well-known South Korean example, Russia, Turkey, etc. see esports as a sport in its own right, while the United States believes that professional players can benefit from the same sports visas as top-level athletes. It is a mistake to try to identify the fact that esports is—or is not—a sport based on legal texts from a single nation or continent. There are many sports practices that are not recognized as sports in France while they are in other countries around the world.

Similarly, while federal institutionalization has for many years been the dominant model for the organization and structuring of sport, it now seems to be increasingly outdated. Since the emergence of so-called "californian" or "extreme" sports in the 1970s (surfing, skateboarding, BMX, windsurfing, snowboarding, etc.), the resistance of traditional sports governing bodies to take them into consideration has encouraged the emergence of a new form of institutionalization of these practices, this time private. This is how the X-Games supervised by the North American media group ESPN, the WCT and WQS surfboards managed by the

company World Surf League, or all the circuits created by the Austrian company Red Bull: Rampage (downhill mountain biking), Cliff Diving, Crashed-Ice (downhill ice-skating), and many others, emerged. These different circuits, although not recognized by public authorities, remain the most legitimate in the eyes of their practitioners and spectators, and are nonetheless the sport.

Thus, if esports is not recognized as a sport by the French government authorities, it does not mean that it cannot be one, especially for some nations in the world.

Nicolas Besombes
NicoBesombes
Nicolas Besombes

medium.com/@nicolas.besombes

CHAPTER 2

GAME / DEMO

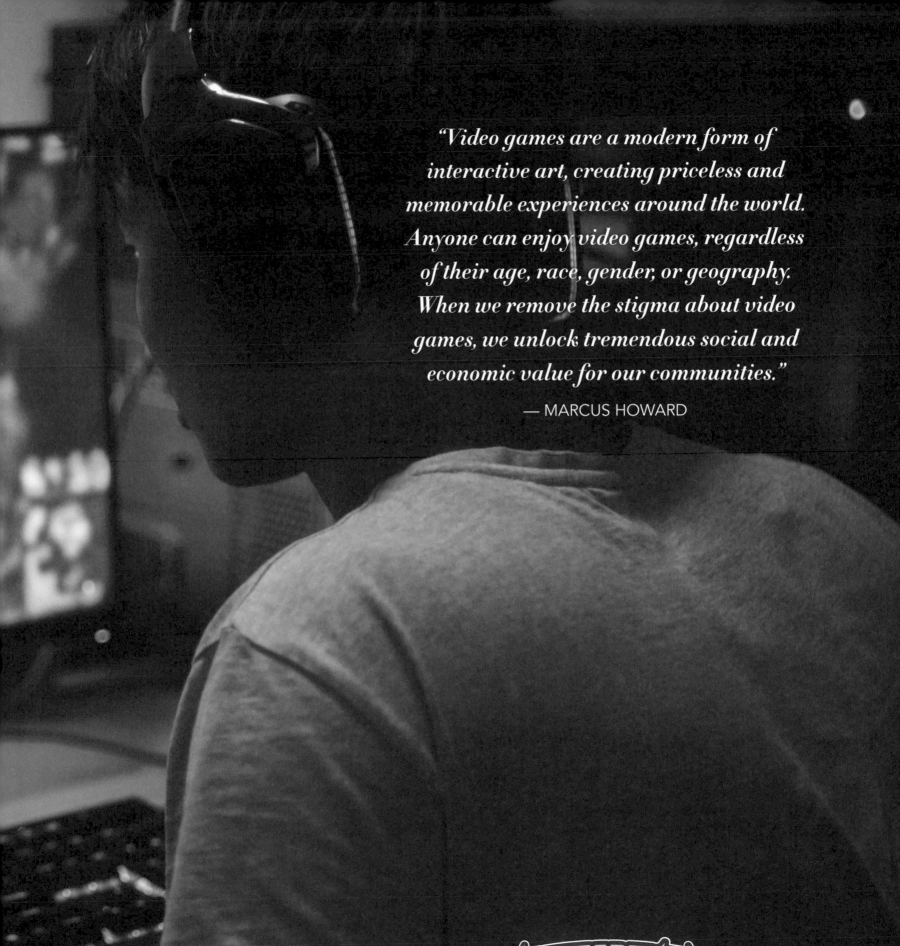

"Video games are a modern form of interactive art, creating priceless and memorable experiences around the world. Anyone can enjoy video games, regardless of their age, race, gender, or geography. When we remove the stigma about video games, we unlock tremendous social and economic value for our communities."

— MARCUS HOWARD

BUILDING THE (INCLUSIVE) BRIDGE BETWEEN WHERE ESPORTS IS AND WHERE IT COULD BE

MetArena provides an easy and positive way for communities and companies to engage using gaming and esports. Democratization and education are the driving forces behind our mission to provide the world with an opportunity to experience all the good games can bring.

If you're working in esports, one of the very first things you must learn to embrace is the art of the meaningful and intentional pivot. The advances made in the gaming industry since its inception are vast, and the rapid changes seen in the esports industry are reflective of exciting developments and pending realities of this social phenomenon. MetArena started in 2013 as a platform to serve the indie game community and help games that would typically go undiscovered gain visibility via educational materials, a supportive community, and a seat at the table. Though our founders pivoted to the world of esports in 2019, the driving forces behind our brand and what it stands for continue to hold: Access, Community, and Education.

Expecting the esports industry to flourish without being inclusive of all communities and providing the necessary access via education, tools, and opportunity is questionable math at best and willful obtuseness at worst. According to MetArena's CEO Marcus Howard, the diverse

fabric of the larger gaming community "creates a universal language and shared social experience that transcends age, race, gender, or geography". This "spicy take" (although it shouldn't be spicy at all) goes well beyond esports organizations, platforms, or brands creating all women's esports tournaments or organizing black and brown community events. It's essential to supply sustained support and understanding, to essentially draw less visible communities in and make them feel welcome in a space that so often feels exclusionary.

We aren't saying all of this to knock esports. Instead, we are committed to making this industry more reflective of its gaming roots by challenging the ecosystem to live up to the potential it promises for all communities -- not just a select few.

To the MetArena team, innovation is challenging ourselves to unearth, walk, and often build a better path for others to flourish in a lucrative, emerging industry.

We started in the indie game community as ProjectMQ, because we saw the power of access that non-AAA titles provided. The wider swath of experiences, perspectives, and relatability that indie games provide offer strong connections to a more diverse pool of players. Though we closed the project, the roots of that journey still exist in MetArena's esports platform, which positions indie games as the future of esports. We now provide tools, educational materials, and ongoing support to significantly increase the pipeline for talent, opportunity, and industry growth.

Drawing in endemic and non-endemic communities and brands is a crucial part of what we do because both are essential to the growth of the esports industry. Opportunities are just beginning to gel as keystone moments in the ecosystem, including blockchain, cryptocurrency, NFTs, and the metaverse. Innovation and progress don't happen in a vacuum, and it's clear that diversity of thought only strengthens what a product or industry could be -- rarely ever does it detract from it.

Over the next few years and the years to come, we are excited to pair curiosity with sustainable change to manifest the very best that esports and gaming have to offer. Whether you're an educator, a gamer, a brand, an advocate for marginalized communities, or someone who wants to know how the tech industry can be better, we'd love to work with you. Let's cultivate the next iteration of esports together.

ProjectMQ founders, Malcolm and Marcus Howard. Photo cred Paul Schnaittacher

MetArenaGG 🐦 in

metarena.gg

ANOTHER CRUSADE

Another Crusade is a brand new RPG with the battle system of an old classic. Enjoy exploration as a platformer game, but experience battles with a timed battle system, where strategy and timing is everything!

Click or use the Global Village App to view the Another Crusade Gameplay Trailer!

MADE IN MEXICO

Click or scan the QR code to access the Game Demo.

AERIAL KNIGHTS

Survive A futuristic Tokyo style Detroit in this 3D runner that tells the story of Wally who has uncovered the evidence that can change his city forever. Explore a game world with a dope-tastic soundtrack featuring the authentic sounds of Detroit Artist.

HEADUP

MADE IN USA

Click or use the Global Village App to view the Aerial Knights Never Yield Gameplay Trailer!

Click or scan the QR code to access the Game Demo.

EPISTORY

Epistory immerses you in an atmospheric action/adventure game where you play a girl riding a giant fox who fights an insectile corruption from an origami world. As you progress and explore this world, the story literally unfolds and the mysteries of the magic power of the words are revealed.

MADE IN BELGIUM

Click or use the Global Village App to view the Epistory – Typing Chronicles Gameplay Trailer!

Click or scan the QR code to access the Game Demo.

NANOTALE

Something is wrong with the heart of magic. Play a young archivist venturing out into a dying world, cataloging its mysteries and its wonders to unearth the truth. Nanotale is the new adventure from the Typing Chronicles franchise and the spiritual successor to the acclaimed Epistory.

FISHING CACTUS

MADE IN BELGIUM

Click or use the Global Village App to view the Nanotale Gameplay Trailer!

Click or scan the QR code to access the Game Demo.

THE RIFTBREAKER

The Riftbreaker™ is a base-building, survival game with Action-RPG elements. You are an elite scientist/commando inside an advanced Mecha-Suit capable of dimensional rift travel. Hack & slash countless enemies. Build up your base, collect samples and research new inventions to survive.

MADE IN POLAND

Click or use the Global Village App to view the Riftbreaker Gameplay Trailer!

Click or scan the QR code to access the Game Demo.

X-MORPH DEFENSE

Unique fusion of a top-down shooter and tower defense strategy. You are the invader! Use destructive weapons or lead your enemies into a maze of towers. Strategize in the build mode by carefully selecting various types of alien towers or throw yourself right into the heat of the battle.

MADE IN POLAND

Click or use the Global Village App to view the X Morph Defense Gameplay Trailer!

Click or scan the QR code to access the Game Demo.

XENRAI

Save the last world in a solar system of living planets being consumed by an invading interstellar army, playing as the world's champion and its goddess. Take on the epic full length campaign and competitive combat focused challenge mode that awaits you in this Sci-Fi spectacle fighter epic.

MADE IN USA

Click or use the Global Village App
to view the Xenrai Beta
Gameplay Trailer!

Click or scan the QR code to
access the Game Demo.

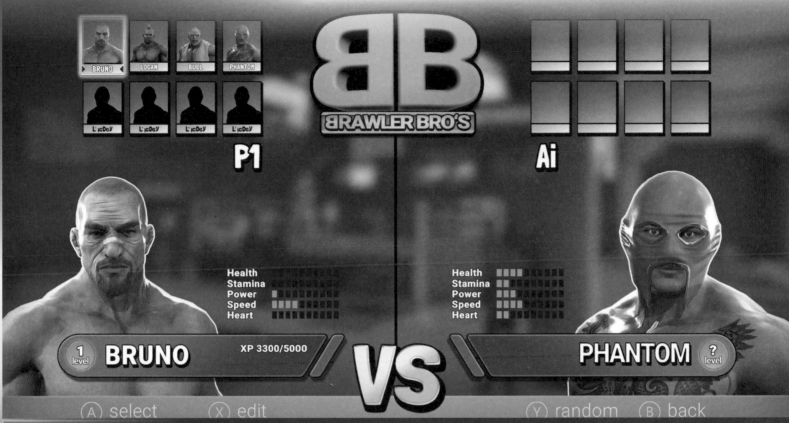

BB
BRAWLER BRO'S

P1

Ai

BRUNO	LOGAN	BULL	PHANTOM
L'ycDeY	L'ycDeY	L'ycDeY	L'ycDeY

Health
Stamina
Power
Speed
Heart

Health
Stamina
Power
Speed
Heart

1 level **BRUNO** XP 3300/5000 **VS** **PHANTOM** **? level**

Ⓐ select   Ⓧ edit   Ⓨ random   Ⓑ back

BRAWLER BRO'S

Brawler Bro's is an arcade kickboxing beat em up title featuring challenging fights against Ai and human opponents. Each fighters stats are dynamically adapting to the situation of the fight leading to challenging encounters which always leave room for a comeback story of the underdog.

PHOS
digital

MADE IN GERMANY

Click or use the Global Village App to view the Brawler Bro's Gameplay Trailer!

Click or scan the QR code to access the Game Demo.

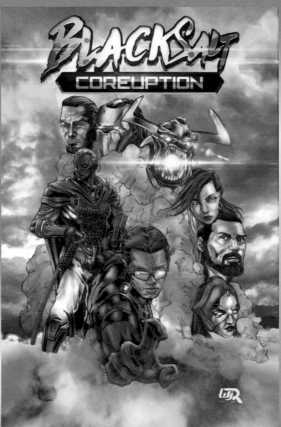

BLACK SALT COREUPTION

Black Salt Coreuption is a one-on-one 3D arena fighting game that allows complete freedom of movement around the arena rather than 3D fighters doing combat on a 2D plane. The Black Salt Coreuption 3D arena fighting game series also combines two action properties.

MADE IN USA

Click or use the Global Village App to view the Triforce – The Black Salt Brand Gameplay Trailer!

Click or scan the QR code to access the Game Demo.

SUPER UBIE ISLAND 2

Ubie has escaped the clutches of the Evil Dr. Terrestrial! But now he's going back to rescue his friends! Jump, roll, and balloon glide your way back through Climate Island to defeat Dr. Terrestrial once and for all!

A GAME BY ANDREW AUGUSTIN
MUSIC BY THAT ANDY GUY & CLAYTON STROUP
CUTSCENES BY EDWARD DENNIS

MADE IN USA

CLICK OR USE THE GLOBAL VILLAGE APP TO VIEW SUPER UBIE ISLAND 2 TRAILER!

CLICK OR SCAN THE QR CODE TO ACCESS THE GAME DEMO

LIFESLIDE

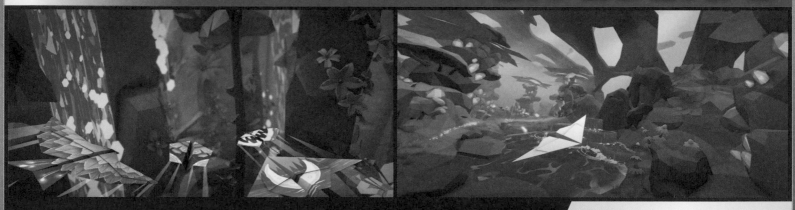

LIFESLIDE

Embark on a journey through life as you master the art of paper plane flight.

MADE IN BULGARIA

Click or use the Global Village App to view the Lifeslide Steam Gameplay Trailer!

Click or scan the QR code to access the Game Demo.

PSYCHOVERSE CITY

STUDIOLEAP GAMES

HQ
High Quality
Video Cassette

PSYCHOVERSE CITY

240 MINS
COLORFUL VISUALS
FAST PACED GAMEPLAY
ADRENALIN-PUMPING MUSIC
GRAVITY SHIFTING PLATFORMER

VHS

AVAILABLE DIGITALLY ON STEAM

PSYCHOVERSE CITY

Dive into the trippy gravity shifted world of PSYCHOVERSE CITY and platform across the rooftops of an ever-evolving cityscape, accompanied by adrenalin-pumping beats!

MADE IN LEBANON

Click or use the Global Village App to view the Psychoverse City Gameplay Trailer!

Click or scan the QR code to access the Game Demo.

MOO LANDER

MOOLANDER

Moo Lander is a 2D adventure platformer, where you take control over your civilization's last remaining spaceship to scour varied environments in search for the source of infinite amounts of milk. Tame the Mighty Cows, discover hidden secrets, solve puzzles and fight intelligent enemies!

MADE IN BULGARIA

 Click or use the Global Village App to view the Moolander Gameplay Trailer!

Click or scan the QR code to access the Game Demo.

STAR EXPLORERS
THE INTERSTELLAR DUNGEON CRAWLER

STAR EXPLORERS

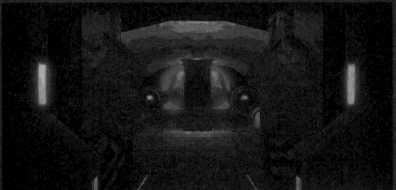

It's the interstellar dungeon crawler. Traverse a randomly generated galaxy in your own spacecraft, landing on planets, fighting aliens, finding resources, upgrading items, exploring caves, all while seeking out a new home for the human race.

MADE IN USA

Click or use the Global Village App to view the Star Explorers 5.0 Gameplay Trailer!

Click or scan the QR code to access the Game Demo.

DWERVE

Dwerve is a tower defense dungeon crawler RPG. It tells the story of a young dwarven tinkerer that adventures into dwarven ruins to unearth the lost technologies of the ancient warsmiths - turrets and traps, the only weapons that can protect the dwarves from Witch Queen Vandra the Wicked and her army of bloodthirsty trolls and monstrous creatures.

MADE IN USA

Click or use the Global Village App to view the Dwerve – NEW PAX West Gameplay Trailer!

Click or scan the QR code to access the Game Demo.

CHAPTER 3

HEALTH & WELLNESS

"A hero need not speak. When he is gone, the world will speak for him."

— HALO 3

GAME QUITTERS

Supporting the mental health of gamers and their families through content, community and coaching.

©creativewerd 2013

Game Quitters provides the best tools, resources, and support for gamers of all ages to keep gaming under control and maintain their health and well-being. We believe there are benefits and risks associated with playing video games and individuals should be equipped to navigate that experience. We do this by sharing educational content on YouTube, inspiring success stories on our blog, and creating a culture of encouragement on our forum. For individuals who need professional help, we have an online directory of specialists available around the world.

Game Quitters began with the vision of creating the ultimate platform for someone who struggles to moderate their gaming. The inspiration for this came from the lived experience of its founder, Cam Adair, who struggled with a video game addiction for 10 years. A talented hockey player, Cam's life took a dramatic turn at the age of 11 when he began to experience intense bullying, leading him to drop-out of high school. He never graduated, and while all of his friends were off to college, Cam was

playing video games up to 16 hours a day. Struggling with depression he got to the point of writing a suicide note, and it was this night when he made a commitment to change. After his recovery, he shared his story online in the hopes of encouraging others who may have been struggling that they were not alone. Almost instantly, the story began to go viral through Google, with tens of thousands of gamers from around the world reaching out for help for excessive gaming. This all led to the launch of Game Quitters in January 2015 and the work we do today with members in 95 countries.

Game Quitters is an innovator. For many years before "video game addiction" or "gaming disorder" was an issue taken seriously by the World Health Organization, media and society at large, people from all around the world were connecting and supporting each other through their gaming struggles on Game Quitters. During a time when mental health can be a difficult subject to talk about, Game Quitters has been on the front lines leading the conversation and creating a space for struggling individuals to receive the support they need. Somewhat ironically, Game Quitters is an online platform for people struggling with spending too much time "online", yet the innovation is to meet people where they are most comfortable. Providing content to individuals searching for help on Google

and YouTube provided us with an opportunity to connect with people seeking answers and then providing them with common sense approaches that work.

For close to a decade Game Quitters has been on the front lines leading the conversation on problematic gaming. Looking ahead to 2022, we are most excited to continue to bring a conversation of mental health to the larger gaming community, especially for individuals pursuing esports. Gaming has so many benefits when played in moderation, and individuals have also shown positive outcomes when they are equipped with the right tools, resources and support to keep excessive gaming under control and focus on their overall health and well-being. 2022 will see Game Quitters continue to innovate and drive this important conversation forward.

cam@gamequitters.com
gamequitters

NUTRI**GMR**

TO EQUIP GAMERS WITH "BETTER FOR YOU" PERFORMANCE BACKED BY INNOVATIVE NUTRITIONAL SCIENCE

Innovative, science-backed product portfolio with cognitive health ingredients for esport athletes, gamers and streamers to consume before and during games and streams, designed to meet the needs of the gaming community.

Our team started studying esports athletes in 2018 and quickly saw a need to provide a healthy alternative to the traditional energy drink space in gaming and esports. Once athletes started asking our Doc what they should be drinking he saw an opportunity and called Josh our CEO and co-founder and together they created NutriGMR.

We understand the critical moment. The deciding factor between victory and defeat that can happen in any game, at any time.

When breathing isn't a guarantee and every nerve is felt for the first time again. The split-second window when we secure hard-fought victories or suffer heartbreaking defeats. These are the fractions of time that form the elite. Those who prove there's nobody better, and never settle for " next time." And in these moments, we must sustain focus and energy. We can't afford to crash. Because the instant we fail, someone else inches closer to our seat at the top. Bur critical moments don't just happen in games. It's bigger than that. We're living in one right now. The moment when we get to decide what being a gamer truly means. We get to choose whether to tolerate negativity or fight tooth and nail for a better community. NutriGMR isn't just about helping you land your shots, it's about giving you the courage to change a culture. It's not just about beating another level, it's about conquering the world in front of you. NutriGMR prepares you for every critical moment because the next one could define your legacy.

We are excited for the opportunity to provide healthy solutions to today's cognitive athletes and bring content and future products to the community that is focused on the mind, improving performance, and are science-backed.

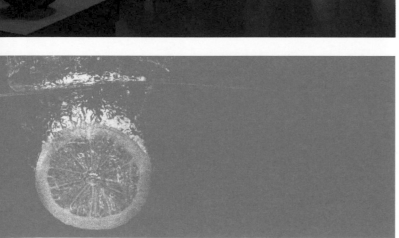

NutriGMR
josh@nutrigmr.com
nutrigmr_/
NutriGMR/
nutrigmr/

nutrigmr.com

Respawn Therapy is a group of Doctors of Physical Therapy that strive to help gamers play with healthier habits and less pain.

We've taken the lessons learned from our extensive experience in working with professional players to teach gamers of every level how to play while simultaneously reducing risk of injury. Everyone plays better when they play pain-free and we want to help them achieve that.

I started Respawn Therapy in 2018 because I wanted to find my niche in physical therapy. I've been an avid gamer since childhood and a fan of esports titles such as Starcraft and CS:GO. Watching many of the matches, I noticed that multiple players sat with terrible posture and this sparked an idea in my head. "Why can't I help them fix that? I see these types of patients every day" I wondered. I immediately began doing research on the common injuries in esports and was shocked to discover how many were retiring in their early 20's due to preventable or treatable injuries. This

made no sense to me as a physical therapist. These young players should be peaking in their twenties, not hanging up the mouse.

I decided to create a resource for gamers on Instagram to provide information on injuries and exercises. From there I connected with a professional esports organization for the first time and began working with the North American League of Legends team, Cloud9. I created Respawn Therapy shortly after as I realized that there were enough teams in the Los Angeles area to possibly create a business around. Over the last years, we have expanded our affiliated teams to include 4 more professional organizations over various titles.

As an organization, we are at the forefront of the new push in esports to improve player health and wellness. We have participated in multiple

wellness campaigns with major companies and colleges as well as continuing to push out health related content for gamers. We've also been the first to work directly with Secretlab in helping them with ergonomic considerations in chair design. We are constantly striving to find new ways to improve the physical health of players at every level. Esports is such a dynamic and evolving space that we have to also be fluid in our approach towards improving it.

We are fortunate to be located at the center of North American esports in Los Angeles and have direct access to some of the biggest organizations in gaming. In addition to the multiple teams within a few miles of our headquarters, we are also in the same area as some of the biggest names in game development including Riot Studios, Activision, and EA. We have unparalleled proximity to dozens of professional players in the hub of esports which makes growth extremely organic.

Other than our obvious goals to provide more organizations with high quality physical therapy services, we also look forward to finding new avenues in which PT can help players around the world. One of our primary goals for the immediate future will be to expand to work with more people in the streaming space because they tend to put in more hours playing than even pros and are often neglected when it comes to physical health. By helping them on public platforms, we also hope to improve the lives of their audiences indirectly thereby increasing the reach of our

Jordan Tsai, Founder, Respawn Therapy

messaging exponentially. We have seen tremendous growth in the last 3 years and are excited to see what we can accomplish in the world of healthy gaming in the future.

Respawn Therapy
jordantsaidpt@gmail.com
respawntherapy 📷
DrJordanTsai 🐦

respawntherapy.com

CHAPTER 4
DEVELOPERS & PUBLISHERS

*"A famous explorer once said,
that the extraordinary is in what we do,
not who we are."*

— TOMB RAIDER 2013

"PLAY YOUR HOMEWORK" WITH THE MECHANICAL WORLD OF DR. GEARBOX BY FLAMEHAWK STUDIOS

Flamehawk Studios is a "games for good" startup that focuses on three main themes: e-learning, diversity and inclusion, and charity.

Flamehawk's first effort is The Mechanical World of Dr. Gearbox. Teachers may consider it a remote learning tool but students consider it a fun game that is clearly inspired by the graphics and features of some of the most popular big-name titles that kids adore.

In addition to Flamehawk's teacher-authored, standards-based educational curriculum, the game redefines the elearning genre by allowing parents and teachers to create their own educational content using a web-based dashboard. The content can then be surfaced to their kids and students during good ol' fashioned turn-based combat. The rules are simple: answer questions correctly to charge up stronger ability spells and tip the loot tables into your favor.

The game also arguably boasts the most inclusive character creation suite ever invented, especially for a kids' game. Players not only have dozens of facial sliders that impact everything from eye shape to lip size, but even the hair styles come in adjustable lengths. The character creator really shines with inclusive options like a wheelchair that converts into a hovercraft over water or during battle, a dozen prosthetic limb options, cochlear implants, heterochromia, alopecia, vitiligo skin patterns, albinism, and more.

As far as gameplay itself, the demo was released on Steam for PC in October of 2021 and allows players to create their character, build a battle party, unlock and collect exotic critters, explore 14 levels, and earn gear that allows even more personal expression. New features in Flamehawk's roadmap include multiplayer modes that not only allow esports style PVP challenging between friends and public matchmaking but plans are in place to allow parents and teachers to be giant raid bosses and battle it out against their kids and students. Also in the pipeline are RPG favorites such as crafting, player living spaces that can be decorated, and a STEM campaign providing a "learning by doing" experience that will teach lessons that can be repeated in the real world.

Flamehawk is also quoted as saying that subscribers will be given a list of approved charitable causes to choose from. Not only will a portion of every subscription be donated to these charities every month, but charity logos can already be found in the character creator with a hotkey that pulls up the charity website to promote traffic for the cause.

Flamehawk Studios, Inc.
973-988-1492
info@flamehawkstudios.com
flamehawkstudios 🄾 f
flamehawkstudio 🄾
flamehawk-studios-inc 🄾
The Mechanical World of Dr. Gearbox ▶

flamehawkstudios.com

SCHELL GAMES

CREATING EXPERIENCES WE'RE PROUD OF, WITH PEOPLE WE LIKE, TO MAKE THE WORLD A BETTER PLACE

In addition to creating original games and learning tools, we count some of the world's most respected brands as clients, including The Walt Disney Company, Google, Facebook, Microsoft, LEGO, Yale University, Universal Studios, Fred Rogers Productions, The Smithsonian Institute, and the US Department of Education.

Our company motto is to create experiences we are proud of, with people we like, to make the world a better place.

We make games strictly for entertainment like *Until You Fall*, a VR sword fighting experience that doubles as a fun and demanding workout, or I *Expect You To Die 2*, the second entry in our VR escape room franchise. Regardless of the intended audience, we work hard to positively impact the people and organizations we serve and make sure they have fun while doing it.

We also aim to show people that educational games can also be entertaining and that VR games are for everybody. We partnered with the University of Pittsburgh to develop a game that reduces diagnostic errors by doctors in the emergency room. We also worked with The Smithsonian National Museum of Natural History and Twin Cities Public Television to create a hands-on, paleontology-based museum exhibit called *Deep Time Detectives.*

However, we couldn't do any of this without the wealth of knowledge, passion, and perspective our employees bring to Schell Games. We live by the principle that "diversity makes us strong." This belief is a core part of our company culture, and it guides the way we create experiences for clients and the gaming public. We embrace diversity because we feel every employee has a voice and that listening to different perspectives leads to lasting change. Studios, organizations, or groups that don't embrace the power of a diverse workforce are missing out. And though we may not have all the answers, we strive to discover the correct answer and act upon it.

Take accessibility, for example. Accessibility in gaming is top of mind when we're developing experiences because if we aspire to create a game with everyone in mind, it expands our potential impact. We created a tool we call "The Accessibility Matrix" that draws from several years of work done at Schell Games. It breaks down accessibility into goals that are then categorized and used to evaluate each project to bring the highest levels of accessibility to our game within scope and budget.

Founded in 2002 by award-winning game designer and author Jesse Schell, Schell Games is the largest full-service educational and entertainment game development company in the United States. We make experiences across various platforms, and we specialize in four vertical areas, including Health and Wellness, Education, Home Entertainment, and Theme Parks and Museums.

Because of this process, we were able to add accessibility options to many of our games. *I Expect You To Die 1 & 2* are seated VR experiences that gamers can play with one hand. *Until You Fall* is a high-energy sword-fighting game with standing and seated play modes (and seated players

don't lose any of the fun). Motion sickness is a significant concern for most people who play VR, so we fine-tune our games to ensure motion sickness is minimized, if not non-existent, for those who tend to suffer from it. From intentional design decisions to groups like our Accessibility Champions, who regularly meet to share best practices and brainstorm solutions, our company culture insists that making games accessible is necessary and achievable.

Creating experiences with everyone in mind wouldn't be authentic if our company culture didn't embrace and support its employees regardless of gender, ethnicity, age, religion, and sexual orientation. We built a recruiting process that draws from the most diverse talent pool possible and employs equitable philosophies and approaches to every aspect of an individual's employment. Some of our methods include:

- Ensuring there isn't gender bias regarding fair pay.
- Actively seeking qualified job candidates outside the games industry norm.
- Developing inclusive teams that enjoy working and communicating with each other during a project's life cycle.

We also work with local advocacy group Vibrant Pittsburgh to expand the breadth and depth of training modules addressing unconscious bias, inclusivity, feedback, and anti-harassment. To date, Schell Games has been a BizJournals Best Place to Work for ten consecutive years, with the most recent achievement being named a 2021 US Best Places to Work by GamesIndustry.Biz, from whom we also received the Diversity Award. The Global Industry Game Awards also nominated Schell Games for our diversity and inclusion efforts.

As we continue to build upon the knowledge, relationships, and creativity that has fueled our studio for the past 19 years and years to come, we look forward to contributing to the growth of the gaming and virtual reality landscape. The power of gaming as a force for good is an idea we firmly believe in, and we're proud to continue growing the space by creating experiences we're proud of, with people we like, to make the world a better place.

Schell Games
SchellGames 🐦 📘 in ▶

schellgames.com

302 INTERACTIVE IS A STUDIO OF GAME DESIGNERS ON A MISSION TO SAVE THE WORLD BY BRIDGING THE GAP BETWEEN ENTERTAINMENT TECHNOLOGY AND REAL-WORLD SOLUTIONS.

EMPOWERING GAME DESIGNERS TO SAVE THE WORLD

Over the last seven years, their mission has been to provide an environment that brings game developers together to build the games of today and the metaverse of tomorrow.

As digital experience developers, 302 Interactive has adopted the best practices of modern game development, product design, lean, and agile methodologies to create a framework to help build metaverse applications across verticals that we call "Everyday Play." From virtual training to education, attractions, and beyond. 302 Interactives' vision to "turn everyday life into a playful experience" is the foundation on which they build digital experiences.

Since the company's founding, 302 Interactive has continued to pioneer in the growing space between games studios and application development and has established itself as a local leader in XR product design and metaverse experiences through its work. Early on, 302 Interactive endeavored to publish their games, but the focus shifted as they continued to find inspiration in the real-world application of 3D real-time game engines and emerging technologies like augmented reality and virtual reality. The team saw an opportunity for the principles of game design and the talents of game developers to be applied to real-world solutions. 302 actively engaged with various industries to identify complex problems that could be solved using the engines to build the most prominent games. In that, the "starving artists" and indies of the games industry could also apply their skills to more than just entertainment.

Today, 302 Interactive operates at the intersection of games, technology, and human experience to "save the world" and empower others to further develop this budding subset of the technology and games industry. Its headquarters in sunny Orlando, Florida, put it at the center of a growing sector in the area. Central Florida is a growing destination for simulation and training. It also features some of the most highly awarded and largest (by enrollment) universities that specialize in teaching game design and real-time 3D development principles. With that, 302 has helped build the local community over the past several years by sponsoring events and pushing initiatives to help support professional development and hiring professionals in the industry.

The industry in which 302 operates is still taking shape; once called digital experience, the term metaverse technology has become a common term to describe the realm 302 inhabits. On the horizon, 302 sees an opportunity to help shape the industry and support its growth by developing an ecosystem for the next generation of companies and developers to contribute to the broadening "metaverse" industry.

302 Interactive
collaborate@302llc.com
407-900-5967
302llc
302interactive

302interactive.com

Freestyle Trampoline
A s s o c i a t i o n

WORLD'S FIRST 3D TRAMPOLINE SIMULATOR
TRAMPOLINE AND GYMNASTICS 'JUMP' INTO ESPORTS
FOR THE FIRST TIME!

Pro Flipper™
#GRT

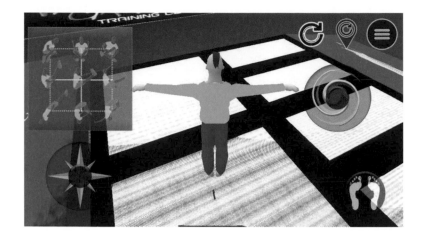

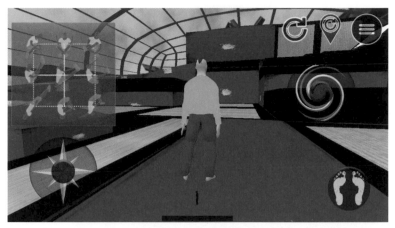

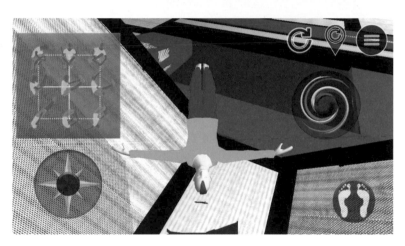

GRT Pro Flipper is a brand new Mobile Trampoline Simulator that takes trampoline to the next level. All other trampoline-based apps on the App stores are all based on simpler 2D game play that does not truly match what a trampolinist actually does in the air at the Olympics.

Developed by the Freestyle Trampoline Association (FTA), an internationally recognized acrobatic brand, Pro Flipper is already turning heads internationally. When the FTA announced they were going to bring acrobatics into the Esports Industry, the Global Esports Federation (GEF) quickly made them an official Federation Member.

Esports as an industry is trying to get into the Olympics and in the Tokyo Olympics it finally happened which means Esports is taking a huge step forward on the world's largest sports stage. With it the FTA believes their Mobile 3D Trampoline Simulator along with one of their Gymnastics PC games can officially bring acrobatics into this booming industry.

Traditionally most Esports are Battle-Royale or First Person Shooter based games. The Olympics is currently only accepting games that are based on real-world sports such as Cycling and Rowing.

This puts the FTA in a great position to be pioneers of both the acrobatic industry by creating an entirely new "Freestyle" version as well as the Esports industry all in one swoop. The FTA has already created dozens of acrobatic Esports teams in Pro Flipper and have started doing smaller Esports competitions in cooperation with their live events. The FTA has made it clear that they plan on using video games to inspire non-acrobats to embrace acrobatics through playing their various games.

There are many members of society who would love to jump on a trampoline or swing around a high bar but for one reason or another are unable to do so. The FTA says that opening up acrobatics to Esports fans will be a great way to target individuals who normally do not get to experience flips and spins on a daily basis.

The FTA will be developing many educational programs within the various acrobatic apps that can be used as an educational tool for real live sports as well. With many great in-game updates, new game concepts and many great partners all over the world, the FTA is a young but hungry association who is one to watch for in years to come in both the Esports industry and the Acrobatic Industry.

FREESTYLE TRAMPOLINE ASSOCIATION

FreestyleTrampolineAssociation.com

inGearProductions.com

TrampolineCoaching.com

GymnasticseSportsOfficial.com

TheRoeShow.com

TheBounceLife.com

GRTProFlipper.com

Innovators rarely consider themselves to be pioneers within their own industry.

And Andrew Augustin is a prime example of this axiom.

Augustin is a graphic designer who, in 2011, founded Notion Games, an Austin-based video gaming company that creates games for people of all ages.

But that brief description fails to mention that Augustin's a self-taught pioneer in the field of gaming who is recognized for being an innovator in the video gaming industry.

When HTML5 technology was released, Augustin was one of the first of the bigger video game designers to use the platform to create video games.

Although HTML5 wasn't really intended for gaming when it was first released, Augustin saw its potential. While some were using it for smaller games and prototypes, Augustin used the platform to make a full length, console-style game.

Being in a previously unoccupied space, and utilizing that technology in such a unique way, provided valuable exposure for Augustin.

It allowed a lot of eyes to see his projects since many people were exploring what HTML5 was and what it could do in the gaming space.

Over the past 10 years, Augustin has created several video games playable on various video gaming consoles.

Super Ubie Island 1 is a game that pays homage to video games from the 1990s and is available on the PC platform called Steam. Augustin took elements of a variety of games from the '90s and mixed them together to create this unique game.

Sheep Herder Nay is a puzzle game that was previously online but it is now back in development for a much broader release. This game allows sheep herder Nay to lead her sheep herd to paradise and requires the player to take a strategic approach since each sheep has a different background and, therefore, a different influence on the game.

Up, Up Ubie is a free game that can be played online via HTML5 technology and is also currently undergoing a much broader development for wider release.

A fourth game, Team Notion, first developed in 2008-09, serves as proof of his innovative mindset. The three heroes in this game are women whose backgrounds are African American, Asian and Latino. Video game characters who are female and people of color were a rare commodity in the early 2000s and Augustin broke new ground in using members from those demographics as his protagonists.

The near absence of female heroes in gaming at that time also reflected the dearth of African American game developers in the industry. Augustin was one of the first African Americans to make the Forbes list of the top 30 under 30 in their magazine's gaming section.

A GAME BY ANDREW AUGUSTIN

With so few people of color in the industry at that time, Augustin stepped aside for three years to teach animation design at a minority majority high school in Houston. That experience led Augustin to decide to develop online courses for young people who can't afford college to nurture their creative talents while they learn independently, just like he did.

An online course he is constructing via Notion Digital Arts Academy is but one of a number of innovations on the drawing board for the graphic designer. Notion Games is also entering other entertainment-oriented avenues that utilize Augustin's talent for graphic design and his love of animation.

Augustin recently signed a deal that has allowed him to expand his company from four to nine people. The deal permits him to have access to resources to "recreate, re-release and remarket" his existing video games while creating new ones.

In addition to finishing Ubie Island 2 for XBOX, Notion Games is also developing an animated comic book series called Middle Skool. The show is about a diverse group of children in an urban setting who are making that always awkward transition from childhood to young adult. Middle Skool is

a show with plenty of diversity about individuals growing up in an urban environment, and represents all colors as well as characters of different shapes and sizes.

With an eye for design for video gaming and animation, an innovative mindset, and development deals in the works, Notion Games is a company on the rise.

Notion Games
andrewa@notiongames.com

notiongamesllc 🐦
notiongamesllc 📷
nin10drew 📷

notiongames.com

CHAPTER 5

INCUBATORS & INVESTORS

LEADER

*"If our lives are already written,
it would take a courageous man to
change the script."*

— EZIO, 'ASSASSIN'S CREED: REVELATIONS'.

STRA

ACCELERATE YOUR GAME DEVELOPMENT

We are dedicated to finding talented game startups around the world.

CREATIVE, SUSTAINABLE FUTURES

GTR is an interactive accelerator program dedicated to supporting independent studios from all over the world. With the development, publishing and fundraising expertise they need to take their content global and towards a more sustainable business.

The interactive era is upon us. Independent developers all over the world are creating exciting content, but often lack the reach or expertise to evaluate their product-region fit or identify the publishing partners they need to launch in a new region.

Through the GTR acceleration program, new studios with great content will receive both funding and the help they need to improve their games and identify & negotiate with potential publishers from all over the world. GTR selects up to 10 games annually for the program, which provides funding, game development, culturalization support, global publisher exposure, fundraising assistance and an extensive global network of professionals to give them the feedback they need to take their studios and projects to the next level.

GLOBAL NETWORK

We want studios to be able to focus on their games and give them access to global expertise. At GTR, we make sure that independent studios can get the insights they need to bring their games to new markets all over the world.

FUNDRAISING AND PARTNERSHIPS

GTR has funding partners who are constantly searching for great content. After receiving funding and graduating from the GTR accelerator, the best performing of our top 10 studios will have a chance to receive proper investment at a reasonable valuation, helping them to grow and focus on making great games.

GLOBAL PUBLISHER NETWORK

Game studios should focus on games! We'll leverage our global network of publishers to help studios identify partners in the markets for which their content is best suited.

Global Top Round
pontus@globaltopround.com
(+46) 721-822181
globaltopround in f 🐦

globaltopround.com

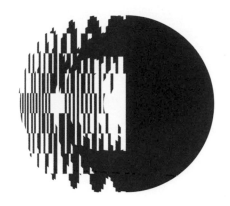

Dreamcraft

We are hands-on venture engineers who support dreamers and crafters building legendary companies.

At Dreamcraft, we invest in European tech-driven companies from pre-seed to series A. We are generalists with a proven track record in iGaming, Gaming, esports, D2C, B2B SaaS and decarbonization. We believe success is created by a team of dreamers and crafters - and we are venture engineers who help the two. The right founders love our engagements that go deeper than just advice.

The Founding partners of Dreamcraft, Jesper Søgaard and Christian Kirk Rasmussen, have co-founded and still manage the company Better Collective A/S.

Jesper and Christian have crafted the company all the way from a two-bedroom apartment startup in 2004 to IPO in 2018 without raising funding from investors and in early 2021 the market cap passed 1bn USD. Jesper and Christian is a great example of a founder team in true Dreamcraft style where you can think of Jesper as the dreamer and Christian as the crafter.

Founder teams that hold both dreamer and crafter capabilities are the type of teams we like and look for.

Eventually, Jesper and Christian became angel investors and one of their investments was in TrunkBird where Daniel Mariussen was one of the founders. They were Daniel's first investors and their startup-investor relationship is what we want to replicate to our founder engagements. After TrunkBird closed down, Daniel was looped into Jesper and Christian's angel setup, which eventually evolved into a traditional VC firm. We have raised $35m for our first fund, and have invested in 19 companies. Furthermore, we have grown into a team of 9 and Carsten Salling became General Partner in Dreamcraft in 2021. We expect to launch a second fund of $70-90m early 2022.

Our mission is to amplify dreams and help entrepreneurs turn dreams into reality. We are all about supporting talented founders and act as an

GRID

innovation enabler through close engagement with founders who are building the businesses of the future. The Dreamcraft team holds an impressive record of learnings from founder experiences from Better Collective, TrunkBird and our portfolio companies. Therefore, we want to make sure that the founders we support do not make the same mistakes as we did. By providing our portfolio companies with knowledge and sharing experiences, we aim to enable entrepreneurs to be innovators.

After nearly 10 years as investors in gaming and esports, there are several reasons for why we are excited about the industry.

First of all, we believe that it is a huge market that will only continue to grow – today over 50% of the global population are millennials and generation Z. Those generations are born in a digital environment with games in the epicenter of their lifestyles.

Secondly, gaming has evolved to more than just the games themselves – it has extended to community, entertainment, as well as social, for the players behind the screens. We see tremendous potential for startups that extend their focus to the social and community elements, and this opens up for exciting investment opportunities. Innovation sparks ways of including the community all the way from production for gaming and esports startups. One of them, Hiber allows for self-expression through user-generated content and the community element is present in edutainment with GamerzClass, as a great example. We think this is just the beginning of how social and community will be included.

With esports, gaming has become a complete entertainment experience, even surpassing some of the major sports leagues around the world in terms of viewership. Esports is however also much more complex than traditional sports with constant server changes, updated content, new gaming IPs, etc, why data is becoming the missing commodity everyone in and around the industry needs. We see great potential in businesses tackling the infrastructure side of things, and GRID esports is a great example of this.

In addition, technology advancements have accelerated the ability to build gaming companies fast and paved the way for new use cases, and new ways to monetize. We are excited to see how NFTs and blockchain technology will influence gaming and esports in the future.

Dreamcraft Ventures
hello@dreamcraft.vc
dreamcraftventures in M

dreamcraft.vc

THE MIX BIOGRAPHY AND IMPACT

The Media Indie Exchange (The MIX) is a platform all about celebrating amazing games and the diverse creators who make them. The organization was started by indie developers for indie developers worldwide in order to provide grassroots networking showcase opportunities to help further their success at a time where it was challenging for developers to find their place in the culture and market. The goal for The MIX was for creators to get press visibility through gaming media outlets such as IGN, Kotaku, Polygon, Gamespot, etc. to bridge the gap between developers and investors, publishers and platform holders such as Microsoft, Sony, Nintendo and to provide a safe place where the amazing developers can connect with each other and other industry professionals.

The MIX initially started out as an untitled, underground networking showcase held in the cafeteria at IGN headquarters in San Francisco during the 2012 Game Developers Conference (GDC). The event was organized by Justin Woodward the co-founder of the indie game studio Interabang Entertainment who was also managing the Gamespy/IGN Indie Open house accelerator. PR consultant and professional games writer, John Polson (Humble Games) also jumped on board, helping to reach press outlets and developers who were looking to find alternative productive opportunities to GDC parties, which typically were laden with loud music, and alcohol. The first event was a success, featuring over 30 games and hosting a myriad of press, publishers, and industry professional guests. Folks such as Namco, Capcom, PlayStation, Xbox, Ubisoft, and more were all present, some of which signed games.

In anticipation of GDC 2013, Woodward decided to start prep on the second showcase, naming it The Media Indie Exchange, The MIX for short as well as branded the event, designing the logo, general aesthetic and the website in order to make things official. The second event was more organized and structured this time around while still keeping the organic flavor and hosting it at IGN HQ. Devs, Press, publishers, and industry professionals signed up for the showcase and the night of the event the word went out and people were lined up around the block to get into IGN. This event cemented The MIX as one of the main events to be a part of during the GDC season, this event opened up opportunities for future events and the growth of The MIX in general.

After the first branded event, The MIX expanded to having a rooftop showcase during GDC Next, and partnered experienced former Lucasarts and Telltale Games marketer, Joel Dreskin after working with CG convention organizers, Siggraph on a showcase in Vancouver, and then set up events at E3 in which The MIX hosted larger indie titles and partnered with companies like Unity3D, Intel, Nintendo, Unreal, Playstation, and Xbox to amplify the developers and showcase their games to larger forums. Through the expansion, the team started organizing and producing events at Evo in Las Vegas and PAX West in Seattle annually.

The MIX has been an intercontinental front-facing event from day one, hosting thousands of global guests and sharing hundreds of international developer's games each year. The international showing increased brand awareness and a demand to produce events overseas. The first international showcase the MIX team produced was in 2015 with Unity3D in Amsterdam at their Unite Europe event, followed by working with the Taiwanese government for a MIX event for the Taipei Game Developer Forum (TGDF). In 2019 the team traveled to Kyoto Japan to team up with partner John Davis and the other co-founders of BitSummit for their VIP press party and ended the year in Cologne Germany for the VIP indie Gamescom event.

The evolution of the MIX has gone from being focused on in-person press events to developing additional marketing strategies to include

broadcasting collaborations and partnerships with Twitch, IGN, and Gamespot on-site and in their studios in order to produce video content and amplify the voices of developers. This experience has transitioned from 4 years of broadcasting production at live shows and pivoting to in-house production during the pandemic leading to the creation of an online press event called the Guerrilla Collective, where The MIX partnered with Kinda Funny, Raw Fury, Larian, Paradox, Humble Games, Good Shepherd, Sega, PlayStation, Xbox/Microsoft, Twitch, IGN, Gamespot, and others as an alternative to E3. The Guerrilla collective ended up becoming one of the most watched gaming events during the summer of 2020 and 2021 and led to a myriad of other online showcases cultivating millions of views.

During the production of the Guerrilla Collective the tragedies of Breonna Taylor and George Floyd exploded into civil unrest shaking the world. With very few Black executives participating in publishing and broadcasting in the game industry, MIX Co-Founder Justin Woodward was distraught by the responses in partnership meetings as he was often the only black executive on the response calls. Forward thinking publisher Raw Fury recognized this and helped to fund the support of an event that The MIX founded, called Black Voices in Gaming which was a showcase that shed light on Black Game Developers who were making a splash in the industry. Black Voices in Gaming has since evolved into a non-profit organization accompanying The MIX and Guerrilla Collective showcases

since 2020, sparked a community and culture of Black Game Developers that can support each other's movement.

Justin Woodward's Bio

With a mixture of over 12 years of independent and AAA development and production experience and a master's in Game Production and Management, Justin Woodward Co-founded and directs an independent game studio, Interabang Entertainment as well as The Media Indie Exchange (The MIX) which is an organization that helps to elevate indie developers' visibility and business opportunities through exclusive indie showcases online and in-person worldwide. Being involved in the development scene has also lead him into the role as a lead advisor with Humble Bundle on the Humble Black Game Developer Fund as well as a consultant for the investment/crowdfunding platform Fig, IGN Prime, and has helped organize the IGN Indie Open House and Double Fine Indie spaces.

Media Indie Exchange
ICJMAN 🐦
indieexchange 🐦
mediaindieexchange 📷

mediaindieexchange.com

*"Hope is what makes us strong.
It is why we are here. It is what we
fight with when all else is lost."*

— GOD OF WAR 3

CHAPTER 6
BUSINESS SERVICES

Smith
Gambrell
Russell

SGRLAW.COM

Smith Gambrell Russell

A FULL-SERVICE LAW FIRM REPRESENTING THE BUSINESS NEEDS OF OUR CLIENTS IN THE ENTERTAINMENT ECOSYSTEM.

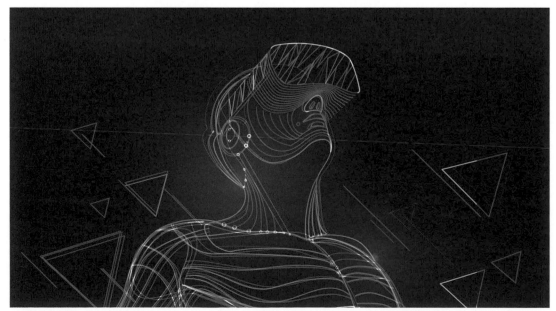

Smith, Gambrell & Russell, LLP's (SGR) entertainment practice includes legal practitioners specializing in intellectual property protection, technology, corporate transactional, tax, and real estate matters.

The Firm's founders began practicing law more than 125 years ago to commit to excellence and attract a wide array of talent dedicated to serving our clients and communities.

The Firm serves as an enabler to gaming companies seeking to innovate and stand out from the market through our intellectual property, emerging company, and disruptive technology practices. Our

intellectual property practice helps emerging companies and founders protect inventions, creative work, products, and design through patent, licensing, copyright, trademark, and trade secrets services.

We also provide technology solutions in the fast-paced industry, including content licensing, licensing of software and technology, venture capital/private equity financings, development and collaboration agreements.

SGR Labs is an innovation team comprised of legal practitioners, engineers, and software developers. We partner with software developers and thought leaders in the legal industry to develop and provide practical legal solutions in a quickly evolving legal landscape. SGR Labs provides a platform for research and collaboration across practice groups, has three initial mandates:

1. Software Implementation: Procurement, development, and education in software ensure SGR attorneys and clients are efficiently leveraging technology in their practice.

2. Data Analytics: Collection and analysis of practice information to better understand how practices and procedures overlap with client value.

3. Automation: Leveraging artificial intelligence, human-machine interfacing, and a new age assembly line to provide the highest quality legal work product in a cost/time-sensitive environment.

Smith, Gambrell & Russell .LLP
Michael J. Riesen, Partner
Atlanta - 404-815-3510
London - +44 (0)20 7084 9262
mriesen@sgrlaw.com
1105 W. Peachtree St. NE | Suite 1000 | Atlanta, GA 30309
London: Birchin Court, 20 Birchin Lane, London, EC3V 9DU

sgrlaw.com

"PERSEVERANCE IS ONE OF OUR GREATEST STRENGTHS, EVEN IF THERE ARE OBSTACLES, WE ARE ABLE TO PUSH OURSELVES FORWARD AND REACH OUR GOALS".

SEAN MENDEZ CATLIN, MANAGING PARTNER, MC & J LAW

Sean Méndez-Catlin is the 1Up Lawyer, giving you a 1Up on the competition and an extra life. He has been playing games since he was a Kid. He started with the N64 and has continued to play as he went through school and now as an attorney. Listening to his mother, Lois, he decided to take this passion and base his business around it.

Sean spends the evenings he is not working playing anything from NBA 2k19 to Red Dead Redemption 2 to Octodad. Sean earned his Bachelors Degree in sociology from the University of Pennsylvania in 2012 and his Law Degree from the University of Miami School of Law. Sean also earned his Masters in Music Business from The University of Miami's Frost School of Music. During his Undergraduate and Legal education, Sean had a large focus on business, minority inclusion and video games. As a Senior he studied multiple games racial depictions and spoke with developers to glean the justification for those depictions.

Sean also learned about business and intellectual property while he completed his Business and Legal Studies minor through The Wharton School of Business at UPenn. Sean continued his interest during his time at UM, where he completed a Masters in Music Business with UM's Frost School of Music. Sean began his legal career at the State Attorney's Office for the Ninth Judicial Circuit in Orlando Florida. With over three years experience at the Office, Sean handled thousands of cases from start to completion. Sean prosecuted simple possession,

battery, misdemeanor traffic, burglaries, firearm cases, and drug trafficking cases. He was awarded the 2017 MADD DUI Prosecutor award of Excellence for Central Florida. However, in 2018, he realized that he was not taking advantage of that passion and after speaking with his mother started MC & J Law, PLLC with his law partner, Sabrina Jadunandan. He took on the mantle of the 1Up Lawyer and focused his practice on esports, video games, content creation, and other forms of digital media entertainment. He currently represents many small businesses and start-ups as well as indie developers and content creators.

Sean believes that "Perseverance is one of our greatest strengths, even if there are obstacles, we are able to push ourselves forward and reach our goals." The firm's one year anniversary was maligned by the start of the pandemic. Relying on digital means, Sean continued to meet people in the industry and furthered his involvement with the academia of the esports and gaming industry authoring multiple articles and evaluating new legislation as a member of the Esports Bar Association (EBA). He spoke at GDC 2021 on a panel about diversity and was a chair of the Intellectual Property committee of the Orange County Bar Association as well as a co-chair of the events committee of the Esports Bar Association. Sean prides himself on pushing for more minority inclusion in the industry. "Diversity forces change, which, as a result, forces innovation!"

MC & J Law, PLLC
407-476-7224
sean@mcandjlaw.com
mcandjlaw 🅵
mcandjlawyers 🅾
Sean Mendez-Catlin (The 1Up Lawyer) 🅻

Mcandjlaw.com

Quiles Law

Quiles Law is one of the world's first esports and gaming focused law firms. Based in New York City and founded by Roger Quiles in 2014, Roger merged his interest in sports and video games to focus the firm on the then nascent esports industry in 2015.

Our firm represents a global clientele of individuals and businesses operating within the esports and gaming industries. The firm's clients include two of the largest esports news media platforms, international teams, world champion players, influential content creators, professional athletes, and the many kinds of businesses who service the space. Our industry-wide focus provides a broad perspective and deep understanding to the many different kinds of transactions that our clients are engaging in, which in turn allows us to provide more effective legal solutions.

POWERLEVELING ESPORTS BUSINESSES AND TALENT SINCE 2015, WE ARE A BUSINESS-FORWARD LAW FIRM FOR THE GLOBAL ESPORTS AND GAMING INDUSTRIES.

Quiles Law is one of the few law firms who are privileged to have represented both an esports and traditional sports clientele. Our practice has assisted professional athletes in their esports and gaming initiatives and advised professional sports teams with respect to planned esports ventures.

Our firm is committed to assisting to foster the development of a more diverse, equitable, and inclusive esports and gaming industry. Accordingly, Quiles Law serves as counsel to Latinx in Gaming, the award-winning nonprofit, to assist with its mission. Roger also serves on Latinx in Gaming's board of directors.

Quiles Law leads with its deep understanding of the business of the esports and gaming industries to provide tailored legal solutions for our clients. As the esports and gaming industries sit at the crossroads of many legal verticals, Quiles Law's work is inherently interdisciplinary. We regularly advise clients on commercial, business, entertainment, corporate, intellectual property, igaming, mergers & acquisitions, and sports law issues.

In 2015, recognizing that many of the individuals creating esports organizations lacked basic business law knowledge, Quiles Law published The Little Legal Handbook for Esports Teams to serve as a reference guide. In 2019, recognizing that the esports industry had matured since the ebook's initial release, we published the Second Edition of the ebook to update the content and include information about basic mergers & acquisition topics. The Little Legal Handbook for Esports Teams remains one of the few, if not only, compiled legal resources for esports organizations.

Internationally recognized as a pioneer of esports law, Quiles Law is regularly invited to speak at conferences across the world regarding esports and regularly serves as a consultant for overseas individuals and businesses seeking to operate in the esports and gaming space.

Quiles Law
roger@esports.law
917 477 7942
rogerquiles 🐦
quileslaw 🐦
rogerquiles 🔗
quiles-law 🔗

esports.law

ONWARD PLAY

WE PUT GAMING TALENT TO WORK

Onward Play is a nationwide game staffing agency specializing in freelance and direct hire. Onward Play's niche is linking up creative, technical and production talent with incredible game, XR, and esports studios.

Onward Play recruits talent for segments like PC, Console, Mobile, VR, AR, XR, esports, toys, casino and tabletop. The benefit to working with Onward Play is we are well connected within the gaming industry. We're aware of the gaming talent that is

looking for work before they hit the market or even start applying. When you work with us, you are tapping into our database of highly qualified AAA gaming professionals, industry veterans, disrupters, and the next generation of game makers.

Onward Play is an innovator in the game staffing space because we invest heavily in diversity sourcing techniques. We have relationships with various gaming associations, nonprofits, and conferences such as Women in Games, ESTA, GAMA, IGDA, Esports Business Network, and more. We can tap into their networks to identify passive talent or pockets of D&I game professional communities. We also have back-channeled marketing and social strategies focused on diverse job boards, HBCU's, social media platforms, clubs, and networking groups. Due to our focus and relationships, we can assist game studios with hiring the top game makers they need to ensure their IPs are on time, on budget, well maintained, and successful. We also have the ability to find direct-hire, project-based, or freelance talent to staff any gaming needs that our studio clients have.

Kimberly Shatzer, Managing Director

Onward Play
40 Danbury Rd, Wilton, CT 06897
213-433-3097
info@onwardplay.com

onwardplay.com

THE **JACOBSON** FIRM, P.C.
ATTORNEYS AT LAW

The Jacobson Firm, P.C. strives to provide industry leading legal services for the entertainment, esports and video gaming industries that are both cost efficient and highly effective.

The Jacobson Firm, P.C. is an intellectual property, entertainment and esports business law firm located in New York City. The Firm handles all domestic and international trademarks, copyrights, and licensing matters for companies and entertainment influencers. They provide services to the esports, video game, music, and entertainment industries, as well as in the sports, fashion, television, motion pictures, jewelry, and visual arts worlds. The Jacobson Firm, P.C. works with professional athletes, musicians, DJs, music producers, record labels, talent managers, fashion designers, professional gamers, streamers, esports coaches, casters and esports teams. Growing up in the music business with a life-long passion for video games, Justin M. Jacobson, Esq., esports and entertainment attorney at The Jacobson Firm, P.C., started on his professional voyage through various internships in the entertainment space. This included stops at MTV,

ASCAP, and the U.S. Copyright Office, all the while, gaming had always been a part of his social interaction and overall daily life. Justin's passion started at an early age with Nintendo and grew into SEGA Genesis, N64; and then, eventually, becoming a daily player of Xbox and now PS4. In addition, he has been a life-long StarCraft and StarCraft II player while also growing in the entertainment space. After college and law school, Mr. Jacobson embarked on his professional journey as an entertainment attorney working with musicians, producers, songwriters, and; eventually, expanding into sports, art, and fashion worlds.

A few years later, he grew into the esports scene. Justin initially began working on the business and legal side of the industry where he has negotiated millions of dollars in professional gamer contracts and has

worked with professional gamers, streamers, coaches, casters, teams, and brands in the space in most major esports titles and with most of the largest esports organizations across the world. Justin has gone on to author the first esports business law textbook, "The Essential Guide to the Business & Law of Esports & Professional Video Gaming" and begun teaching esports business courses at University of North Carolina Wilmington, among other higher educational institutions. The sky is the limit, and the story is just getting started for The Jacobson Firm, P.C. and Justin M. Jacobson, Esq. The Jacobson Firm, P.C. is uniquely positioned as both an innovator as well as an innovation enabler. The Firms acts as innovators through its establishment and global growth of its world-class esports and video-game legal and business law firm. They were one of the first firms working in the space on the East Coast and one of the initial ones to expand from traditional entertainment, music, and sports into the esports realm. In addition, by fusing practical entertainment industry experience and extensive business and intellectual property knowledge, The Jacobson Firm, P.C. has provided new perspectives and insight in the contract negotiations on behalf of its client in the space and they have begun revolutionizing the existing agreement structure. In addition, The Jacobson Firm, P.C. acts as innovation enablers by helping and advising innovators on the best practices to achieve their goals in the right and legal way.

This includes advising these individuals and companies on the proper legal and business structuring, such as LLC and corporations, on intellectual property protections, including copyrights, trademarks, and patents, as well as any other relevant legal and business consideration that must be examined when operating an innovative venture. We have been one of the first law firms to begin building up the East Coast esports and video game professional scene. This was done to be a more natural bridge for transactions and communications between European countries and the U.S. as well as being able to smoothly interact and conduct business with the rest of North America and other neighboring nations. We are also able to identify and understand the new trends and where pop culture will move as we sit at the center of the culture aligned with music, fashion, sports, and art as they merge into the gaming space. We are excited about the next clients we sign and the next talent that we work with. We are always looking forward to expanding our imprint and getting more viewers and readers on our content. It will be amazing to see how the esports scene continues to grow, especially in the non-professional scenes and in the ancillary professional careers. The Jacobson Firm, P.C. are very

excited about the future growth of high school, college and recreational esports and our position within these worlds as industry leading educators, curriculum innovators and talent advisors to the professional gaming world's top innovators.

The Jacobson Firm, P.C
212-683-2001
justin@jacobsonfirm.com
jacobsonfirm 🐦
justinjesq 🐦 📷
justinmjacobson 💼
thejacobsonfirmpc 📘
justinmjacobson 📘

thejacobsonfirmpc.com
esportslaw.biz

espat®

CHANGING THE WORLD, ONE PIXEL AT A TIME.

Dante Simpson (L), Mario Prosperino and Ed Brooks (R) are the co-founders of ESPAT

ESPAT (Esports Pixels and Technology) is a technology company that is utilizing the legacy digital media licensing model to help gaming and esports IP holders monetize their digital assets. Through computer vision and machine learning technology, the company is converting traditional licensed assets into interactive, commerce-enabled experiences for viewers / consumers. As the first photo and video licensing platform dedicated solely to the gaming and esports industry, ESPAT has photographed the biggest esports events around the world, with its images generating more than one billion impressions globally. ESPAT's global distribution partnerships with gaming organizations like Riot Games, Misfits Gaming and Talon Esports provide an opportunity for content owners to scale the consumption of their content. With its content commerce offering, ESPAT is disrupting the legacy licensing model, shifting from licensing pixels to licensing commerce and consumer data. In doing so, the company is arming licensees (editorial outlets, brand marketers and independent content creators) with the tools to generate new advertising and affiliate marketing revenues through their platforms.

ESPAT was founded in 2018 by Ed Brooks, Mario Prosperino and Dante Simpson, each of whom bring a unique perspective from across the creative, licensing and sports/entertainment landscape. Ed Brooks is the visionary of ESPAT, with a strong background in design, technology and innovation at companies like WPP and the NFL. He is driving the future of ESPAT's growth as Chief Product Officer. Mario Prosperino is a digital media licensing veteran, having spent more than 20 years at Getty Images and AP Photo, building and managing licensing partnerships with properties such as NASCAR and the NFL. Today he serves as ESPAT's Chief Revenue Officer. Dante Simpson brings a wealth of business development and marketing experience from his previous career at blue chip companies like Sony BMG and The Gucci Group. He now leads ESPAT's marketing efforts as CMO. Finally, Matt Hill joined the team as

CEO in February of 2021, after 20 years in the sports and entertainment world with the NFL, Major League Soccer and GMR Marketing. Matt's background in business development, partnerships, marketing strategy and communications will help ESPAT achieve new heights. Together, they are carrying out ESPAT's mission to unite the world, one pixel at a time.

ESPAT
espatmedia 🐦 📷

espat.ai

"We learn through play... The games we play on computers, consoles, and phones are simply the newest iteration of how we have used games to teach and learn for thousands of years."

— ESA & HEVGA

CHAPTER 7

GAMING: GREAT FOR SCHOOL

FOREWORD

We learn through play. Whether it's chess, playing with dolls, or a digital game of solitaire, play inspires critical thinking, creativity, and connection. For children, play shapes and improves their social and psychological development. It is an important and necessary way for them to experiment with the world.

Each game we play teaches different lessons. Chess, for example, emphasizes planning, problem solving, and complex thinking. Playing with dolls emphasizes imagination and role playing. Board and card games can teach strategy. Memory games can teach facts. Storytelling games help children remember and appreciate the past and connect with shared cultural and collective experiences. The games we play on computers, consoles, and phones are simply the newest iteration of how we have used games to teach and learn for thousands of years.

Teachers use video games in their classrooms to help students think through creative approaches to complex problems. These practices promote the development of digital skills and competencies in this important media form. Understanding how teachers use games in the classroom and how students learn through play will inform educators and policy makers in developing a curriculum that positions students for success after graduation.

Our organizations believe in the power of video games. This report represents a unique collaboration between HEVGA and the ESA to explore and highlight the important role of video games in today's educational ecosystem.

It carefully examines current practices and trends regarding the important contributions that teachers are making through the use of games in the K-12 environments of today and tomorrow.

Through playing and creating games, students develop problem-solving skills, promote critical thinking, and create meaningful relationships with their peers. Virtual worlds help students learn about the real world. They learn through play.

- **Andrew Phelps**, *President, Higher Education Video Game Alliance*

- **Stanley Pierre-Louis**, *President & Chief Executive Officer, Entertainment Software Association*

"Nothing brings out kids' thinking better than gameplay."

— MIDDLE SCHOOL SCIENCE TEACHER

EXECUTIVE SUMMARY

Video games are ubiquitous. In the United States alone, nearly 227 million people play games every week, and video game revenues reached nearly $57 billion in 2020 according to NPD. Worldwide, there are three billion video game players, and global revenues reached nearly $180 billion in 2020 according to Newzoo. Video games are not, however, just a source of entertainment. Increasingly, video games are becoming valuable tools across a broad range of sectors, from healthcare to industry to education.

The use of video games in the classroom is not surprising considering that 80 percent of Americans believe that video games can serve an educational purpose. As described in the ESA's 2021 Essential Facts About the Video Game Industry report, most Americans believe that video games can improve both cognitive and creative skills. Our report underscores these same potentials.

This report outlines how today's teachers are using video games in schools from kindergarten to grade 12. The report is written for a general audience that is interested in the uses of video games to augment the K-12 learning environment. It is based on an extensive review of academic literature on video games in K-12 education and draws on in-depth interviews with experienced teachers on their use of video games to extend and enhance student learning. These teachers work in public, charter, and independent schools in big cities, suburbs, and towns across the country. They teach chemistry, physics, math, history, English language arts, Spanish, and a host of other subjects. They use big budget games, free mobile games, text adventure games, game engines, and more.

This report finds several important, high-level benefits to the use of video games in education:

- **Video games create networks of playful learning,** which facilitates increased engagement;

- **Video games meet students where they are**, which connects students to the educational material;

- **Video games enhance problem-solving skills,** which enables students to work within systems and make meaningful choices; and

- **Video games help teachers accommodate different learners,** which provides students opportunities to engage with materials at their own speed and in their own way.

When utilized in schools, video games provide real, tangible benefits to the education process in the classroom and beyond:

- **Video games are dynamic**, which gives teachers opportunities to tie current events to curricular objectives;

- **Video games promote engagement and resilience,** which improves students' attitudes towards learning, as well as increases social and emotional well-being inside and outside the classroom;

- **Video games stimulate collaboration,** which promotes leadership and cooperation opportunities within the school;

- **Video games develop technical skills,** which offers students new career pathways in game design and development; and

- **Video games encourage participation,** which generates opportunities for students who do not otherwise participate in extracurricular activities through games clubs and esports.

The report concludes with a discussion of how teachers have successfully integrated games into their teaching and their recommendations for anyone interested in games as educational tools.

2021 ESSENTIAL FACTS

ABOUT THE VIDEO GAME INDUSTRY

Millions
a sense

There are
227 mi
players across all

Games provide entertainment and stress relief

90%
of players say video
games bring joy
through play

87%
say video games provide
mental stimulation

87%
say video games
provide stress relief

77%
play with others online or
in-person at least weekly
(up from 65% in 2020)

74%
of parents play games with their children
at least weekly (up from 55% in 2020)

+ Data Source: The ESA's *2021 Essential Facts about the Video Game Industry*
Learn more at https://www.theesa.com/resource/2021-essential-facts-
about-the-video-game-industry/

eople find joy, connection and
elonging through video games

n the US

The average video game player is

31 years old

ACROSS ALL PLAYERS & AGES

55% **45**%

Identify as male   Identify as female

And during the pandemic, games were a
welcome break and a source of connection

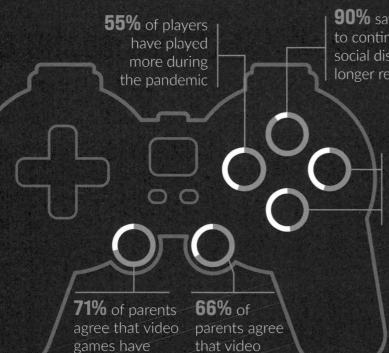

55% of players have played more during the pandemic

90% say they are likely to continue playing after social distancing is no longer required

For players during the pandemic, video games have been a welcome source of stress relief (**55%**) and distraction (**48%**)

71% of parents agree that video games have been a much-needed break for their child

66% of parents agree that video games made the transition to distance learning easier

esa entertainment software association

BEYOND THE CLASSROOM
Game Clubs and Esports

Learning occurs at a nexus of interest, relationships, and opportunities. Students who feel connected to their school do better in school. Extracurricular activities such as esports and game clubs provide authentic learning opportunities that can improve literacy, skill acquisition, and peer cohesion.

Even without specific pedagogical goals, design clubs, game jams, and student groups that focus on simply playing games can also bring students together and promote social cohesion. Coding clubs for girls, for example, can lessen anxiety about participation in STEM-related disciplines, providing students an alternate avenue for success in disciplines from which they have traditionally been excluded.

Esports is a growing cultural phenomenon that benefits many K-12 students. One of the oldest and most popular competitive games is League of Legends (2009), which has over 115 million active monthly players worldwide. In recent years, the number of people who watched the various League of Legends World Championships has exceeded the number of people who watch the final game of the NBA Finals, the World Series final, and the Stanley Cup finals combined. The esports industry includes not just athletes and coaches, but also managers, sponsors, physical location staff, concessions, merchandising, advertising, streaming platforms, and more. As such, after school activities may prompt students to pursue a viable career in esports.

There are hundreds of North American colleges and universities that have varsity-level esports teams. Many of those institutions offer scholarships and financial support for esports players. In fact, colleges and universities provide millions of dollars annually for collegiate esports players.

Increasingly, K-12 institutions are creating formal esports leagues with the help of partners such as the Varsity Esports Foundation, the High School Esports League, and Play VS. This new kind of extracurricular activity provides students who may not normally belong to any other school teams an important opportunity to be part of the fabric of the school.

"I tell them all the time, 'You belong here. You're supposed to be here. This is where you should be. And yeah, it's difficult, you're going to get stuck, but there are many ways to get yourself unstuck. We have everybody here in the classroom who can help us and you can do this.' I think the whole point behind these extracurricular clubs is to reinforce that sense of belonging, which is pretty crucial I think, for young women and marginalized peoples."

— MIDDLE SCHOOL SCIENCE TEACHER

For the full report, visit
bit.ly/k12videogamebenefits

Creating OPPORTUNITIES for STUDENT PARTICIPATION

Creating opportunities for more students to be a part of school teams benefits individual students and the entire school community. Students who participate in extracurricular activities tend to have more lasting positive memories about school. Esports provide space for students with differing physical abilities to build connections with teammates, coaches, and the school at large.

Esports can teach soft skills to students as they become personally invested in the success of their team. Students learn to relate with one another while developing communication and problem-solving skills. They become more aware of themselves and others. Presenting esports teams as opportunities to improve student experience and performance may be a successful avenue towards garnering support from parents, teachers, and other stakeholders in school communities.

Esports can be a safe space for students to experience passionate disagreement. Coaches have an important mentoring role in esports and traditional sports alike. Good coaches moderate communication, model the proper ways to handle stressful situations, and demonstrate active interest and care for students' development. These skills and connections help build student success and happiness in schools.

IMPROVING Student Outcomes

Through esports, students may improve their academic achievement in more traditional subject areas. For example, students who participate in esports improve problem-framing skills such as asking better questions, defining problems, and analyzing and interpreting data.

Participating in esports can give students additional extrinsic motivation to do well. By allowing students to participate in something that is both challenging and fun, esports provides an opportunity for students to excel both inside and outside the classroom. The academic standards required of varsity athletes in high school can encourage attendance and scholastic achievement.

The benefits associated with esports activities seem most profound with disaffected and marginalized students. There is measurable improvement for students in school when providing mentorship inside and outside of a classroom setting, especially for those not likely to receive such guidance elsewhere. Those most at-risk often receive the greatest benefit from after-school programming, offering increased social interactions with peers in a safer play space. These opportunities provide an often low-pressure environment where students and teachers can interact outside of environments associated with summative assessment. These activities offer increased flexibility for parents who may now be able to work a full shift instead of leaving early to pick up their child. These activities also tend to be much cheaper than formal after-school care.

"I had a robotics club. And one of the things I did was I offered a girls robotics club by itself. I find that girls, when it's just them together, they will engage in a different way."

— MIDDLE SCHOOL SCIENCE TEACHER

entertainment® software association

HEVGA

HIGHER EDUCATION VIDEO GAME ALLIANCE

Making GAMES WORK
Considerations for Educators

Video games can seem infinitely complex. Integrating games into the classroom might seem daunting to any educator. Although there are no nationally recognized curriculum standards for video games, there are teachers, education research groups, and advisory organizations that offer guidance for those seeking to insert games into classrooms. Based on the advice provided by those interviewed for this report, teachers looking to effectively bring games into their teaching may consider the following suggestions.

Be MEANINGFUL and RELEVANT

Games must be coherent and internally consistent with the learning objectives. Care must be taken not to simply replace traditional rote learning exercises with irrelevant game-like activities. Many teachers see gamification as a superficial way to address a flawed curriculum, and students have become fatigued with poorly designed rewards systems that have no meaningful connection to the material. As one student said to a teacher with respect to badge and point systems that were not actual games, "They're lying to us. They're pretending this is a game, but they're lying to us."

Students should see themselves and the issues they care about in the games they play in the classroom. Games provide a space for students to grapple with learning material as part of a playful community of learners. Students will understand the course content better if it is relevant to their experiences and the experiences of their peers.

START SMALL and Pick the RIGHT TOOLS

No game will satisfy all the social, cultural, and curricular needs of a group of learners. Rather, games are rich sites of pedagogical potential to be integrated within a larger classroom ecology of teachers and learners. Short excerpts from games, such as the introduction or a single mission, can be more effective as a teaching tool than having students play an entire game. These brief gaming moments can be supplemented with supporting materials — such as a reading, a video, an historical document, or a reflection document — that provide additional context for the lesson. Keeping gameplay short also creates space for the inclusion of a wider variety of games, each of which might offer a different perspective on a topic.

> "Start at a point that you feel you can be successful. Start someplace small and someplace where you feel will do the most good. And if it completely fails ... well cool."
>
> — ELEMENTARY SCHOOL TEACHER

While it can be tempting to jump on the newest technology, these often have a steeper learning curve for both students and instructors. The engagement incited by novelty does not last.

The most important consideration when choosing technology is to choose games and tools that will not add barriers to learning.

OBTAIN Administrative and Parental SUPPORT

The majority of the teachers interviewed identified administrator support as absolutely essential to success in integrating games into the curriculum. Administrators help secure the financial resources necessary to bring games into the classroom. A supportive administration provides legitimacy to the entire exercise, reassuring parents and other teachers that learning outcomes are being addressed. District administrators are also instrumental in introducing game-based learning at a larger scale. They connect teachers between schools and create a community of teaching practice where ideas, resources, stories, and solutions to common problems can be shared.

Clear and consistent communication with parents is key to securing their approval. Parents are more likely to accept game-based learning when teachers demonstrate clearly how such efforts meet curricular outcomes. Parents seem reassured by explanations of curriculum research that underpins the use of games.

Be FLEXIBLE

Game-based learning experiences, whether focused on playing games or building games, should emphasize discovery and exploration. Creating space for student exploration and curiosity allows students opportunities to find new avenues for learning and promotes intrinsic motivation. Too much planning can curtail these efforts.

A teacher's most crucial role may be modelling the learning process. If a teacher works through a new game puzzle alongside their students, for example, the teacher can model positive learning and troubleshooting practices. Problem solving is an iterative process that requires embracing uncertainty and failure. Good game-based learning experiences reflect this. It's okay to not know how things will turn out — it may even be better that way.

> "You just use a 10-minute segment of the game; you don't have to play the whole thing. You put it in front of the class, and you arrive at this kind of juncture. And then you get them to go off and choose a school of moral philosophy to justify the decision they're going to want to make at that particular moment."
>
> — HIGH SCHOOL LANGUAGE TEACHER

BUILD Scaffolding to PROMOTE LEARNING

Instructional scaffolding guides students through unknowns by introducing skills and knowledge as required. It is essential to game-based learning as it bridges the gap between limited content knowledge presented by a video game and a broader, more contextualized understanding of a topic defined by the curriculum. Teachers should provide internal and external scaffolding.

Internal scaffolding is integrated into the flow of the game. It caters to the needs of different learners by providing students with just enough help navigating content or mechanics to let them advance through the game at an appropriate pace.

External scaffolding involves teachers helping students make explicit connections between game concepts and their "real world" counterparts. External scaffolding connects game expertise (knowing how to move around the game world, for example) and content expertise (knowing the history depicted in the game). The challenge is to offer additional context in a way that isn't divorced from the game, as students retain more information when external scaffolding meaningfully informs in-game experiences.

Ideally, the level of scaffolding should be such that students still feel challenged during play but have access to enough support and feedback that the perceived challenges seem manageable.

Scaffolding should provide enough help that the tools used to play and build games are not a barrier to learning or expression, without eliminating the learning that comes from failure.

DESIGN for EQUITY

In deciding what tools to use and how to use them, every teacher interviewed was above all focused on equity. School budgets often don't allow for expensive consoles or games. Teachers favored lightweight games as they were more likely to be able to run on widely available devices, such as phones. Teachers were careful to keep gameplay in class, with the school or teacher providing the required technology.

Freely available games and tools were preferred.

"At the beginning, things were very simple... simple tasks, simple things. We kept building upon those kinds of game skills as we went through. And while building on these game skills, I found they grew in combination with the Spanish skills."

- HIGH SCHOOL LANGUAGE TEACHER

CONCLUSION

With millions of players nationwide, and the majority of Americans convinced of their educational value, it's no surprise that video games have made their way into today's K-12 classrooms.

Teachers leverage the interactivity of games to create structured learning experiences that engage all types of students. Playing games in the classroom as part of a community of learners increases students' engagement with the curriculum and broadens their digital literacy. Building games in the classroom engages students in complex problem solving and introduces them to increasingly important technical skills. Beyond the skills needed to play and build games, game-based activities teach critical thinking as well as soft skills such as self-awareness and teamwork.

Games amplify student agency in learning. Students make meaningful choices allowing them to see how their decisions impact the game world. In doing so, students are prompted to connect these game experiences to the real world.

Games are a community activity. They create space for a diversity of skill sets — programming, art, music, etc. — fostering a culture of collaboration and peer mentorship. Esports teams may offer a sense of belonging to students who often feel they don't have a place in the school community.

With no nation-wide curricular guidelines, game-based learning in the American school system is currently practiced and promoted by small communities of teachers. This report summarized the efforts of these teachers to use games in the classroom and to connect those efforts to larger communities of practice. It showed a small glimpse of the potential of games to cultivate a playful learning environment that can benefit a diversity of students across America.

For the full report, visit
bit.ly/k12videogamebenefits

"It's not a vision that looks to completely overhaul an English curriculum and just play games. I think it's part of a repertoire of relevant narrative techniques and manifestations they should be exposed to, because part of consuming narratives is having the critical tools to think about the narratives that you actually consume — the way that narrative is playing out in the 21st century."

— HIGH SCHOOL LANGUAGE TEACHER

Entertainment Software Association
@TheESA

TheESA.com

Higher Education Video Game Alliance
@theHEVGA

HEVGA.org

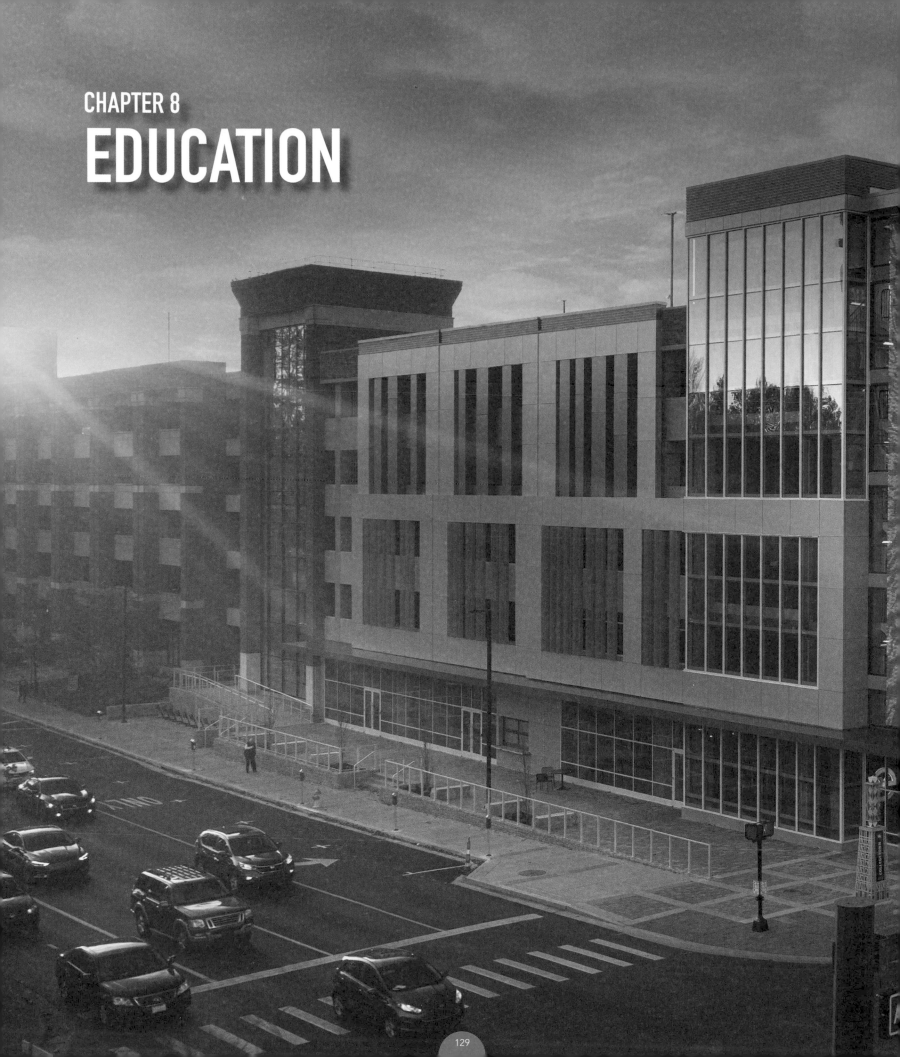

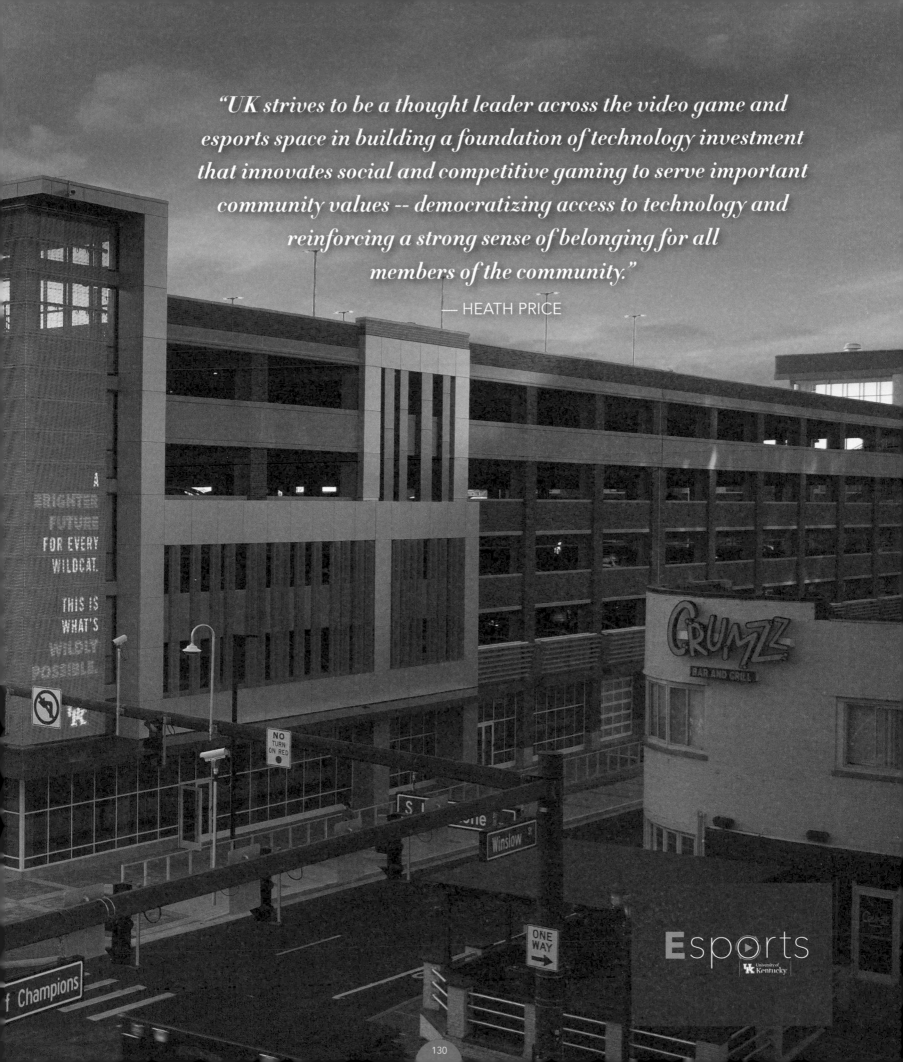

"*UK strives to be a thought leader across the video game and esports space in building a foundation of technology investment that innovates social and competitive gaming to serve important community values -- democratizing access to technology and reinforcing a strong sense of belonging for all members of the community.*"

— HEATH PRICE

TO ENGAGE WITH OUR COMMUNITY OF STUDENTS, FACULTY, STAFF AND PROSPECTIVE STUDENTS WITH GAMING AND ESPORTS TOPICS WHILE PROMOTING EDUCATION AND CAREER DEVELOPMENT IN THIS SPACE.

As is common with many of the great things that universities do, it all started with the students. The UK Esports Club was organized around 2017 by students that were interested in growing the community and helping different clubs that were focused on individual games to pool their resources and better leverage their resources. The club has developed a great community - they compete actively in a wide variety of games and they have developed an active Discord.

Against this backdrop, UK spent 12 months (late 2018 - fall 2019) researching and learning more about the esports landscape. More than 200 colleges and universities across the United States currently have implemented some level of committed esports student programming, classroom learning, competitive gameplay, and more than $15 million in scholarship investment focused on the most popular esports games. These numbers continue to rise annually.

Early on in the learning process, the University of Kentucky has leaned heavily on one of our key campus partners - JMI Sports (UK's media rights holder for Athletic and Campus Marketing Rights) - to identify industry

leaders in the esports space that the University can collaborate with to more aggressively achieve the goals laid out above. After detailed dialog and research, the University and JMI formed a partnership with Gen.G, the only leading esports organization that owns and operates top teams in the world's three most important gaming markets -- China, South Korea, and the U.S.

Among the world's leading esports organizations, Gen.G stands out for its trailblazing advocacy of the community values that form the core of UK's vision. Namely, Gen.G has pioneered: (1) diversity through its #TeamBumble platform for the empowerment of women in gaming, featuring the world's best all-female Fortnite team; (2) academic advancement through its international Gen.G Elite Esports Academy; and (3) talent development through its historic partnership with the NBA 2K League and its player wellness platform.

o   Gen.G is the only major esports organization that owns and operates top teams in the world's leading esports markets — China, South Korea and the United States.

o   Gen.G's core mission is to help fans and athletes use the power of gaming and esports to get ahead in and beyond the competition.

CREATE

o   UK students can work with us to create streams on the UK Twitch channel based on topics that they are interested in

o   UK students can be a part of programming and events that UK and Gen.G put on - participate as a caster, behind the scenes in production, etc. Recent examples include:

o   Hoops at Home - Annual NBA2K tournament with 64 participants across brackets for current students, future students, alumni, and Big Blue Nation; the 2nd annual Hoops at Home event ran from April 9-11 2021.

o   Give Health – we partnered with the UK Children's Hospital to raise money through a week of nightly streams. Generated around $20,000 in funds that went directly to the hospital's mission.

o   Virtual Governor's Cup – since the 2020 football rivalry between UK and Louisville couldn't be played, we put on a virtual event pitting the rival schools in a few different Esports titles during the week. It was a fun time – Louisville won the inaugural championship in 2020.

o   UK's Wrigley Media E-caster space and Production Suite provide a broad set of tools and resources that students can take full advantage of - with opportunities to gain experience both in-front of or behind the camera. Streaming events like Cornerstone Commentary and weekly streamers like Captain Donnie provide the opportunity for UK students to learn how to coordinate a live-stream, develop interviewing skills to engage with subject matter experts, and build their own brand.

COMPETE

UK students can join the UK Esports Club and participate/play with the game/team that they want to join

UK students can work with current teams to provide coaching if there is a good fit

UK students can organize teams within the UK Esports Club

UK students can organize esports tournament events that they would like to hold at the UKFCU Esports space

COMMUNITY

We are excited about the open of The Cornerstone space on campus. This space will serve as gateway to an emerging innovation district that will further link the university with the city of Lexington.

The Cornerstone houses the new UK Federal Credit Union Esports Lounge, a gaming space that has been designed to invite UK students, campus constituents, and community visitors into the campus to experience PC gaming on high-end gaming machines in a comfortable and welcoming environment.

o   4,500 sq ft space

o   ~100 seats on retractable risers for tournaments and classes

o   Esports gamers lounge will include at least 50 PC-based gaming units and multiple console-play areas

o   Team rooms where UK Esports Club teams can practice and sharpen their skills

As opportunities to be back in-person continue to increase in the future, we look forward to having the UKFCU Esports Lounge as a place that welcomes current students, prospective students, and people from across the community to come and gain gaming experiences that will serve to broaden their personal relationships.

University of Kentucky Esports
cornerstone@uky.edu
UNIVERSITYOFKY ▶
ukyesportslounge 📷
ukyesports 🐦 💬
university 📺

uky.edu/esports

EsportScholar is located at the intersection of esports and education, and is home to the future of learning and competition.

Our after school league coalesces in-game coaching with STEAM instruction into a dynamic, engaging program for organizations, schools and school districts. We're in the business of building vibrant esports communities with the goal of being the highlight of our students' days. We believe in recognizing abilities that have (for far too long) been underappreciated and teaching skills that lead to academic and professional opportunities in their futures.

It should come as little surprise that kids love gaming. A recent Pew Research study revealed that 97% of teen boys and 83% of teen girls consider themselves regular gamers. At the moment, a vast majority of those kids are gaming without guidance or structure. That's exactly what we're looking to remedy.

As a school, why not meet students where their interests lie? Taking a stance against esports is like attempting to hold back a tide of change that is quickly sweeping across the globe. Instead of fighting the inevitable, or taking up Don Quixote-esque fight against a windmill of our day, there's a chance for schools to embrace this change and use esports to their advantage.

Our program uses gaming as a Trojan Horse to teach STEAM skills like graphic design, video editing, broadcasting, and other esports tangentials. These are elements of a knowledge base that prepare students for modern workplaces and scholastic endeavors; a set tools they can employ throughout their lives.

EsportScholar was born of necessity during the throes of a global pandemic. In a time where traditional sports and after school activities came to a grinding halt, we took on the challenge of establishing a place where students could forge a creative community, find solace and social interaction through mutual interests. Over the course of the pandemic, esports were one of the few competitions that schools were able to participate in, and many took this bold step into the future with us.

Our crew of dedicated instructors and gamers have helped teams from coast to coast (and in between) become better gamers, learners, and friends. As one can imagine, it was almost impossible for students to connect with classmates while quarantined at home and some who participated in our program hadn't even had the chance to meet each other in the real world. Only through esports were they able to establish these bonds.

Beyond satiating a craving for community, we saw an opportunity to provide something that others hadn't already. Obviously, there are other players in the Scholastic Esports space, among them High School Esports League and the $300 Million behemoth PlayVS, however these companies serve largely as a league platform software to facilitate games between schools. For those who can afford their hefty seasonal price tag, and have the means to staff coaches themselves, those services work well. What we found was that many schools do not fall under that category. Many school administrators face the challenge of trying to cross a steep generational divide and aren't sure how to go about establishing a team or the practicalities of how to run it. Moreover, finding a teacher who is a Challenger rank in League of Legends or who has over 4,000 hours invested in Rocket League is incredibly rare. That's why our expert game pros who boast such credentials are key to developing a competitive program. Especially when some games (like League of Legends) require a depth of understanding that even a somewhat familiar player would struggle to pass on to another. We saw the opportunity to differentiate ourselves with this expertise, and through other instructors with their industry specific experience to teach our STEAM related courses. Matching teams up against each other in a league format is truly only half of the battle.

In this way, we at EsportScholar, do consider ourselves innovators in our own right, but our true focus is to enable future innovators who will define the esports landscape of tomorrow. We are firm believers in constant improvement, and have taken an agile methodology approach in constantly adapting our program to match the needs of students and maximize their ability to participate and create.

Though we are headquartered in Boston, Massachusetts, our team is found scattered across the country. We believe strongly in the ability of our dedicated staff to accomplish their goals while working remotely. Though our schools are likewise nationwide, we hope (in the near future) to cement local connections in New England and the North East where esports is less adopted than in other regions.

Moving forward we hope to spread the scope and reach of scholastic esports, reaching new demographics, and further expanding our curriculum (which has been accredited by STEM.org). Our successes will be measured by the number of students who receive esports scholarship opportunities, employment in the esports industry, and the portfolio of work that is produced through our program. We, as always, continue to introduce more students to the levellest playing field that has ever existed: esports.

EsportScholar
hello@esportscholar.com
617-797-7104
Boston, MA, USA
esportscholar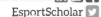
EsportScholar

esportscholar.com

"IF YOU BUILD IT, THEY WILL COME..." THIS MISQUOTED LINE DERIVED FROM THE MOVIE, FIELD OF DREAMS, IS OFTEN ASSOCIATED WITH STARTUP DEVELOPMENT. IT SOUNDS GOOD BUT UNFORTUNATELY IT IS NOT REALISTIC.

What does work is the act of providing a reason for why they should come. That is the central theme of Oakwood University's Entrepreneurship Center, OU Launchpad, and it is why gaming is at the heart of the center's success.

OU Launchpad is structured around ideation and microentrepreneurship. These two areas are rarely prioritized within entrepreneurship supporting organizations due to the intangibility associated with idea exploration and the lack of focus on scalability with microenterprises. Microenterprises make up 92% of businesses in the United States, and one of the fastest growing groups of microentrepreneurs can be found in the gaming industry. Did you know that experts expect the number of online streamers of online games to rise to one billion in 2025? That is equivalent to one in nine people this year. George Kneller, author of The Art and Science of Creativity states that, "creativity, as has been said, consists largely of rearranging what we know in order to find out what we do not know. Hence, to think creatively, we must be able to look afresh at what we normally take for granted." In order to find new solutions to new and old problems, we have to be creative and that starts with ideation. One of the best tools to maximize creativity can be found in gaming and at OU Launchpad, we prioritize accessibility to the resources needed to harness that creativity.

Before joining the ranks of Oakwood as a faculty member, Professor Julian Waddell, Executive Director of OU Launchpad, was the CISO for the university. During that time, he learned that one of the largest uses of the network was connected to gaming within the dorms. Whether students were streaming to Twitch, setting up NBA 2K tournaments or participating in LAN Parties, it was clear that gaming ranked high among the student body. Regardless of areas of study, gaming was the connective chain among these diverse sets of students and for most of them, the lessons and skills they were obtaining seemed to better prepare them for life after college, especially as entrepreneurs. These students became experts at logistics, marketing, user experience, scalability, risk management and technical support. When it came to pivoting to account for unforeseen issues, their lean model was near flawless and replicable, but this phenomenon is not new. From Golden Eye to Smash Brothers to Command and Conquer to Madden, students have continuously built an entrepreneurial ecosystem with gaming at its core. And so in 2020, Oakwood University decided to embrace and enhance that ecosystem.

During the pandemic, OU Launchpad established a partnership with Unity Technologies to develop a train-the-trainer game development initiative for aspiring microentrepreneurs, as well as built out a content creator support infrastructure for the center's recently formed esports program. With assistance from Cxmmunity, OU Launchpad has been able to dedicate 5000 sqft to esports, leading to the creation of multiple startups from individuals that never realized they had a business in them. OU Launchpad then helped these aspiring entrepreneurs get access to funding while supplying them with specialized training from subject matter experts to take their idea to the next level.

As an entrepreneur, you must be focused and patient because there isn't a one size fits all model for success. An entrepreneur must know how to learn from failure and keep going until they overcome the obstacles in their way. At OU Launchpad, our mission is to guide our students, faculty, staff and community entrepreneurs from the tutorial level of starting a business and that's why they come, now that we've built it.

Oakwood University
256-726-7080
7000 Adventist Blvd., NW
Huntsville, AL 35896
Oakwood University 📘 🐦
oakwoodu 📷
oulaunchpad 📷

oakwood.edu

How an EdTech startup is reinventing esports and providing a competitive platform for creative coders.

At the start of 2021 we launched the CodeCombat AI League. Built on the foundation of our annual CodeQuest competitive coding hackathon, this new and innovative esport was born. The CodeCombat AI League is the first of its kind, part AI battle simulator and part code engine for learning real Python and JavaScript. We are redefining what an esport can be and giving the next generation of engineers a platform to showcase their creative coding abilities.

Founded in February of 2013, CodeCombat was born from a simple idea: make learning to code engaging and accessible to all. The game-based learning platform teaches real typed Python, JavaScript and C++ coding languages through the power of play. The dungeon crawl gameplay is paired with a scaffolded curriculum to allow self-paced learners the ability to master foundational programming concepts before moving on to the more complex. Each level challenges the player to type the code necessary to advance their hero and achieve the level goal. With the basics down, the competition can now begin.

"Coding competitions or hackathons are not new," said Nick Winter, CodeCombat's CEO, "but our drive to evolve the format has led us to develop the CodeCombat AI League, a unique esport that turns competitive coding into the spectacle it deserves to be."

With a basic knowledge of coding, anyone can step into the arena to compete. In this league, your code powers the strategies and tactics in battle. So instead of directional keys or a joystick, players write the code that informs what heroes to summon and what they will do. Need resources? Program a thief to snatch them from your opponent. Want to protect your base? Code your soldiers to form a wall.

When a player is confident that their code is ready to compete, they enter the arena and challenge tens of thousands of other coders from around the globe. Players can run test matches against any competitor, then allow the AI to simulate hundreds of asynchronous battles on the global leaderboard in seconds. When a match completes, the platform adjusts its Bayesian estimate of each player's skill and updates the rankings. Players can refine their code at any time, rerun the battle, and position themselves for the season final championship.

"The creativity we've seen out of these young coders is incredible," said Valentin Briukhanov, AI League Design Architect. "I designed these

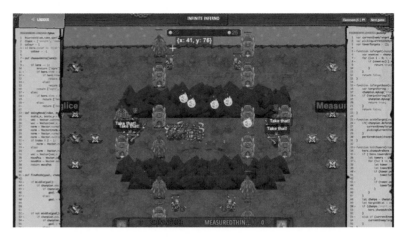

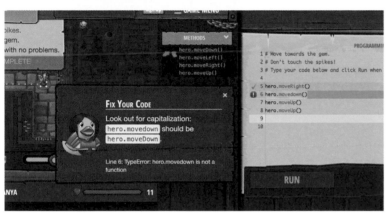

arenas, but the code that some of these players are generating, I never could have imagined."

With three seasons per year and two new themed arenas each season the intensity and creativity in competition continues to grow. Tens of thousands of players participate in the competitive head-to-head arenas each season with more than just bragging rights on the line.

Nick Winter, CEO, CodeCombat

Endemic esports mainstays RESPAWN and HyperX are proud partners of the CodeCombat AI League, and along with great prizes, they offer confirmation that competitive coding has a place in the esports landscape.

Just like every other sport, competition drives innovation. Competitors are continually looking for ways to gain an edge. Without the limitations of defined interfaces like directional keys and joysticks, there is an immense amount of control and flexibility that comes with using code in competition. We believe that we've only just scratched the surface of what competitive coders can achieve and are excited to see what future seasons of the AI League will evolve into.

CodeCombat
Brehan@codecombat.com
codecombat [in] [O] [f] [y]
codecombat

codecombat.com

JOHNSON C. SMITH UNIVERSITY (JCSU) ESPORTS AND GAMING TRIFECTA, THE FIRST AT AN HBCU

Dr. BerNadette Lawson-Williams, JCSU Esports and Gaming Trifecta Founder/Advisor

In February 2019, a mere conversation that I had with a JCSU athletics administrator about the paucity of Historically Black College and Universities (HBCU) that possessed structured on campus esports programming became the impetus behind my development of a proposal later that day for an esports and gaming academic program. The proposal gained the immediate approval of several campus administrators. Six months later, fellow JCSU colleague and esports business maven, John Cash and I merged efforts to both launch and institute JCSU's Esports and

Gaming Trifecta, the first at an HBCU. At the time, collegiate esports and gaming programming, whether clubs, varsity teams, or academic programs, was prevalent at PWIs, but nearly non-existent at HBCUs.

Johnson C. Smith University's Esports and Gaming Trifecta consists of: academic/Certificate programs in Esports and Gaming Management, a state-of-the arts Esports Lab, and a Game Development Club/Esports Club. Our establishment of partnerships and collaborations with global

endemic and non-endemic corporations such as: Riot Games, Epic Games, POINT3, and the CEV Collection, a Black-owned premier eyewear company based in Dallas, Texas, among others, was an instrumental component in solidifying the Trifecta's brand as a premier collegiate esports and gaming dynasty.

Another notable strand of success accomplished by JCSU's Esports and Gaming Trifecta during its first year of operation was its highly competitive Esports Club, which made history by becoming the first HBCU Esports Club to advance from its inception to League Playoffs six months later. Its long list of victories against many well-known esports clubs and varsity teams across the nation, including, but not limited to: Virginia Tech, the University of New Haven, California State University of Los Angeles, the University of North Carolina – Charlotte, Virginia Commonwealth University, Barton College, and Shenandoah University helped to position its prowess as a formidable force in the collegiate esports and gaming ecosystem.

producing the first ever HBCU Esports Conference and Career Expo to be held in a blockchain ecosystem. JCSU's Esports and Gaming Trifecta has become widely recognized as a blueprint for HBCU Esports. Together, with industry esport/gaming community leaders, we are working passionately to transform the collegiate esports and gaming ecosystem, one controller at a time.

JCSU's Esports and Gaming Trifecta has been featured in over 20 local, state, regional, national, and international publications such as: the Washington Post, Esports Observer, ESPN's Undefeated, HBCU Digest, Diverse Issues in Higher Education, Inc Magazine, and EdTech Magazine, among many others, as well as televised segments on NBC and CBS affiliate channels. However, most notably, in collaboration with MetArena, a technology company, JCSU's Esports and Gaming Trifecta assisted in co-

Johnson C Smith University
Email: blwilliams@jcsu.edu
DrBLW32 🐦
JCSUEsports 📷

jcsu.edu

FULL SAIL
UNIVERSITY®

Every single degree that we have is touching esports in some capacity. We're seeing it everywhere.

For Full Sail University, esports came naturally. Since the school has offered gaming degrees for over 25 years, it came as no surprise when esports culture became widespread among Full Sail's students. The wildly popular degree programs have made gaming just as prevalent on campus as music or film. And with esports, the combination of gaming and live entertainment was a perfect fit.

The university's Career Development Department also began to see a shift in where alumni were finding work. Graduates from programs like Show Production, Entertainment Business, and other live-event focused programs were building careers in esports – not just grads with gaming degrees.

"Suddenly a lot of folks were going into the world of esports," says Sari Kitelyn, Director of Esports and Project Development at Full Sail. "And because of the way live events were working with esports – it's high-energy, it's high-technology – there was a strong need to understand all the moving pieces, from sound to stream capabilities and technology to computer setup."

Full Sail needed an esports initiative that was well-rounded for the world of entertainment, and a space that was adaptable. The Fortress, Full Sail's collegiate esports arena, would be just that space with ten million pixels of LED walls, all-LED lighting rigs, concert-level PA systems, and capacity for 500 people. It's the largest collegiate esports arena in the US, and it's built to be flexible. The removable LED walls, mobile stage and caster areas, and adjustable audience views allow The Fortress to optimize for an ideal event experience, no matter the game. It would also become home to Full Sail's collegiate esports organization, Armada, with varsity teams in games students choose and try out for themselves.

As a classroom, The Fortress gives students unparalleled opportunities, not just with Full Sail's Armada, but as a venue for real-world experience. Organizations like Red Bull and NBA 2K have hosted esports events in The Fortress allowing students to shadow production or take part in roles like camera operation.

Alumni also bring opportunities to The Fortress. "We have grads that have worked on pretty much every title that would field an esports team," says Sari. "We've had grads that have been in the industry for quite some time, and we have brand new grads that just went into the industry, and all are already coming back."

Matt "Burns" Potthoff is one of these grads. After his eUnited team won the Call of Duty World Championship, Matt came straight to The Fortress to host a Call of Duty collegiate invitational with Full Sail. He and other grads have come to campus to talk to students about breaking into the industry and how to transition from player to working in the business of esports. Justin Burnham, Global Creative Director for DreamHack, the world's largest gaming and esports conference, has also hired grads and given students internship opportunities.

Blizzard Entertainment's Lead Project Manager in Esports and the first woman to graduate from Full Sail's Game Design master's program, Erin Eberhardt, brought a Hearthstone tournament to The Fortress. Students served in project manager positions, managed schedules, and provided logistical support. Long after the event, Erin still serves as a mentor and gives these students advice.

"We have to assemble all the cohesive parts for a program that reflects the esports industry together at once," says Sari. "We're optimizing the students' benefits, we're optimizing their opportunities, and we're giving them the full experience."

Full Sail University
FullSailUniversity
fullsail

fullsail.edu

EDUCATION AND ESPORTS:
How esports can be used to reimagine Business and Multimedia Classrooms.

STEM Fuse is a developer of digital K-12 STEM and CTE curriculum and PD, working with 12,000+ schools across the country. We were founded in 2009 with the mission to help schools deliver engaging STEM programs to prepare students for the fastest growing career opportunities. The Founder, Carter Tatge, was a recruiter for the MN State College System responsible for raising student enrollment in STEM degrees. He noticed the existing High School curriculum and course offerings weren't doing a good enough job of getting students interested in STEM related careers, so he knew something had to change.

Carter found that using video games was an excellent tool to get students actively learning a multitude of technologies, programming skills, Math and Science formulas and concepts, and digital art, design, and simulation. So, with the help of educators in central Minnesota, Carter developed STEM Fuse's first course- Game:IT. Due to its ease of use and success with raising student engagement in crucial subject area, Game:IT has become a leading Computer Science curriculum taught across the country.

Fast forward 12 years, and esports has presented another tool that should be used to maximize student engagement with skills related to highly demanded career opportunities. STEM Fuse developed two semester long esports courses that are aligned to educational standards in Business and Technology and designed to introduce students to sales/marketing, graphic design, event planning, A/V hardware, streaming and communication technologies, data analytics, and project management all focused on the esports industry. However, the skills and experience students develop throughout the esports courses are highly demanded across all industries providing students with a meaningful foundation to build upon no matter their next steps.

STEM Fuse is now bridging the gap from High School to higher-ed and career opportunities for students. We are working with colleges and companies nationwide to create dual credit, internships, certifications, and entry level positions for our students as they build their digital resumes and explore "what's next" within STEM Fuse courses!

Stem Fuse
sales@stemfuse.com
stem-fuse in
STEMFuse f
stemfusc

stemfuse.com

Teaching With Video Games

Hey Listen Games was born out of my passion for gaming and my desire to find ways to best teach my students. I teach at Ellis Preparatory Academy, a public high school in New York City dedicated to a one hundred percent immigrant and ENL (English as a New Language) population. Through my experiences teaching here, I have founded Hey Listen Games; an online resource for free curriculum and lesson plans for educators who are interested in teaching with video games.

Teachers currently have more opportunities than ever before to introduce diverse texts and media into their classrooms. Books, movies, tv shows, video essays, comics, manga, graphic novels, music, poetry and so much more are all resources that have steadily become more commonplace in many schools. Go back fifteen years and it would be very unlikely to find a teacher assigning a comic book as a text or allowing video essays on YouTube to be utilized as a legitimate resource. Walk into any school library today and there is a decent chance you might find an entire section dedicated to comics and manga. Schools are starting to catch on that it is in all of our best interests to begin tapping into the prior knowledge and experience of our students. It makes sense to bring their own passions into the classroom in order to make school a more enriching experience.

Video games today are where comics were a decade ago. You are still unlikely to find a teacher playing a video game with their students in class. It might be difficult to find teachers willing to even consider using a video game as a text in a unit. Video games however contain some of the best examples of storytelling out there. They are a massively untapped resource. When I originally started teaching seven years ago, I knew that I wanted to make gaming a part of my classroom's culture. Originally, that started off as a video game club that met during lunch every day. Eventually however,

I recognized that the passion my students have for games demanded a space in my curriculum and teaching practice. I've always played games myself and I knew that my own educational experience would have been enriched by the presence of video games in class. So I started scouring the Internet looking for lesson plans from other teachers who might have taught with video games before. Specifically, I wanted to find lessons focused on the use of entertainment games instead of educational games. I found nothing.

This began the journey that eventually led to the creation of Hey Listen Games. When I went to my principal with the idea of bringing games into my classroom, the first thing they said was show me the lesson plan. So I started making detailed lessons for each and every game that I wanted to bring into my class. And the lessons went just as well as I had anticipated. They were and remain some of my most fun and engaging lessons each year. When I shared what I was doing with other teachers, they expressed interest in the lessons' executions and results, as well as whether I'd be willing to share my resources with others. Hey Listen Games was born out of these conversations. I put together a website where I can freely share all of my curriculum. I want to make game based learning as accessible as possible for those interested in trying.

Hey Listen Games has also evolved into a personal blog of sorts where I can provide full rationales for each of the games added to the site. It is also a space where I share my own experiences teaching with video games. I write up a post whenever I teach with a game in one of my classes. I detail the effectiveness of the lesson based on my experience and provide student samples so that other educators can get a sense of student learning. Hey Listen Games was immediately successful. Teachers are constantly

Zachary Hartzman, Founder, Hey Listen Games

reaching out to let me know that they've tried some of the lessons on the site. Conversations about teaching with video games have noticeably increased online since Hey Listen Games' inception. Because of this work, I was even chosen as an inaugural member of The Game Awards Future Class.

Bringing games into my history class has vastly increased engagement, but most importantly it has helped build incredibly strong relationships with my students- gamers and non gamers alike. Passion is contagious and students perform better when a teacher is truly passionate about the content they are teaching. The success of these lessons has led me to pioneer a new class at my school where we exclusively play and analyze video games as literature. It is currently the most asked for class by students at my school. There are gamers in every classroom and teaching with video games has the potential to engage students in unique ways not often found in traditional education.

Hey Listen Games
HeyListenGames 🐦

heylistengames.org

THERE IS A GAME FOR EVERYONE

GIA STORY

"What if learning felt like a game?" This initial question was actually the starting point for the Games Institute. When Thomas Kunze stumbled over the topic of Game Based Learning in 2010, it was a question that never really left his thoughts again. Learning, especially in a digital world, needed more interactivity, more differentiation and more playfulness. As every game is actually only a set of problems, it felt right to bring games to learning or to at least apply the successful learning principles of games in educational settings. Though the topic was controversial in the beginning, over the years more and more studies and data supported the effectiveness of this approach. And there were a number of actual use cases (in Human Resources and VET as well as in traditional education) and soon the first products and services were developed. From the use of Escape Room games to assessment with digital games and the application of the strengths and the potential of games and Esports culture, the Games Institute Austria developed a comprehensive portfolio and a world-wide network to bring the benefits of gaming to education and life-long learning in the digital age.

ACHIEVEMENTS

The Games Institute developed its own Escape Room case for education called Best Case and is constantly inventing new Escape Room games for schools and VET. Beyond that, the method of learning through playing and designing Escape Room puzzles applies well for a number of settings around learning, brand development and communication.
In collaboration with the federal chancellery of Austria, we developed an assessment tool with digital games that assesses skills in an action-oriented way. It has been further developed and is an exciting tool for job orientation and vocational education training in Austria and beyond.

Over the years, we developed an expertise in Esports education and created a network of specialists all over the world. We participate in international projects in Esports, gaming and digital education and partner with companies and agencies in this field all over Europe (e.g. the European Erasmus+ project Games in Basic Skills Teaching). In these projects, we are the innovation partner and bring in our expertise to help educators understand the potential and the use of games and also help to create manuals and blueprints for successful game based learning.

Beyond that, we also help design educational games and are booked as experts for game based learning and Esports for talks and seminars.

VISION

Games are going to be the one medium to change education and life-long learning in the 21st century and beyond fundamentally. They are the blueprints to show us how successful learning works and how to create a growth mindset in learners, to be open to new digital tools and games and tinker with them and thus create situated learning by doing and help develop the skills of a society of prosumers who actively take part in today's digital world. We help people understand how they can benefit from games and what this culture offers to enrich more traditional processes of education, personal and professional development. We would like to bring games to every educational institution and every company and thus change the way we communicate and collaborate because there is a game for everyone and soon there is going to be a game about everything. And the Games Institute is the one partner to help you understand the potential and guide you along the way.

Thomas Kunze has been playing games all his life. With a faible for communication and a degree in linguistics and literature he started out to become a teacher. After having finished his studies he soon realized the potential of the world of gaming for personal development and life-long learning. "Games are the medium to revolutionize education in the digital age," he says and following this conviction he started the Games Institute Austria in 2015. Since then, the company's portfolio has grown considerably, including game design, game based learning, Esports education, consulting, international project collaboration and the like.

GAMES INSTITUTE AUSTRIA
KunzeGIA 🐦
GamesInstituteAustria 📘
tkgamesinstitute 📷
games-institute-austria 💼
Games Institute Austria ▶
thegamesinstitute 🟣

gamesinstitute.at

LEARN2ESPORT'S MISSION IS TO HELP YOUTH LEARN VALUABLE LIFE SKILLS THROUGH ESPORTS.

Their core product, Gameplan, helps players of all ages acquire real-world skills that aid professional development, cognitive abilities, promote healthy habits, and more.

Rasmus Sandstöm and Dan Andreasson started Learn2Esport in 2016 with the vision of engaging students through esports, and teaching them valuable life skills to prepare them for future success. Their background as semi-professional esports players in CS:GO, and their passion for education, fueled their desire to offer something meaningful to the esports landscape.

Their story began in 2011 at Keita Gaming, a non-profit tournament organization founded by the two entrepreneurs. Through this venture Rasmus and Dan hosted tournaments for Swedish youth and built an academy program. Their roster of over 25,000 members was filled with pro-teams, pro-streamers, and academy members.

Through this experience, Dan and Rasmus found that the world of esports lacked an esports management and educational platform. They wanted a way to bring the lessons they learned at Keita Gaming to a bigger audience, and provide an easy way to deliver these lessons to players.

This led to the creation of Learn2Esport, and the birth of their core product - a robust and scalable esports management and learning platform known as Gameplan. The full suite of features available in the platform enable anyone, of any skill level, to effectively grow and manage their esport program. The platform is now the backbone of esports curriculum, summer camps, academies, and more.

Gameplan is led by a strong team of educators, coaches, researchers, analysis and professional players. While the Learn2Esport office is founded and headquartered in Uppsala, Sweden, the company benefits from the expertise provided by it's employees around the world - all of whom are gamers themselves.

Gameplan offers over 500 hours of content across multiple game titles. The expanding content library is maintained and updated with each new game patch, so the lessons are always accurate.

Players can hone their skills through perfectly timed practice drills that are integrated into the learning content. Both coaches and players can take advantage of unique features such as gameplay reviews, which provide the ability to offer direct feedback in the video using annotations, captions, drawings, and more.

Features within the platform also serve to mitigate a common struggle in the esports world; getting parents to understand the value behind gaming. Features such as player journals were created to provide students the opportunity to reflect on their skills, what they have improved upon, and their emotions. This allows parents to see how esports encourages critical thinking, self-reflection and more.

The core goal behind all lesson material is to ensure students are learning skills they can apply to a variety of real-world situations. The curriculum within Gameplan also serves to ensure students maintain a focus on important subjects like nutrition, proper sleep schedules, fitness, and more.

Lesson material around complementary subjects in esports are continuously being added, this gives students who enjoy esports but don't necessarily want to become pro-players, a path to a career in the esports industry. Partnerships like that with Twitch, provide content around subjects such as developing and honing skills as a streamer.

With its constantly expanding library of content and features for managing esports players and teams, Gameplan offers the esports world an opportunity to focus on building best-in-class programs by harnessing the power of the Gameplan platform.

Learn2Esport
gameplanggtv 📺
ckEt6pMgs7 💬
gameplanesports 📷
info@learn2esport.com

Gameplan.com

CHAPTER 9

TEAMS & ORGANIZATIONS

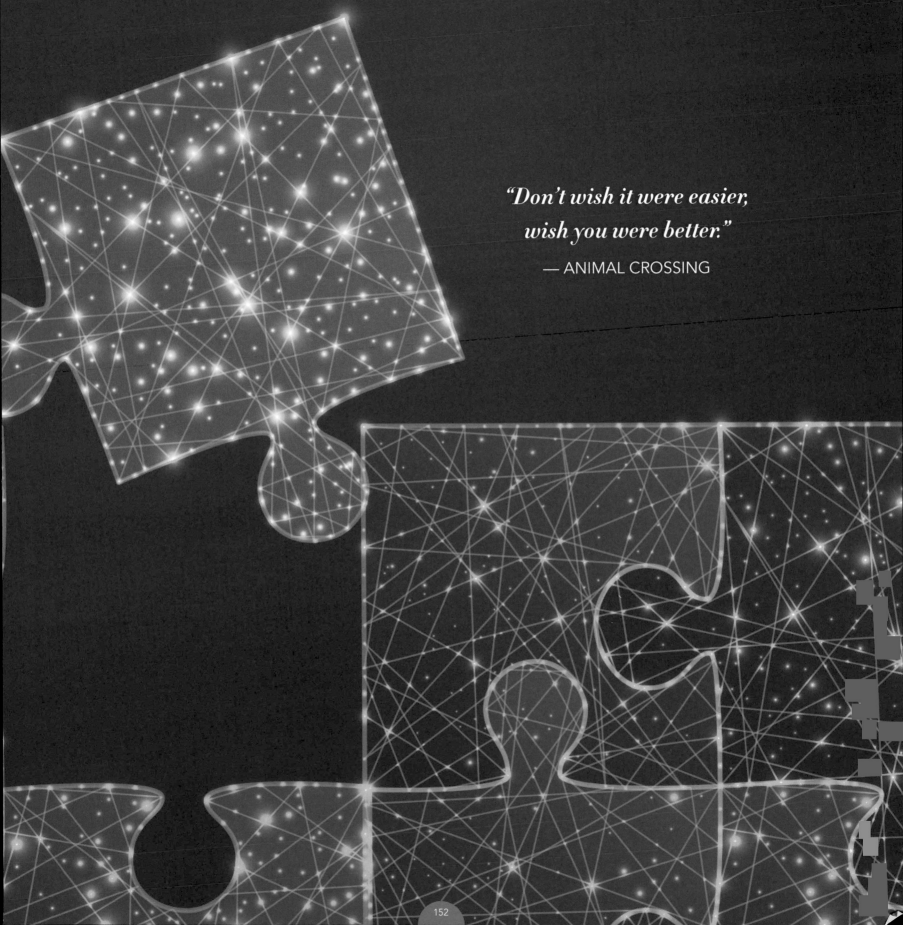

"*Don't wish it were easier,*
wish you were better."
— ANIMAL CROSSING

Putting the "Florida Man" in gaming with Tampa local esports company FMG

Florida Man Gaming is a Tampa, Fl-based esports organization that has brought innovation to the community through partnerships with like-minded local businesses intending to help bridge the gap in our community.

Florida Man Gaming is an American esports gaming community founded in 2019 with the vision to bring a community of gamers together. Not allowing the Covid 19 pandemic to hinder the growth, FMG decided to pivot and deliver to its community on a virtual platform. Through virtual tournaments, FMG has seen success and amassed over 500 registered members in the gamer discord. The discord serves as the primary means of communication for the community. It enables the members to share stats, progress, learn of FMG sponsored tournaments, other tournaments, solicit members to join their gamer party, etc. Florida Man Gaming opens its doors to all who share the passion of gaming, streaming their games, and those who want to be a part of their gamer community. While focused on Florida, FMG is open to all who are interested in subscribing to the community.

FMG serves as an innovation enabler as it encourages its members to curate their own experience while leveraging the FMG community. FMG is recognized for its varying tournament offerings that nurture a platform for the community to grow through unique paths. FMG's vision of growth provides flexibility for those who subscribe to the forum. FMG has a subset that follows and manages content creators with the primary objective to grow their social platforms by providing weekly coaching sessions and providing

honest feedback on streaming sessions. This service is on a subscription basis and has seen an uptick of interest as content curators seek an avenue to grow their brand while receiving the guidance and support to stay abreast in the esports world. At FMG, we take pride in even the most minute progressions, and we are looking forward to continuing to grow our subscribers to help propel them to higher grounds.

Florida Man Gaming LLC
flamangaming@gmail.com
813-335-1194
FloridaManGaming
fmg.gg
FlaManGaming

fmg.gg

Most Vicious Players (MVPs) is a stylishly unstoppable Call of Duty team that displays its community's talents through esports events.

Most Vicious Players is now the parent company of the Amateur Esports Union (AEU). But before the AEU was created, MVPs has been most well-known for its individual players having live streamed over 1000 wins in a row on YouTube, in which this live stream record has not been broken to this day worldwide (5 years running). After being highly competitive and delivering top notch content for 5 years, MVPs decided to expand their brand to event hosting which included hosting tournaments and clip contests. MVPs tournaments ended up having a global presence right away; teams that won were from places such as India, Canada, the United States, Nigeria, Ghana, and more. Furthermore, MVPs clip contests consisted of anywhere between 200-400 clip entries per contest with millions of views on the MVPsTV Instagram stories alone where the voting took place.

The Founder of Most Vicious Players, Jordan Taylor AKA J Jonah, was a high-level basketball player having played with and against over 20 NBA players throughout his career in high school and college. There came a time when he simply didn't have time to go to the gym and play basketball anymore, so began playing Call of Duty Ghosts. J Jonah realized that often he was the best player in the matches he played, but he didn't win every single game like he felt he should have been. This prompted J Jonah to create the Most Vicious Players clan, and the standard was no one could join unless he felt they were at least as good as him.

5 years later, J Jonah received a direct message from William D. Simmons III on Instagram. Having received thousands of DMs from peers and fans, J Jonah thought it would be another person he would most likely give advice to and show support or even just show appreciation that they reached out to him. To his surprise, William immediately began speaking to him with enormous business savvy and proved that he was far from the average person in J Jonah's DMs, and the two quickly became close friends and Will was soon named the Chief Strategy Officer of Most Vicious Players. J Jonah and Will decided to build a business based on the holes they felt needed to be filled in the Esports industry. A big reason for this master plan was the fact that despite MVPs major accomplishments, there was

still no effective path for them to take their players professional or get scholarships to play at colleges. This master plan is now a company called the Amateur Esports Union, which is a global Esports consortium that supports global sanctioned tournaments, global rankings, and partnerships for the purpose of domestic and international recruitment for high schools, institutions of higher learning and the amateur level.

Through the partnerships MVPs has developed, the company now created a path for Esports players to get recruited whether it's on the professional, collegiate, or amateur level by delivering players' content like never seen before as well as bringing players from different geographies across the world to compete against each other both directly and indirectly.

Most Vicious Players
info@aeu.gg
MVPsTV 📷
MVPs_TV 🐦

AEU.GG

Creating local and digital activations at events or on streaming platforms to help promote your product or service

Dynamik Focus was Founded in October 2016 By Aziza Brown. After varying experiences with previous esports teams, and seeing a need for representation and structure in the growing esports space, she partnered with former teammate Devin Harris, and Dynamik Focus was born. Soon after the organization was founded, Dynamik Focus added its first few members to the #birdsquad, and began competing in fighting game tournaments.

Over the years, the "focus" of Dynamik Focus has shifted to place more importance on Content Creation, building a lifestyle brand, and building a platform to show millions of people of african and latino descent that there is a space for them to thrive in this industry. The #birdsquad does all of this in addition to continuing to compete in gaming tournaments at a very high level: we help foster world class talent and encourage them to hone their talent on and off the sticks so that they can build a future for themselves in the industry they love even after they can't play any more.

APPAREL

Since late 2017, Dynamik Focus has partnered with Akquire Clothing to help produce our clothing for our esports team, and in 2020 we are looking to expand our line from just esports-centric clothing, to a full on lifestyle offering so that fans can rep our brand in comfort and style. This will be achieved through the launch of seasonal capsules highlighting the designs of east coast based artists based off of our mascots, logo, and word mark.

ACCOMPLISHMENTS

- Saiyne got 7th place in Soul Calibur 6 at EVO 2019

- Grr twitch partnership, featured on twitch rivals, and multiple appearances on the twitch.tv front page

- Multiple appearances on the twitch.tv front page for Cresta starr

- Aziza has been on multiple panels talking about diversity in the gaming space

- We launched an ad campaign on our social channels for our Akquire gear

- Expansion of content creation services and team

- Stream production services for Li Retro convention in 2018

- Saiyne got 2nd place at the Soul Calibur 6 world championships LCQ in 2019

- Rome_Himself will be a commentator for SNK would tour for 2020 season

- Uchi became a brand ambassador and commentator for power rangers battle for the grid

- Uchi hosts a regional tournament series "Catch me inside" for the southern NJ and Philadelphia area

- SakiSakura is the producer of the Queen of the Hill Series, an event to celebrate the women and non binary competitors of the esports community. We are the creators of the apparel to the series.

- SakiSakura has been featured on the Playstation Network for the Women of the FGC

- Queen of the Hill is probably the first Fighting esports tournament supported by Urban Decay, a cosmetics company.

- Uchi was a commentator for the season finale for the Battle for the Grid League

- Rome_Himself has done a series of online tournaments called Regime Royale. These are coop tournaments for the SNK titles.

- Aziza Brown (NNZ) and George Foulkes Jr. (Grr) did interviews in the Netflix Documentary, "Not A Game."

Dynamik Focus
DynamikFocus 🔲 📘
Team Dynamik Focus 🐦

dynamikfocus.com

the*gameHERs is the first and largest media platform, social networking community, and lifestyle brand for women who game and who work in the gaming space.

WHERE WOMEN WHO GAME CONNEC

The global gaming market is forecast to be worth $257 billion by 2025 and of the 2.7 billion gamers worldwide, 46% of them are women. The majority of these women experience hate and toxicity while gaming, simply for being women. In fact, in an effort to avoid harassment, 75% of women have gamed with their voice commands off to mask they are women. Because of this, many women gamers are eager for an easy way

to find other women to meet and game with based on shared experiences. With our first of its kind women-led social networking and game matchmaking web and mobile app that launched this year, coupled with our community generated content, the*gameHERs amplifies women in the gaming space and enables them to easily and safely find other women to socialize and game with. the*gameHERs also host the*gameHERs Awards,

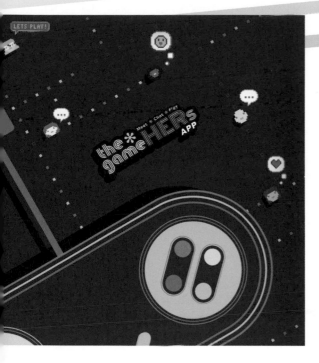

professional development bootcamps, charity gaming streams, collegiate esports tournaments/chapters and other live and virtual events. These will all be migrated to the app which will truly be the hub of the entire the*gameHERs community.

the*gameHERs app!

the*gameHERs offers a gaming community that centers women. Connect with other players in real-time, join live events and chat with others in a fun and inclusive space.

The number of gamers who are women, femme-identifying or non-binary is growing strongly, which is why we want to create a safe space for gamers of all backgrounds to meet and connect. Let harassment and trolling become a thing of the past by meeting other like-minded gamers who share a similar passion.

Chat for hours, play favorite games and build real-time connections with other gamers. the*gameHERs is a sexist-free space for the casual players, the hardcore gamers, the techies, the streamers, the designers, the cosplayers, the developers, the programmers, and more. The app allows gamers to participate in live events and connect with others by joining communities that fit their interests.

By respecting others and honoring the achievements of all gamers, we can foster inclusivity and ensure that everyone feels comfortable to express themselves.

the*gameHERs app Features:

Women Focused Gaming Community
- Escape daily harassment and trolling as a woman gamer
- Connect in real-time with other like-minded gamers
- Become part of a supportive and uplifting community

Play & Chat With Other Gamers
- Find other gamers who love playing your favorite games
- Use the "Play Now" tab to connect with others instantly
- Direct chat and make new friends in an open-minded gaming community

Join Unique Communities & Live Events
- Input personal preferences, including games, interests and consoles
- Find social groups that share your passions
- Meet and bond over shared interests and gaming experiences
- Participate in live events on your favorite games and topics

Our mission is to advance the role, voice, image, and power of all the*gameHERs in the gaming world.

** While this app is created for women and femme identifying people of marginalized genders, we welcome everyone! Whether you identify as a woman, femme, trans, nonbinary, man, masc, or another gender, connect with other like-minded people who prioritize geeking out about video games in an inclusive way! We do not tolerate illegal, hateful, or other inappropriate behavior. Therefore, to support a diverse and safe environment for all genders, we require all users to abide by our terms of use and community guidelines.

Testimonials:

I love this app! The aesthetics are gorgeous, and it's easier to converse/follow than Discord.

I love what you all have done with the app so far. I think this whole thing is a marvelous idea!

the*gameHERS
thegamehers 🐦 📷 🎮 📘 ▶

thegamehers.com

AQUATIK ESPORTS, CREATING AND FOSTERING A COMMUNITY UNLIKE ANY OTHER!

With a mantra of 'Esports for Everyone,' Aquatik Esports is truly unique and has propelled an abrupt tidal wave of followers, fans, and participants spread across multiple channels and touchpoints across the world.

By providing approachable spaces, opportunities, and platforms for amateur competitive gamers, creators, and streamers to launch their gaming career regardless of their skillset, available time, or age. Aquatik's approach is all-inclusive and makes it the ideal organization for anyone looking to jumpstart their career in esports or content creation.

Aquatik Esports was founded in March 2020 by our parent company Horizon Cloud; a firm focused on technology for events, eCommerce, and related verticals. Our organization puts a particular focus on the areas of climate change awareness and ocean conservation efforts as part of its mission, fusing those elements within its various competitive and community offerings. Esports and gaming are also growing at an unprecedented rate. Businesses and individual creators alike are struggling to grasp how to take advantage of the industry. It's why we created Aquatik, to help both sides of the fence get a better understanding of the segment and create rapid and meaningful growth. What started as a pipedream, today Aquatik Esports brings the latest in technology, gaming, and virtual reality to the screens of many.

Aquatik Esports is always looking for the most innovative ways to transform the esports industry by providing a platform for gamers and streamers of every level worldwide to interact, compete, and share their passions. With the growth team that consists of Andrew Bouley, Matt Dolan, and Sarah DeToma, their primary objective is to support the larger team in success in the growth of their burgeoning new venture. This is evident by our hosting of two Collegiate conferences featuring Valorant among the Big10 and SEC conferences. In addition to the immense amount of organic growth the team was able to accomplish on our social channels to over 150k+ in just over a year, we used the latest trends in esports and marketing in inventive ways.

Aquatik Esports is located in Naples, Florida, where our parent company, Horizon Cloud, is headquartered. Since the start of this venture, we have realized that we are benefitting from being in Florida; whereas, there is no large esports footprint established within the state just yet. The consistent influx of people allows us to reach more of them on a local level, as demonstrated by their rapid and sustainable growth.

The future of Aquatik is bright! We are all very excited about our software, Kontrol. Kontrol creates B2B and B2C opportunities using stablecoin cryptocurrency and payment technology to disrupt social gaming. Kontrol gives creators one platform to control all their gaming and esports variables while empowering businesses to navigate the challenging but rapidly growing $37B industry of gaming/esports.

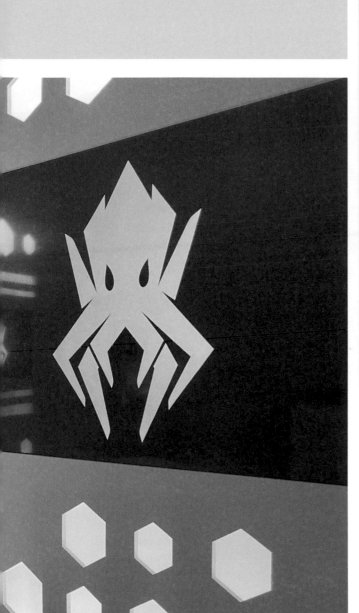

Aquatik Esports
hello@aquatikesports.com
neptjungaming
aquatikesports
Aquatik Esports
aquatikesports
neptjun
aquatikesports

aquatikesports.com

We are also very excited about our partnership with the Orlando area's 2022 Special Olympics USA Games. Aquatik Esports will explore the engagement between esports, the athletes, and fans; whereas, the organization intends to learn from the events while engaging with the passionate esports community from around the United States. To make this successful, we have recently partnered with Epic Games to run Fortnite tournaments on the Special Olympics behalf to raise money and awareness for the games.

WE WILL HELP YOU POSITION YOUR BRAND INTO THE GAMING & ESPORTS INDUSTRY WITH THE MOST CREATIVE CAMPAIGNS ACCORDING TO YOUR BRAND

"At the beginning of this pandemic, during my free time, I started consuming video game streams, and on one of the many channels that Facebook Gaming has I met again with Jose Vargas who had just started streaming # Dota2 content from Amsterdam. In the coming months we understood how big and how much digital audiences had evolved, especially in the gaming sector, which went from being a niche market to a mainstream one. It was then that we began this adventure with a Dota2 tournament, which had more than 1,200 people registered and the request for a second edition by the Peruvian community" – Andres Villagomez, CEO & Cofounder of Basher Agency

"This month we celebrate a year in this industry working with specialized marketing campaigns in #esports & #gaming in Latam, Europe and Asia for more than 15 clients: with operations in Peru, Brazil, Bolivia, Mexico, Portugal the Netherlands, Philippines and starting some projects in Africa. We manage more than 50 influencers in the region, and we have partnerships with professional esports teams, streaming agencies, esports platforms, payment providers, blockchain companies, betting companies,

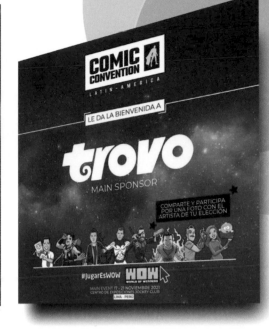

etc. We currently have more than 15 employees made up of Account Executives, Marketing Specialists, Community Managers, Designers and more. In addition, this month we attended our first #TheInternational Dota 2 in Romania, one of the largest esports event, in the company of our partners Thunder Awaken Esports; and #IGBlive in Amsterdam, the largest iGaming convention" – Jose Vargas, CFO & Cofounder of Basher Agency

Since its founding in 2020, Basher has grown into one of the leading agencies in esports in Peru and South America. We've worked with some of the biggest names in the industry, including Beastcoast, Thunder Predator and SG esports. From representing esport players, streamers, influencers and artists to working on marketing campaigns that raise awareness about esports, we've done it all. Our clients can expect us to always go above and beyond what they ask for when it comes to creating an amazing product.

Basher is not just an advertising company. We are a group of professionals with competent areas who share experience and knowledge in order to develop integrated communications campaigns for our customers.

What makes Basher so special? The professional background and the passion of our co founders.

Jose is a Civil Engineer with a Master's degree in The Netherlands. Since then, he has been working in complex engineering projects applying the Project Management philosophy. This knowledge has been implemented on Basher's methodology to execute different projects. He is also an Esport Agent in SEG International, based in Amsterdam. SEG is one of the biggest representation agencies and it is well connected with the biggest teams in the world, including esports organizations.

Andres has more than 10 years of experience as Key Account Manager of The Coca Cola Company. He operates with excellent performance, the most complicated marketing campaigns for Coca Cola and their hundreds of clients expanded all over Latam. This methodology is also applied to Basher's deliverables. He has also completed an International Esports Diplomacy in Peru, where he acquired a big network of the esports leaders in Latam.

Merging Jose and Andres skills, experience and network from Latam and Europe, Basher is a leading agency. The 15 employees so far expanded all over the globe have an excellent coaching from the cofounder, being the next esport leaders in the region. Basher is not only bringing potential clients to Latam, but also, they are empowering the esports community. Basher is changing the game and putting LATAM in the scope of the big investors, giving back to the esports community tournaments, events, competing teams, you name it.

Basher
basheresportspe
basher-esports

basher.agency

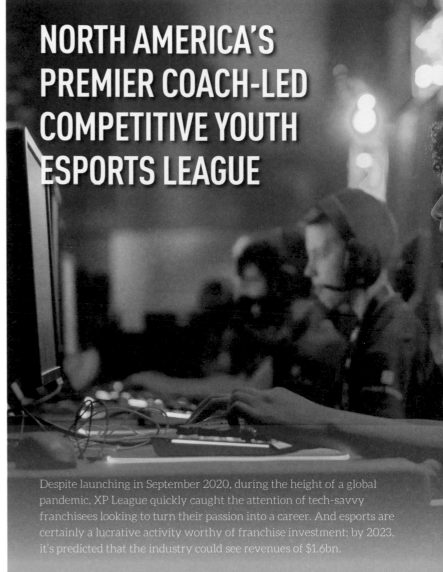

NORTH AMERICA'S PREMIER COACH-LED COMPETITIVE YOUTH ESPORTS LEAGUE

Despite launching in September 2020, during the height of a global pandemic, XP League quickly caught the attention of tech-savvy franchisees looking to turn their passion into a career. And esports are certainly a lucrative activity worthy of franchise investment; by 2023, it's predicted that the industry could see revenues of $1.6bn.

XP League is the bridge between youth sports and competitive gaming. It's an opportunity to build a positive healthy ecosystem where school age kids will build valuable lifelong skills while doing what they love," says Jay Melamed, co-founder. "Our dual focus on positive coaching and conventional youth athletic formats create a unique experience for gamers to engage in social and emotional learning while building on the meta and skill needed for competitive play."

Esports has been gaining traction over the last decade and the current pandemic has only added fuel to the fire for this growing industry," added Melamed. "XPL is easy-to-run and nomadic, so a local civic center or empty office or retail space can quickly become an esports hub. There is vast white space available for entrepreneurs interested in monetizing a career in esports."

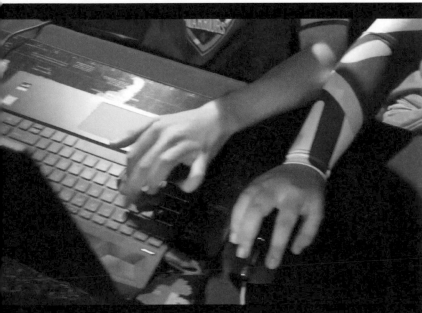

XP League
919-752-7385
xpleaguehq
XP League
xpleague

xpleague.gg

CHAPTER 10
CONSULTANTS & AGENCIES

*"We are the sum of our deeds,
not our names."*

— FINAL FANTASY TACTICS: THE WAR OF THE LIONS

SUGAR GAMERS

MEET THE **NEW** *FACE OF GEEK CULTURE*

GAMING APPEALS TO OUR INNATE SENSE OF HUMANITY. IT INSPIRES CREATIVITY, PLAY, CONNECTIVITY, AND COMMUNITY.

These also happen to be the fundamentals of today's video games. This wasn't designed by accident, either. Playing video games empowers people no matter their backgrounds, religion, politics, race, gender or location. Sugar Gamers exemplify this. Sugar Gamers advocates for inclusivity and diversity across race, age, gender, orientation, or gamer type.

The origin story of Sugar Gamers began with Keisha Howard in 2008 and has grown full circle with community support and collaboration and a strong team with a unified strategy to advance a version of the gaming industry that is inclusive and innovative. As a lifelong gamer, Keisha understood the benefits (social, emotional, cognitive, and physical) and value of video games in her life. Southside Chicago isn't known as a breeding ground for gaming talent - be that playing or game development. It is a rough and tough community – with masses of untapped potential. Searching for an outlet for her gaming passion, she realized they represented very few people of color and women in the wider gaming community. A proudly Southside Chicagoan, she founded Sugar Gamers in 2009 as a platform for female gamers in Chicago to connect and interact. Sugar Gamers' mission was – and remains - to provide a space for these underrepresented groups in the gaming community. On another level, Sugar Gamers created innovative pathways for community development through gaming.

Today, Sugar Gamers hold an influential position within the gaming space and not only in Chicago but across the United States. Sugar Gamers have partnered with brands like HBO, Netflix, Microsoft, AT&T, Syfy, NBA, and more, to bridge the divide between the wider gaming community and marginalized groups.

Initially founded as a gaming community platform for people of color and women, it has grown to be the biggest black video game community – yet its biggest success has been transcending those groups through inclusion and diversity across race, age, gender, orientation, and gamer type. Sugar Gamers' mission is to build a thriving ecosystem for all gamers, gamer types, and underrepresented people through community, opportunity, and advocacy. Since its formation, Sugar Gamers have navigated the gaming industry to sidestep gatekeepers, solved problems in unorthodox ways, and fought to share information so that others won't have to experience the same difficulties in gaining opportunities in the gaming space.

This company – and social movement – believes gaming has the power to inspire and influence people and communities into spaces where real-life characteristics and behaviors from gaming (such as critical thinking and problem-solving) are taught as life lessons and to form communities. Through nurturing a community of inclusiveness and accessibility, Sugar Gamers believes mentoring and supporting marginalized groups by providing them with the skills and tools to build video games and navigate the gaming space will help them gain employment in the gaming industry. Partnering with brands and companies will ultimately broaden the diversity of the gaming culture as a whole.

There are four aspects to Sugar Games' advocacy goals. The first level is consulting, research and development: Searching for areas to innovate and introduce new ideas and services to the gaming industry. The second level is to study how games are made in terms of the narrative; Sugar Gamers consult with game developers on methods to connect different markets: the gaming community represents a wide variety of people and gamer types. The third level: to understand the technology and tools of game development so that they can share those with communities to build better and different games. Last, Sugar Gamers advocates for the education of communities on technology and gaming so that no people in societies are left behind in opportunities or accessibility to create wealth or learn skills.

To achieve its mission, Sugar Gamers applies a grassroots approach to develop and foster communities. In Southside Chicago, Keisha and her team advocate for video gaming and the benefits of video gaming through education initiatives. Sugar Gamers hosts school camps across Chicago's Southside on technology and gaming – and these have proven effective at illustrating the opportunities the gaming industry provides in life skills and career choices available to the youth. The outcome of these camps is: children learn that their video game ideas – with tools and technology Sugar Gamers share – can make a game to teach others something they wish to share. For a marginalized group not socialized for the opportunities in gaming, this creates a potential for positive social impact.

Gaming has the power to enact meaningful change for society. Empowering the underrepresented voices broadens the diversity of gamer types, games, and builds stronger communities based on inclusivity. Gaming is pro-social and pro-community. Social upliftment is Sugar Gamers' unique approach to improving the gaming industry and culture.

Sugar Gamers
sugargamers 🟥 🟦 f

sugargamers.com

![HPG](HPG logo)

HIGH POINT GAMER

High Point Gamer is a premier Esports consultant group for forward-thinking gamers, brands, and organizations.

High Point Gamer (HPG) was founded in 2015 by two military veterans, Derek Watford and Dion Wrenn. HPG was the first black and veteran-owned Esports consulting company in the world.

They established their presence in the Esports industry early on by producing competitive video game tournaments. These competitive tournaments allowed skilled gamers to earn clout and prizes. Due to tournament production being their entry into the Esports industry, they were able to gain valuable insight into how to streamline the production of live tournaments, how to integrate influencers, how to authentically include brands, and how gamers conducted themselves during tournaments. This made HPG a proven thought leader in the space.

HPG was the first in Florida to produce a scholarship gaming tournament series entitled, STIX-to-GLORY. This tournament was the first of its kind to give high school students the opportunity to use their gaming skills to fund their continued education.

Esports was rapidly evolving at the time thanks to the advances in technology. Mobile technology played a vital role in speeding up the adoption and popularity of Esports and HPG was on the frontlines championing it.

Growing the industry and creating real economic opportunities became the focus of the High Point Gamer team.

Their commitment to the gaming industry and the community helped pave the way for others to find careers in the space. Their work ranged from tournament production, consultancy, headlining on speaking panels, authoring books, product creation, facility design, and more.

Their early pioneer work landed them the opportunity to study the National Basketball Association's rollout and execution of the NBA's

Esports initiative - the 2k League. HPG provided valuable insight to newly drafted professional gamers and newly appointed esports staff.

HPG evolved into providing brand-enhancing advice, content, and support to success-seeking gamers. HPG also develops Esports programs and activations that aid in a brand's or organization's business or community engagement goals. They worked with professional athletes and celebrities throughout their career; producing an impressive amount of Esports and gaming events.

Their expertise has been put to use on projects ranging from league development, scholastic development, facility design, and event production. They have worked with many notable NBA, NFL, and entertainment figures.

HPG believes Esports promotes economic empowerment, social inclusion, diversity, and STEAM interests. They ultimately want to build an Esports facility that can support the development and growth of the local gaming ecosystem as they continue to pioneer the innovation of the Esports industry.

High Point Gamer
info@highpointgamer.com
727-619-9355
highpointgamer

highpointgamer.com

RFLX | ↗

❝ WE'RE A CREATIVE AGENCY DEDICATED TO ESPORTS, SPORTS AND LIFESTYLE MARKETING CONTENT." — RFLX

RFLX is an integrated suite of content marketing expertise, dedicated to the eSports, sports and lifestyle industries in North America. Our purpose is to create online and offline experiences that are both captivating and exhilarating and allow brands to increase or establish their notoriety.

RFLX was born out of a growing demand for the eSports, sports, and lifestyle markets within TAKEOFF Creative, a content marketing agency focused on the video game industry. It is only natural that RFLX would connect the dots and fulfill the expectations of these markets. Located in Montreal, one of the cradles of video game creation, its commercial activity is directed towards the North American market.

Therefore, we've drawn heavily on our clients' universe to create the RFLX brand identity, to denote its commitment to the eSports, sports, and lifestyle industries. We are a one-stop shop for the sports & gaming industry leaders. Our creative team specializes in crafting a wide range of high-quality and exclusive print materials, video productions, digital campaigns for passionate fans, and real-world activation events.

VIDEO PRODUCTION

Nothing gets fans hyped up like exciting videos! We offer a full range of video production services, including (but not limited to): gameplay footage capture, VFX, motion graphics, video editing, voice recording, 2D/3D compositing, sound design, CGI, scriptwriting, and storyboarding! We've got what it takes to handle your trailer, 3D, and live-action video needs!

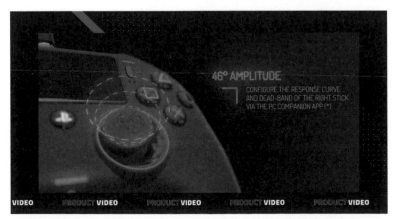

DIGITAL: Product trailer for the NACON Revolution Pro PS4 controller (NACON)

VIDEO: Gameplay trailer for the game Valorant (Riot Games)

CUSTOM PROMOTIONAL ITEMS

Capture the attention of the media with fully customized promotional items! Conceptualized and built directly in our workshop, we can design figurines, custom video game consoles, buzz kits, limited editions, life-sized replicas, and more exciting custom items to match your brand or IP!

DIGITAL

We provide digital design services ranging from logos, brand images and brand guidelines to social media content and web banners. Whether you're looking to rejuvenate your brand, start from scratch or create highly clickable content, we've got tons of creative ways to maximize your audience conversion!

EVENTS

We love designing thrilling live experiences for all types of events to bolster interactivity and audience engagement! From pop-up stores to roadshows and booths, we can handle the design, set-up, custom booths, and tear-down of any activation event you could envision in North America.

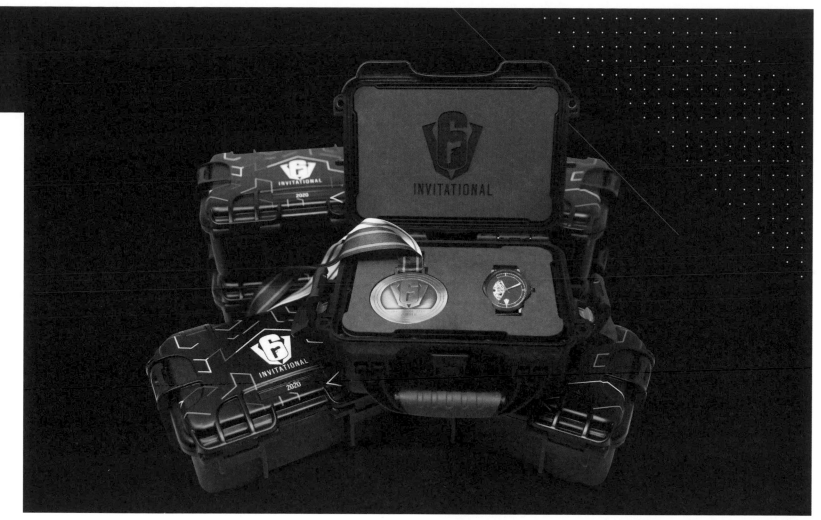

CUSTOM ITEMS: Esport winner giftpack for the Six Invitational (Ubisoft)

We've had the pleasure of working on projects such as the Six Invitational custom Winner prize packs for Ubisoft for several years, as well as for smaller enterprises on projects mixing sports and video games. It's always exciting to see the boundaries between our industries blur to further excite and engage their communities! Subsequently, we have collaborated with brands such as V-Rally and Valorant on enticing game trailers. It seemed only natural to create a devoted brand for these clients, to further immerse ourselves in their industries and push our suite of integrated services even further.

We work with some leaders in the sports, esports and lifestyle industries, but we also collaborate with smaller companies that bring so much innovation and energy! No matter what your needs and resources are, we can adapt our creative content and maximize profit and engagement!

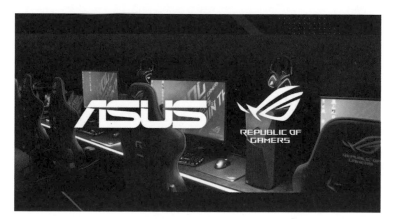

EVENTS: ROG tour truck, roadshow (ASUS ROG)

We strive to be innovators and innovation enablers: we continuously take our craft further through our creative processes and artistic production practices. We push our clients to broaden their vision, thereby creating larger-than-life outputs that make a mark on their industry. Our innovation also lies in our ability to customize ANY product — be it hardware, consoles, customer products, press kits and more! — to meet our clientele's needs.

We constantly seek and develop new creative processes and techniques to raise the dimensions and quality of the projects we undertake. NO project is unachievable for us!

RFLX-TO
contactus@rflx-to.com
1 (514) 271-4445
showcase/rflx-to **in**

rflx-to.com/en

WELCOME TO PHORCE MANAGEMENT GROUP - WHERE WE SHOWCASE THE BEST TALENT AND CONTENT IN GAMING

As a Sport Management professor, I sat and spoke to my students about the various aspects of gaming. Knowing the majority of my classes were filled with gamers, we would have countless discussions about the business and possibilities of esports. From these conversations I saw first hand how limited the knowledge was in this booming industry. With a limit of knowledge comes a limit of opportunity. My students had no clue that they could make a living in the gaming industry and did not have the guidance of how to make it happen. Seeing the lack of guidance made me realize if my students had no idea how to capitalize, how many other gamers, streamers and content creators were faced with the same issues. Majority of professional athletes in sports or entertainers of all kinds, have one thing in common, management.

I feel those trying to breakthrough in the gaming industry needed agents or management as a whole to be an assistance to truly maximize their potential in the field. At the time I found there were very few agencies focused solely on gaming culture so I was able to contribute to the industry in my own way. As I ventured into management, I wanted to make sure to effect diversity in the gaming space as well. Being a teacher at an HBCU (Historically Black College and University) I was very aware of the lack of awareness from my students who are majority african american. Being in the industry I saw the stark difference in diverse representation on different stages in gaming but I knew even though not always seen, African Americans were not only involved in the industry but were also change agents in gamings history. This led me to creating the Black Gamer League.

The Black Gamer League was created with the objective to connect and create a networking community to contribute to the growth and development of all Black gamers and those in the industry near and far. The BlkGL is focused on building connections to assist as many underrepresented individuals on their journey in the gaming industry as possible. In gaming, you face the need for a more diverse and inclusive environment on multiple fronts as in other industries. The esport and

gaming space has an opportunity to stand out in these areas as there are many more places and situations where minorities can find their footing. Esports itself is in its infancy stage so the growth leaves areas to not only improve on but also innovate in. This is the perfect situation for minorities because the race in gaming space doesn't have a long standing history or gatekeepers at every turn, leaving the potential for a beautifully diverse and enriched industry where all are accepted.

Phorce Management Group and the Black Gamer League will continue to place a focus on developing the next game industry standouts while promoting the importance of diversity and inclusion. Everyone should have the chance to be great, no matter where they are from.

Phorce Management Group
Black Gamer League
Chrisdavis@phorcemg.com
Phorcemgnt - BlkGamerLeague 🐦 📷

Phorcemg.com

ANY GAME. ANY GENRE. GO FOR GOLD.

DRAMATICALLY INCREASE YOUR SALES BY UNLOCKING THE TRUE POWER OF THE ESPORTS & GAMING INDUSTRY

Starting as an esports talent agency in 2017, Gold Standard Gaming has become a full-service marketing company that caters to brands, influencers and corporations worldwide. The founder, Sebastian "Chosen1" Burton is a former professional gamer and spent many years as a consultant to some of the largest brands in the esports space. This passion for gaming and its ecosystem is the catalyst where the company name was developed from.

In 2017 GSG became a small agency managing both talent and production for it's first client IMG LIVE, supporting its partnership with Turner

Broadcasting Studios on a production called ELEAGUE. At the time. Eleague became one of the most-watched esports shows of all time (2018) and was one of the channels (TBS) Highest viewed shows of the season.

By 2019 GSG was fortunate to have partnered with companies across the globe on various different activations and partnerships. Companies like EA Sports, Iheartmedia, SuperCell and many more AAA studios, publishers, and developers in the esports arena. However, nothing could prepare the company (Or any of us) for the Covid-19 pandemic that shut down economies worldwide. With resilience, the company made a pivot from

exclusively executing and managing experiential marketing events to creating robust digital advertising and marketing campaigns for not only gaming companies but businesses that had no choice but to relocate their marketing to digital platforms.

In 2021 GSG has become one of the top choices for entrepreneurs, intrapreneurs, and brands to partner with when looking to grow their reach and utilize the esports and gaming space to activate their audience. We look forward to working with you on your next large esports event or digital advertising campaign.

Gold Standard Gaming
ochosen1o 📷 🐦 📘
sebastianburtonthechosen1

consultgsg.com

NFT

"Boolien unlocks multi-usability of NFT in real life"
— TEAM BOOLIEN

booliennetwork.com

180

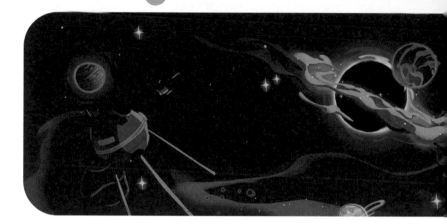

AN ENTERTAINMENT STUDIO FOCUSED ON CREATING STORIES THAT TRANSCEND MEDIA - INTER-KNIT NARRATIVES AND CHARACTERS ACROSS FILMS, VIDEO GAMES, AR, VR & BEYOND.

PUSHING THE BOUNDARIES

Stories are fascinating, timeless things. They existed long before you and I made our entry into this world, and will forever remain long after we've become grains of sand drifting in eternal winds. Each story is complemented depending on when told in different media or platforms but also stands out on its own.

We strongly believe that storytelling needs to be pushed to untouched boundaries - How we experience stories independently or together on multi-branched media as games, AR, VR, novels, or beyond.

LIMPIDFROG AHEAD

Having worked in the multi-faceted entertainment industry, we are moving into a conversion phase where LimpidFrog is solely focused on creating cross-platform and independent storytelling I.P's.

We are currently working on our first I.P. - House Party. It's an experience like never before. Additionally, we are working on a gaming product, imbued with blockchain. Our teams utilize a wide range of technologies, always learning and adapting processes to be as efficient and data-driven as possible. At Limpidfrog, we strive to work as a closed group and be as fearlessly creative as possible.

THE INCEPTION

Founded in 2014, LimpidFrog emerged as an Art & Design service to gaming companies. In the beginning, our office was a 1-room apartment with a cooking stove for a table. A team of innovative minds and the common goal to take design to the next level got together to cook art and provided services to small-size and Indie gaming companies across India, Chile, Hong Kong, France & Utah.

After a few months, we initiated Palette69 that provides experience design services for brands. LimpidFrog has evolved over the years in team-size, passion, and methods for creating entertainment I.P. never experienced before. In a way, yesterday has acted as a foundation for our tomorrow.

LIMPIDFROG

INTRODUCING HOUSEPARTY

Website - *https://housepartyuniverse.com/*

House party is Limpidfrog Cross-platform narrative IP, which is launching soon from as a TV series to Games and anything in between.

The story is set in a surreal environment loaded with dark comedy and humour. Featuring seven orphan teens, and their dark, adventurous life events.

Check out some of the cool images that would introduce you to the world of the House party.

House party is the one of a IP launching within the Boolien Ecosystem.
Here is a sneak peak of Boolien network.

Website - *https://booliennetwork.com/*

A lot of fun and madness dropping in soon from the team Limpidfrog. Stay tuned and reach out to us for any business collaboration

Email - *info@limpidfrog.com*

LimpidFrog
info@limpidfrog.com
limpidfrog 🎮 in 🐦 f ▶ 📷

limpidfrog.com

AlturaNFT

Altura's mission is to provide gamers with the ability to control and own their in-game items and the ability for game developers to integrate blockchain technology in their video games seamlessly.

Maxim Sindall, Co-Founder

Majd Hailat, Founder

Altura's NFT Project The current state of NFTs is comparable to that of the web in the 90s; static and boring. Altura is pioneering the concept of Smart NFTs. Smart NFTs have properties that can change, for instance, a video game sword that gets stronger as you use it or an in-game pet that evolves. Altura is developing APIs and SDKs for game developers to create and easily integrate NFTs into their video games. Additionally, we are also creating a digital asset marketplace for transacting Smart NFTs.

Other products we provide include verifiably random NFT loot boxes, Altura Guard, a blockchain verification system for authenticating yourself in-game without needing a web3 wallet connection and perpetual royalties for game developers. Altura earns revenue by taking a 2.5% cut from every transaction on the Altura marketplace and taking a 5% cut for all NFT loot box interactions.

Majd Hailat - Before my journey into the crypto world, I was a student in high school, learning as much as I could about programming. In 2 years I learned Python, Java, data structures, and algorithms. Using those skills I taught myself iOS development and launched a few successful apps onto the App Store. From learning how to release and create products, I ventured into web development working on the frontend with React and backend with Nodejs and Express. My cryptocurrency journey began as an investor in Bitcoin. I was intrigued by its technology and seemingly impossible traits such as digital scarcity. I then decided to look into how Bitcoin works in detail. With that knowledge, I learned about smart contract development and the amount of the space which was left undeveloped. I saw the value in tokenization of in-game assets and the ability to implement dynamic NFTs within games. These aspects helped me form what Altura is today.

Maxim Sindall -My foray into cryptocurrencies began in late 2016 when I discovered and started mining cryptocurrencies. I saw it as a no-hassle way to make some passive income, but soon became incapacitated of the endless opportunity in the space. In the following years I traveled through Canada and the United States educating young students on the mining aspect of cryptocurrencies, while giving them a simple introduction into the space. This helped me build a diverse network that built my presence in crypto further, eventually leading to the launch of Altura NFT.

I think Altura can be both thought of as an innovator and innovation enabler. We are innovators through the creation of a new standard in the NFT industry through Smart NFTs. These dynamic NFTs are able to change with events occurring outside of the NFT world. This is a much needed change and an addition of utility unforeseen by regular (non-changing) NFTs. This technology added with our marketplace allows for the free trading and creation of these Smart NFTs by anyone. How we enable innovation is through what these Smart NFTs can provide in application. For example, in gaming we can allow items to be NFTs themselves and allow them to be upgraded when certain events in-game occur. This brings in a new precedent within gaming by first giving value to gaming items, and secondly allowing gaming items to have a progressive increase in worth through gameplay. We have been able to do this by centering innovation at Altura. In terms of crypto and gaming we look to do things that haven't been done before, and it has helped us to create more value within both crypto video-games and non-crypto games.

Altura NFT
alturanft 🐦 Ⓜ
Altura.nft 📷
Altura 💬
AlturaNFT 🤖
altura_nft 🎵
alturanft.com
app.alturanft.com

POWERING THE GAME

"THE WORLD IS RUNNING OUT OF COMPUTING POWER ..."
WE HAVE A SOLUTION.
GAIMIN DELIVERS SUPERCOMPUTER DATA PROCESSING POWER

Clive project explanation in Switzerland

Martin Speight, Gaimin CEO being interviewed

Swiss Lawyers Wadsack, father & son Hans & Lukas

THE WORLD IS RUNNING OUT OF DATA PROCESSING POWER...

GAIMIN has developed a PC-based app that utilises, in the background, the processing power of the GPU in a gaming PC to create a decentralised data processing network with the power of a supercomputer.

GAIMIN utilises this processing power for a number of data processing applications, currently focusing on powering blockchain computations for cryptocurrency transactions and video rendering services.

Downloading and installing the app provides GAIMIN with immediate access to the gamer's device and the gamer with the immediate ability to start earning passively.

THE GROWING GAMING COMMUNITY

The gaming market is growing rapidly with over 1.5 billion PC gamers globally. Gamers are focussed on improving their gaming experience all the time and are constantly investing in their gaming devices to improve their gaming experience. However, these costly devices are only used for about 20% of the day for game play and remain unused for much of the time!

GAIMIN rewards a gamer for the passive use of their device and processing power. Rewards are in the form of GAIMIN's own crypto token - GMRX which are stored in a gamer's own wallet and can be used to purchase in-game assets, NFTs, accessories and merchandise or even converted to cash or another cryptocurrency.

Advisor, Alexander Shulgin

Buki our CTO signing our Agreement

Clive Aroskin, Gaimin COO with Swiss token buyers

UK Accountants Sedulo, Paul Cheetham & Dan Wilson

GAIMIN FOR THE GAMER

Downloading the app and registering with GAIMIN enables the gamer to become an active user of the GAIMIN platform and start earning an immediate passive income. Running in the background, the app does not impact the gaming experience at all and when the gameplay stops, passive earnings start!

Building up a GMRX balance allows the gamer to utilise their rewards for the purchase of in-game assets, NFTs, accessories and merchandise, or even convert their rewards to cash or a different cryptocurrency, ultimately replacing the need to purchase these items with real cash.

GAIMIN FOR THE INVESTOR

Passive earning for a gamer is not always about spending your GMRX!. You can use GMRX for investing and trading assets. A holder of GMRX can retain their GMRX and track its value on decentralised exchanges (DEXs). GMRX can be converted to other cryptocurrencies or it can be used to purchase NFT assets which can be rented in games or sold on NFT exchanges. A gamer can use this passive earning capability to purchase their rewards.

This is not financial advice and use of GMRX is completely in the hands and control of the gamer/GMRX owner!

DOWNLOADING AND INSTALLING THE GAIMIN APP

The GAIMIN app can be downloaded by anyone for free. However the amount of GMRX earned depends on the performance of your GPU. Older and slower GPUs will not work - a 4Gb GPU is a minimum! An active device is immediately incorporated into the GAIMIN network and rewards are proportional to the hashpower provided by the device to the GAIMIN processing network.

DATA PROCESSING USE CASES

GAIMIN currently focuses on two data processing use cases - powering blockchain computations (crypto mining) and video rendering. Powering blockchain computations is about pure hashpower, video rendering is more specialised and requires the same GPU models allocated to the processing application.

The GAIMIN AI Engine assesses the immediate requirement, available devices and utilises the network for the most profitable application at the current time. For mining, the AI Engine also selects the most profitable crypto to mine at the current time, thereby maximising earnings for the gamer.

Gaimin
Gaimin.io
GaiminIo

gaimin
gaimin_io

gaimin.io

früitlab™

FRUITLAB IS A COMMUNITY PLATFORM FOR THE BILLIONS OF PEOPLE IN THE WORLD THAT ENJOY SMILING OR GAMING OR SMILING AND GAMING

Imagine a social platform built especially for gamers that enabled users to earn cryptocurrency from their content and from playing their favourite games. Now imagine being able to use that cryptocurrency to buy games and in-game upgrades, purchase NFTs of content from top Content creators or to compete against other players for value.

This is fruitlab.

The original vision for fruitlab was to build a digital nation for gamers and game developers that brought content, social connectivity and competitive esports to the members of the community all powered by a universal reward mechanism that users could earn from posting content, being active in the community and by playing their favourite games. Essentially bringing the play to earn model to content and games for all users whilst providing an esports framework that doesn't rely on large corporate sponsors. To solve this, we created the PIP, a proprietary Ethereum token that provides both utility and a means of transferring value.

This vision was driven by the desire to make gaming more equitable. In both gaming content and esports, the vast majority of financial reward is concentrated in the hands of a tiny minority with a long tail that is monetised by the platforms but not by the value creator. This seemed unfair and motivated the creation of fruitlab.

Fast forward 3 years and today fruitlab is a thriving gaming community of 650k players who have posted over 2 million videos that have been

watched over 1 billion times generating over $1million of PIPs to users of the platform. In addition, hundreds of thousands of esports events have been played that have been funded by players.

The fruitlab esports model aims to provide up and coming esports players a career pathway to help them achieve their goals. In the same way that online poker helped numerous poker players forge a career without needing to qualify for the World Series, the fruitlab esports platform aims to provide regular player funded esports events that enable esports players to earn an income and raise their profile for the large esports organisations.

The journey until now has been exciting but things are about to go up to another level completely. The next phase for fruitlab is bringing the ability for content creators and game developers to create NFTs around their content and in-game items. Humans have an in-built desire to collect and own things and the fruitlab NFT platform will help address this. Content creators will now be able to sell the ownership of a video they make to one of their fans, who would then earn all the royalties from that video on the

fruitlab platform. We see an exciting opportunity here for fans to support their favourite content creators early in their career and watch them grow knowing they own one of their earlier pieces of work- much like buying a Picasso painting before he became known.

The developer tools that we are currently building will enable game developers to build in both the social & esports features of fruitlab into their games along with our cryptocurrency and NFT solution. This will open up and connect together individual game ecosystems enabling players to be able to seamlessly move between titles whilst still having access to their PIP balances and network of friends providing games developers the opportunity to build in native competitive esports for PIPs whilst allowing the development of new game economy models such as Play to earn. On top of these exciting new features, the fruitlab ecosystem allows the building of communities around specific game titles, genres or publishers. This provides game publishers a way to interact in an authentic way with their player base and tie together players from different game titles that they may have.

Until now, our user growth has been entirely organic, word of mouth from existing users to their friends. We are soon to embark on a period of rapid growth fuelled by closing some key partnerships and a significant marketing effort. We are genuinely excited of the opportunity ahead of us and we can't wait to realise the vision of fruitlab- the digital nation for gamers of all types.

fruitlab
fruitlabuk [f]
Fruitlabuk [Twitter]
fruitlab [Instagram]

fruitlab.com

GAMERS HAVE WANTED TO DO MORE WHILE GAMING. NOW THEY CAN.

READY PLAYER ONE

"What if I actually owned my digital games and in-game items?" That's been the question on most gamers' minds.

With limited solutions and some gamers resorting to the shady second-hand grey market to make use of their content outside of the game, David Hanson and Nicolas Gilot, Co-CEOs of Ultra, knew something had to be done. They noticed how blockchain technology could revolutionise the games industry and they got to work.

In 2018, Ultra was born, with the mission being to create an abundance of opportunities for gamers and game developers around the world. Ultra aims to move the games and entertainment industry to the next level, by giving gamers the chance to sell, buy, and trade their games assets and providing a fair and equal playing field for everyone to enjoy in Ultra's world.

Ultra's ecosystem currently consists of three main apps: The games store, Ultra Games, a native blockchain wallet, Ultra Wallet, and the NFT Marketplace. With their technology constantly being enhanced, the opportunities are endless and more apps will be developed and integrated to mature the ecosystem even further.

GAMERS WANTED MORE SO WE GAVE IT TO THEM

Ultra isn't changing the way gamers play. It's reshaping the current perception of gaming and providing new solutions so players can interact with their games, in-game items, and the wider ecosystem in the way they've always wanted.

Ultra's key component, a highly specialised NFT standard, opens up the gaming world to a ton of new possibilities. With this technology, Ultra is able to provide players with unprecedented gaming experiences that haven't been accessible until now.

Tokenized games and in-game assets mean that players around the world can enjoy playing games, with the added opportunity to sell and trade them to others once they're done. Because these digital assets live on the blockchain, there is an unmatched level of transparency and conditions set by the developers that allow all parties involved to benefit from the first-hand and secondary markets.

Ultra's ecosystem is designed to reward users for interacting with the platform and they can earn through watching live streams, participating in beta tests, watching ads, and promoting 1 content. Ultra removes the middleman and makes it simple so players and game developers can both be rewarded for their participation and time.

GIVING GAME DEVELOPERS MORE FOR LESS

With millions of games to choose from, gamers are spoilt for choice and platforms aren't doing enough to cater to all developers, whether AAA, AA, or indie.

Ultra is here to change that. Distribution fees on Ultra are at a comparisingly low 12%, giving developers the freedom to spend their time, money, and resources on what matters most: game development and community building. Developers can now break away from the existing monopoly and use Ultra's tools to gain visibility, earn more from each game, advertise their games effectively, and provide more to their communities.

Developers receive the tools to seamlessly and easily interact with influencers and communities through Ultra's robust promoter program. No contracts or back and forth is needed, just a hassle-free marketing tool that allows developers to easily promote their games and focus on their community.

Ultra's SDK helps developers take advantage of blockchain technology and provide more utility in each game they create. Ultra helps developers take

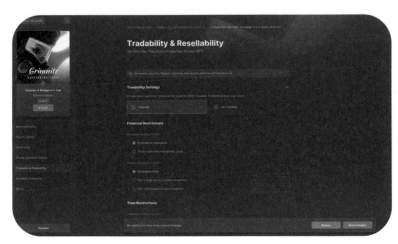

advantage of the secondary market and monetize content, even after users have made their initial purchase. Ultra essentially provides developers with an equal playing field and more opportunities than ever to display their games in front of potential players while monetizing their existing content.

THE BEST THAT BLOCKCHAIN HAS TO OFFER

Ultra's blockchain is specifically designed to bring blockchain technology to mainstream gaming and entertainment.

To do so successfully, they've made it as simple as possible for players to create blockchain accounts and start using the platform. Users don't even necessarily notice they're creating blockchain accounts but can benefit from all that blockchain technology has to offer.

Ultra's users have the choice of using its utility token, UOS, or fiat money (for example, U.S Dollar, Euro, British Pound) to buy games and NFTs, giving everyone the opportunity to use the platform however they'd like.

Ultra's blockchain is fee-less, meaning that users around the globe can use UOS for free to buy games on Ultra Games, purchase NFTs on the marketplace, and more. Better yet, Ultra's blockchain has unprecedented transaction throughput, benchmarked at 12,000 transactions per second.

And last but not least, Ultra's blockchain is carbon neutral certified, making Ultra one of the only sustainable blockchain projects in the world.

The games industry has always been the first to embrace technological changes and this time it's no different.

Ultra
contact@ultra.io
Ultra_io 🐦
Ultra_platform 🐦
t.me/ultra_io ✈️
ultra.platform 📘

ultra.io
onultra.io

H_{ELICON} NFT

OUR MISSION IS TO DELIVER A SUSTAINABLE NFT GLOBAL MARKETPLACE, WHERE SAVING THE METAVERSE ALSO SAVES THE PLANET IN REAL-LIFE.

HeliconNFT is a new online universe, combining a gaming metaverse with a NFT buying & trading platform that provides real rewards where you can play, mine and earn to become the master of a new market. Ultimately, HeliconNFT bridges the gap between centralised games and decentralized NFTs for a true inter-gaming experience, allowing gamers to monetise their in-game assets across different games. HeliconNFT has been inspired by ancient Greece, where Mount Helicon was a source of inspiration for all the art and culture, and the well from which the fabled 9 Muses drew their vision to ignite the world. In the same respect, HeliconNFT will have a unique ecosystem of 9 liquidity mining pools in order to reflect the 9 Muses.

HeliconNFT is both an innovator and an innovation enabler. We are innovators as this is the first all-encompassing ecosystem of its kind. HeliconNFT not only lets you monetize in-game assets, buy and sell NFTs, and integrate these NFT's into blockchain games, we are also the first platform to aggregate other games for a true inter-gaming experience. This is how we are also innovation enablers. Our game-add-on system facilitates third party developers to tokenize their games on the blockchain, giving them a whole new revenue stream. HeliconNFT wishes to completely disrupt the gaming and blockchain industry. We are the Amazon of the metaverse. Everyone is welcome on our platform to truly change the game!

Claire Cawthorn, Chief Marketing Officer

HeliconNFT is a global foundation, with offices across North America, Singapore, Australia and the United Arab Emirates. We have partnered with the leading minds of blockchain from around the world to create a hub that will attract influencers, artists, gamers and game creators. The team launched Insomnia Gaming Festival in Dubai and Saudi in 2019, and bearing in mind that MENA is the fastest growing gaming market in the world with 25% y-o-y growth, we find ourselves in rather perfect circumstances to launch a gaming NFT platform globally. HeliconNFT is most excited about launching our very own blockchain game, Helicon Titan, along with enabling third party developers to tokenize their games and mint their in-game assets into NFTs to be sold and traded on Agora, our marketplace. We look forward to being a key figure in the metaverse landscape allowing gamers to build, design and grow the metaverse as they please.

HeliconNFT
971-521-673826
marketing@heliconnft.com
Helicon- **f**
NFT-102049948901999
heliconnft 📷 🐦

heliconnft.com

CHAPTER 12

METAVERSE

"The Metaverse is truly the final digital frontier. What has been promised to society for many decades has now finally arrived. Over the coming years the physical and virtual worlds will merge through a seamless economy that will open up new opportunities for every sector of business existing today."

— JASON CASSIDY

GAME CREDITS

CREATE YOUR LEGACY

GAME Credits and the Metaverse, the true final frontier of gaming GAME Credits has a long history in the cryptocurrency and blockchain world. Initially launched as a proof of work chain back in February of 2014, As a company, GAME has experienced many ups and downs, bull and bear markets and seen many new technologies come and go. One thing that has been consistent throughout the entire time has been the focus and desire to improve the state of gaming through blockchain technology. Being the first gaming cryptocurrency in history, that is a duty that we take rather seriously. GAME itself is a testament to this, being one of the first cryptocurrencies created after Bitcoin many years ago. Before there were blockchains that focused on supply chain, sports, entertainment, shopping, health, real estate or many other key sectors, there was gaming. It has and will remain one of the most relevant applications for blockchain technology and cryptocurrency.

GAME's evolution over the years has seen the company grow from focusing initially on the esports industry to embracing and leading in the areas of NFT (non-fungible tokens) and the Metaverse. That journey has come with some impactful lessons that we carry with us as we move forward. One of the most critical parts of this journey came in the summer of 2020 when GAME Credits moved off of its historical Proof of work blockchain and migrated over to Ethereum. This also meant that the GAME coin also moved over and became an ERC-20, which is what GAME exists as today. The decision to migrate over to Ethereum was one that was not made lightly. Careful consideration was given to the short, mid and long term impact of making such a large economical

and technological move. Today, that decision has been validated as a wise one as Ethereum has blossomed into the defacto source for innovation within the blockchain gaming, NFT and Metavese sectors. GAME is proud to be standing at the forefront of these innovation pockets and the move to Ethereum has opened the door to explore the possibilities of the ERC-721 and ERC-1155 token standards. A large reason behind the move to Ethereum was due to the belief in the future of NFT's. GAME Credits, as a company, has a high IQ for both all things NFT but also virtual real estate and the concept of what a blockchain-based Metaverse can be. First off, it's probably a good idea to identify what exactly a Metaverse truly is. The Metaverse is a virtual space, often created with unique aspects that do not resemble the physical world. Metaverses are much more than simply a futuristic looking virtual world - they are the final frontier of all blockchain gaming.

The best real-world example that exists today for what a Metaverse could be is the film 'Ready Player One'. In the movie, a futuristic virtual world co-exists with people living out their lives in the physical world. While the Metaverse is not yet ready to deliver on the entertaining take that is Ready Player One, the underlying message is still very accurate. The Metaverse is a place that extends beyond gaming, it embraces commerce, entertainment, education and a host of other key areas of day-to-day human activity. Metaverses challenge the strongly held notion of what constitutes a 'game'. Second Life is another example of a virtual world that played more like a simulation of the real world than it did a game at times. Metaverses take this concept and expand it greatly, allowing for true business that normally takes place online, to happen within the confines of a shared virtual space. This opens the door for concerts to be held in the Metaverse.

What about education via universities and college campuses? Online learning becomes more engaging the moment you are able to interact with your classmates and instructors again. Shopping can also become an engaging and interactive experience once more when applied to the virtual world. Adding blockchain and cryptocurrency to the mix greatly enhances this effect. GAME Credits has always believed that the Metaverse will be where all NFT's eventually find their true homes. Utility is something that the blockchain and NFT space are lacking, often falling short of offering much more than a graphical image and / or a sound bite. But things in the blockchaiin space evolve much faster than normal industries, demand to tap into the innovation vein that is blockchain is growing by the day. Allowing NFT's of all types to enter into and have a functional home in the Metaverse is a priority for GAME. And it is in this ethos of giving the NFT world true freedom that GAME decided several years ago to begin building out its own Metaverse. This would be a virtual space that would allow for both personal freedom but also provide a measure of purpose and direction. Once the seed was planted the idea grew and took on a life of its own. The team at GAME Credits has well over twenty years of NFT and Metaverse experience despite these sectors only being a few years old as of today. This knowledge, coupled with a passion to do things differently, is what spurred GAME to create our own Metaverse. Enter, Genesis Worlds. Genesis Worlds is GAME Credits Metaverse, being released Q4 of 2021. Built on the Ethereum network, Genesis Worlds is a series of unique and distinctly themed planets that offer land owners and casual gamers alike an experience unlike anything they have encountered before. The goal of Genesis Worlds is to become the first 100 year Metaverse.

This is not just a catchy sales pitch but a true goal that has been thought out carefully. To that end, a governance system is in place along with a realistic roadmap that allows for a mixture of both company oriented and community based input. The Genesis treasury will be run by the Genesis Foundation, a not-for-profit organization that is tasked with building and growing Genesis, and by the Genesis community. When the community (or a community group) needs funds for a project, they make a request to the Foundation. The Genesis Hub holds both the up-to-date vision for the entire Genesis project, and the governance tools to make changes to that vision.

Any community member can make a proposal, and, with enough support, make a fundamental change to any part of Genesis Worlds. Players will find they can visit any number of worlds and that each has its own distinct look and feel. What players can do in each world will depend both on GAME's creative input but more importantly, on the communities. Building out land with the freedom to go in many fun directions is a quintessential part of the Genesis Worlds experience. Whether you are looking to explore, bring business into the virtual space or build something truly special. Genesis Worlds allows you to do that and much more. The Metaverse will also allow players to engage in quests, some community inspired and some delivered as unique content from the game studio itself. In this sense, there is truly no limit to what a player can do within Genesis Worlds, Cooperation and working in groups is strongly encouraged in Genesis Worlds and you will find many group oriented quests that reward those that are willing to work towards a common goal. The Genesis Metaverse runs on two tokens: World Stakes (erc1155 NFTs) and GENESIS Tokens (erc20) World Stakes allow their holders to manage individual worlds, with each stake represented by a 3d model of the world itself. Holding World Stakes over time enables holders to mine GENESIS Tokens. GENESIS Tokens are the governance and economic token for Genesis, allowing holders to guide the direction of the game, and make transactions within the game. World Stakes are bought and sold in GAME Credits using a bonding curve. This limits the total supply possible for each World, and ensures a fully liquid market for them. Owning a World Stake NFT lets you:

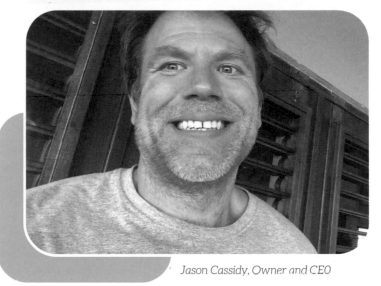

Jason Cassidy, Owner and CEO

- Mine GENESIS Tokens for yourself and the Foundation
- Participate in governance for the World
- Share in the economic activity in the World Worlds also contain plots of Land, which can be sold to players, used for community spaces, and granted to top content creators.

As you can see, we've put a lot of thought, passion and creativity into Genesis Worlds. As each day unfolds, more and more of our physical life ends up somewhere in the virtual space. And each day that unfolds, more

of that virtual existence is finding its way into the Metaverse. We envision a robust future economy with Genesis Worlds, where students are taking online classes while down the street someone is seeking legal advice and using a practising lawyer to complete a business deal. The possibilities become endless when you build something of value and ensure you are able to scale that solution to the masses. The concept of what a Metaverse is today will take some time to catch on, no doubt. It's a novel offering to many still and blockchain and crypto are on their own a rabbit hole many have yet to venture down. All that being said, nothing can stop an idea whose time has come. This idea is the Metaverse, and Genesis Worlds is our way of offering value via in-game item ownership, creative freedom and the foundation to build a thriving digital economy. I hope you take a look at what we are doing and perhaps even show up virtually as a guest, we'd love to have you1

See you all in the Metaverse - Jason Cassidy, owner and CEO at GAME Credits

Game Credits
GAMECredits [in] [X] [f] [O]
info@gamecredits.org

gamecredits.org

BEYOND THE POLYGON:
Making The Metaverse Real

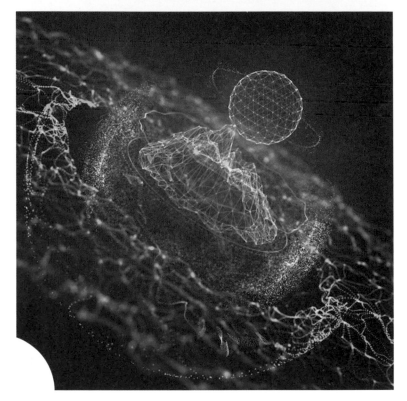

Transmira is the innovative company behind Omniscape™, the first true Metaverse platform that blends augmented and virtual reality (AR/VR) together in a unique synthesis while connecting the real world and digital information, data layers, and holograms together.

Transmira goes beyond simply creating 3D spaces and games like most other "metaverse" projects. Omniscape's direct link to the real world gives context and relevance to various experiences, and the unique blending of AR and VR together adds an entirely new dimension of immersion, interaction, experience, and capability.

Imagine being able to explore anywhere in the world with your digital avatar and being able to interact with local people...they see your avatar's hologram in AR, and you see their avatar in VR. Imagine walking down the street and invisible layers of data and information are instantly at your fingerprints and responsive to who you are, where you are, what is around you, and who is around you. Imagine working and collaborating with people around the world in entirely new ways, or education, sports, entertainment, shopping, and so much more. This is what we are developing Omniscape™ for on a global scale.

Amazing graphics and pretty visuals aren't enough though. Omniscape™ is a framework that anyone can build upon, and it is designed to be monetized for businesses, brands, content creators, and consumers. This deep focus on monetization and Omniscape's patented virtual goods technology, make it easy for anyone, anywhere in the world, to create value and generate revenue. Building upon this, Omniscape™ is developing Artificial Life Intelligent Agents (AI-driven avatars and MetaPets™), blockchain, 3D NFTs, IoT integration with smart buildings and smart cities, virtual real-estate ownership, and much more.

We have been inspired by Neuromancer, Ready Player One, Diamond Age, Snow Crash, Dennou Coil, TRON, Minority Report, .Hack, Rainbows End, Summer Wars, and many more. We believe that the Metaverse can only realize its full potential to change the world and our daily lives when it is directly linked to the real world, and experienced through AR and VR together. It must also be dynamic, extensible, and interoperable across many systems.

We are driven to innovate constantly and challenge preconceptions of what is possible. We regularly try to shift our perspective to look at things

from different angles, to find new solutions, insights, and ways to do things that are often overlooked. We have an amazing vision for creating the Metaverse in a way that will change the world and change lives, and we can't wait to share it with you.We are building the future, today, for a better tomorrow.

Transmira Inc.
robert.rice@transmira.com
(919) 607-4124
omniscapexr

omniscape.com

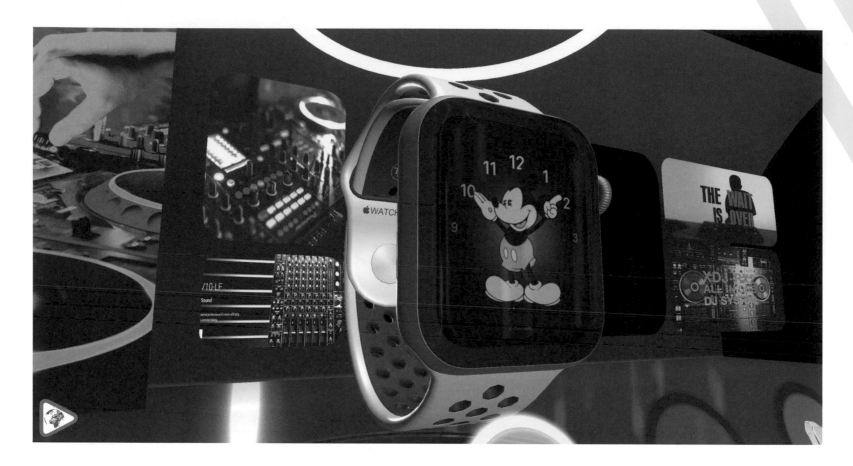

METAⅦRSE

MetaVRse is on a mission to unlock the power of XR for everyone.

MetaVRse is a proprietary, code-optional, web platform that makes it easy to create & share interactive 3D/XR experiences instantly to over 7b compatible devices from a one-click publish.

In 2010, we introduced Emulator, the world's first touchscreen performance system for DJ's. After being invited to perform at Curiosity Camp (Eric Schmidt, Google), I had the opportunity to try virtual reality in 2014. I had the instant 'AHA' moment when I realized that this technology would become the next human communication paradigm. In 2015, we started building solutions for enterprise clients across health, mining, food, media, consumer electronics, pharma and more.

In 2019, MetaVRse acquired a 3D deep tech platform called Cherry3D which would become the basis for the MetaVRse Engine, a new creation platform to quickly and easily build and share XR experiences from the web to any device. Since launching the product in June 2020 amidst the global pandemic, the company has provided solutions built on the platform to companies such as Samsung, Mastercard, JP Morgan, Hilti, Siemens and others.

Forbes called MetaVRse 'a game engine that means business' and Oracle's head of XR said 'MetaVRse is 3X faster and 2X simpler than Unity'

MetaVRse is both an innovator and enabler. Our studio is constantly pushing the limits of what is possible for our clients, but the code-optional web-editor is also unlocking possibilities for creatives who are interested in creating robust XR content without the hassle of App Store permissions or commissions.

Innovation is at the heart of everything we do. Just in the past few months, we have pushed updates to the product that have decreased load times by 300% while increasing rendering speeds up to 200%. Building the future requires massive innovation and the MetaVRse team has been leading the enterprise XR revolution for the past 5 years and will continue to do so long into the future.

The ability to create and share interactive XR or 3D content without the need for any apps and delivered over the internet is a unique feature of the MetaVRse platform. Our next generation of the software will also include workspaces, a new system for remote collaboration on projects in real time (like Google Docs for the 3D world).

As a self-funded organization, we pride ourselves on delivering the best product and projects to our clients while remaining steadfast to our mission 'to unlock the power of XR for everyone'. Our sales have increased 3000% since last year and are growing exponentially, but when it gets really

Alan Smithson, Co-Founder & CMO

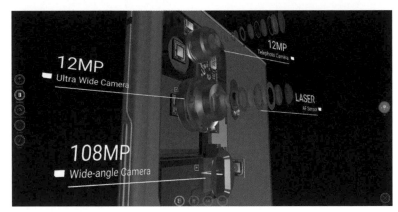

interesting will be when we hit 1 million creators on the platform building solutions we never would have imagined. This is the most exciting part of building a creative tool is watching what the world builds as a result.

MetaVRse
647-545-0610
alan@metavrse.com
metavrse in 𝕏 f

metavrse.com

CHAPTER 13
PLATFORMS

"*Success is not final, failure is not fatal:
it is the courage to continue that counts
– 'Call of duty.'*"
— MODERN WARFARE

KARTRIJ

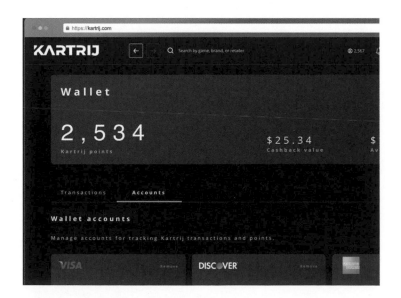

Kartrij is a free platform that helps gamers discover brands through cash back offers. Gamers earn cash back automatically by securely linking their credit card to the platform and shopping at the stores they already do. Kartrij enables gaming brands to effectively advertise through real-time customer insights and custom offers.

With the pandemic in full stride, our founders stayed connected through their passion for gaming. They found that there were hundreds of amazing games and brands that had yet to be discovered because of tough competition and expensive advertising costs. Driven by this realization, they quickly started working on a prototype to help gamers earn cash back on gaming through their credit cards. Excitement quickly grew and Kartrij was founded. Most gaming brands find themselves lost in retail and online stores with an ocean of competitors. With small marketing budgets and little brand awareness, gamers rarely discover some of gaming's most creative brands. Kartrij's cash back platform provides a real alternative to gaming's traditional retail advertising options. The platform gives control back to the brands allowing them to directly

TO UNITE GAMERS THROUGH THE DISCOVERY OF AMAZING BRANDS THAT CELEBRATE THEIR LIFESTYLE.

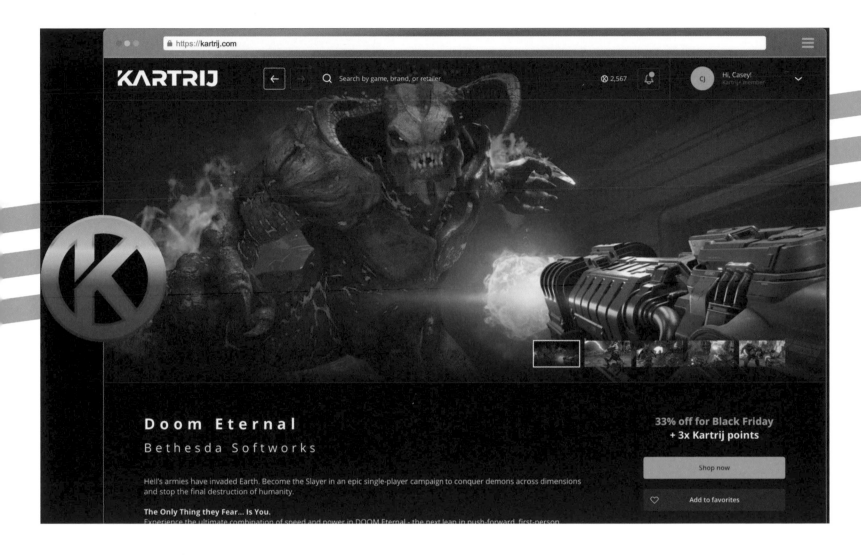

and efficiently market to the gamers they want. Kartrij's card-linking technology allows brands to leverage transaction data to personalize offers for each customer.

This allows every brand to competitively engage new and existing customers. The platform's real-time analytics allows brands to easily quantify their marketing spend down to every transaction and benchmark performance. Brands using Kartrij will experience an overall increase in customer spend and frequency, while reducing their bottom line. With its launch, the platform supports one of the largest gaming brands, Microsoft. Kartrij will continue to introduce new brands, bringing a diverse collection of games, hardware, and merchandise for every gamer. However, the cash back platform is just the beginning, Kartrij is going to curate an entire experience that captures the gaming world from member perks to exclusive events to esports. Kartrij will be in every app, game, and event. Kartrij will become the cultural voice for the gaming community.

Kartrij
contact@kartrij.io
get.kartrij
get_kartrij
get.kartrij
kartrij

Paddy Markham, CEO & Founder

Connect, Engage, Compete! CAPSL disrupts the esports scene with BAASH to ignite the next generation of esports heroes.

CAPSL is the developer of BAASH, the mobile social gaming platform helping game influencers engage and monetize their fans via competition. Starting out in Southeast Asia, BAASH targets the 300 million mobile gamers in the region. By using a combination of chat and integrated competitions, BAASH reduces operational efforts by over 60% while providing influencers a path to monetize their fans across any mobile game.

Started in 2016, CAPSL was always committed to redefining how esports fans compete in and spectate online tournaments. Founder & CEO of CAPSL, Paddy Markham started reaching out to game influencers, interviewing them about the issues they were facing in the mobile esports scene at that time, and whether they would be interested in using a tournament platform that could assist with tournament management, as well as monetizing their fans.

At the beginning, only five responded to the request. However, over the course of two weeks, the passionate nature of the Southeast Asian game communities sprung to life. Word spread like wildfire and soon, there were over fifty game influencers sending CAPSL requests that they wanted to use BAASH, which, at the time was still pre-development. The signals were clear; CAPSL had struck a chord, discovering a pain point that was clearly not being addressed. Confident that they were on the right track, BAASH was born.

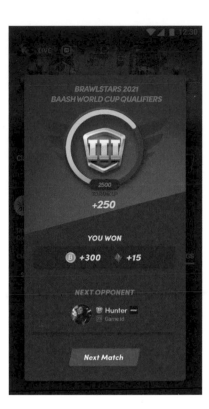

BAASH AS AN INNOVATION

BAASH is a content creator platform that is focused on mobile gaming & mobile gaming influencers. With it's cutting edge technology, BAASH enables grass root tournament organisers to fluidly operate small to medium sized mobile game competitions supporting up to 1024 players automatically.

Using computer vision technology, BAASH is able to achieve a 95% accuracy in match results extraction, helping tournament organisers saving hours of operational costs when running tournaments.

WHAT CAN CAPSL DO IN OUR REGION THAT CANNOT BE DONE ELSEWHERE?

In Southeast Asia, there are over 311 million mobile gamers who generated over 3 billion dollars in 2020 alone. This is paired with game influencers operating over 10,000 tournaments on a daily basis in the region. This is why CAPSL has dedicated themselves to Southeast Asia, servicing BAASH to users of all levels within the region.

Although mobile gaming is on the rise in the West, adoption is still far behind Southeast Asia's 29.1% YoY growth. To a large degree this is, because in Western countries, access to PC and consoles has been established for several decades, whereas in SEA, a mobile device is likely the only device that players will be able to game on. That's not to say that Western markets are not significant, and the CAPSL team expects mobile competitive gaming to increase significantly over the next 3-5 years.

MILESTONE & THE PATH AHEAD

Since soft launching, BAASH has grown organically at tremendous speed, holding over 1,400 tournaments in the first 6 months of operation. While having launched only in the Philippines, early and mid-term retention rates have eclipsed industry standards. Paired with the launch of the BAASH influencer program, over three hundred influencers collaborate on BAASH as their goto mobile esports tournament platform.

At the time of writing, BAASH was in the early stages of growth. BAASH is due to launch across the rest of Southeast Asia in the coming 12 months, while supporting the top fifty competitive mobile titles, and igniting a new generation of esports athletes.

CAPSL
capslentertainment [f]
_CAPSL [🐦]
capsl-entertainment [in]
capsl.ent [📷]

capsl.cc

Livewire

Livewire is focused on being the global leader in gaming marketing and gametech that works horizontally across all gaming verticals.

Livewire is a global gaming marketing and gametech company that leads major brands and agencies into the gaming ecosystem.

We create bespoke gaming strategies based on proprietary research and knowledge that build authentic and culturally relevant brand positions within the gaming audience and deliver results that build brands fame and cultural relevance through people's shared passion of gaming.

Our company was formed by the combination of backgrounds of Co-Founders Brad Manuel and Indy Khabra. Brad's esports partnerships, gaming content and gaming talent management experience combined with Indy's extensive digital and programmatic highlighted an opportunity to agnostically help brands market to the gaming audience utilising experience and a fresh, engaged mindset.

Livewire is an innovator as one of the first companies globally that solely focuses on creating ways for brands to engage the gaming audience in a way that authentically engages generations of digital natives who have lost touch with traditional media.

We are focused on creating innovative marketing products across research, strategy, gametech and gaming marketing, partnering across the gaming ecosystem to create unique brand positions in gaming.

Our goal is to continue to drive innovation for the brands we work with in gaming, requiring us to be on the cutting edge of creating new ways to engage with, provide experiences to and talk to the gaming audience. Livewire has expanded across APAC and EMEA within our first seven

Brad Manuel, Co-Founder and CEO, Livewire

months and are currently building APAC's largest gaming contextual advertising marketplace. This enables us to work with brands and major advertising bodies alike, providing a range of gaming advertising formats to target the gaming consumers and audience where they are most engaged.

The global nature of gaming and our business provides borderless opportunities to engage with brands and marketing agencies, while our position as thought and practice leaders enable us to work across the gaming verticals based on what strategy dictates.

Livewire is excited about the continual growth of the gaming industry and the opportunity for marketers to gain further exposure and education on ways to utilise gaming marketing and gametech to talk to the gaming audience.

We believe the continual growth of technology, AR, data and gaming as a marketing platform will position the gaming ecosystem as one of the major marketing battlegrounds for brands of the future decades.

Indy Khabra, Co-Founder and CEO, Livewire

Livewire
+61-439-411576
brad@livewire.group
Livewire_Group

livewire.group

INDIE CLUSTER

Inspiring the untargeted, promoting the unseen, and supporting the unfunded!

The Indie Cluster is a platform providing opportunities, resources, and services centered around supporting indie game developers. We focus on quality assurance testing, discoverability, hands-on production, and curating a traveling booth for our games. As our digital future demands more interactive experiences, sustainability is crucial for these small businesses. We've created a modular studio for our members, allowing each developer to focus on their game while still staying connected and succeeding together!

The Cluster was created by indies, for indies. The experience of fighting to complete your project, wearing multiple hats, building a community before launch, while simultaneously feeling alone when pitching your ideas are feelings we know all too well. In this volatile space, we love seeing projects thrive, and learning how they did it. We decided to commit ourselves to sharing resources and opportunities to help developers grow their businesses. We also wanted to create a model to supply those needs directly, dealing with the logistics so members won't have to. For years now, we've been the pulse of the indie gaming scene here in Atlanta, Georgia. It took some business finesse, some bootstrapping, and some friendly connections to have a recognizable platform today. Our traveling booth created opportunities for developers to network at local conferences, meet potential customers, and gain much needed feedback on their games.

We use our Twitch channel as a tool to not only promote indie games but to talk UX design, find bugs, and host playtests live for those that may need it. With our new membership strategy, we are excited to be giving QA support, coaching, social media management, and start up advice to a global market. Most other online game communities are just websites, however we provide directed services. This has never been done before so we're super proud of our team and the heart of our partners. In the community we've been able to foster, there's so much talent and enthusiasm for creativity and the future of games. Through the hard times, it was their

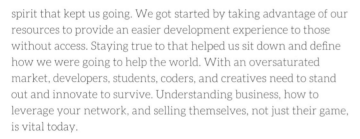

spirit that kept us going. We got started by taking advantage of our resources to provide an easier development experience to those without access. Staying true to that helped us sit down and define how we were going to help the world. With an oversaturated market, developers, students, coders, and creatives need to stand out and innovate to survive. Understanding business, how to leverage your network, and selling themselves, not just their game, is vital today.

In teaching and serving this community, our mission is to never let a passion project die because of a lack of resources. I can't speak highly enough of the family environment we have cultivated here in Atlanta. It's become a core part of our company's culture, and something we want to offer those indies without a network. Game development is at the intersection of art and technology. We create artistic expressions in a rapidly growing medium that changes constantly. If you're not innovating and iterating, it's easy to get left behind. For developers, the setbacks from becoming a starving artist are magnified as development time for one project often lasts years. This is where our system comes in, enabling that innovation and fueling those iterations. Indies already have the experience in creating something out of nothing. The Indie Cluster provides the buffer for these game makers to become successful entrepreneurs. Game design theory is experimentation, encapsulation, discovery, and presentation. Start ups suffer through the same process as games do during production. By automating the common things, we're able to show more love to the product. The product being, great games by our clients. We built our website with this in mind, presenting our members and their games professionally. We're excited to expand our outreach projects, building arcade cabinets and teaching minoritized students how to make games. We plan on hosting more community oriented streams and building a library of game dev content. Even blockchain technology is on our radar as we prepare our developers for a sustainable future.

Indie Cluster
IndieClusterAtl

IndieCluster.com

Quickscope is a new social networking platform for video game developers.
Development and creation talents to can connect with like-minded individuals, create professional industry-specific portfolios, and speak with recruiters regarding employment opportunities. We offer our users innovative industry-specific features such as advanced search filters and networking tools to ease the everyday hassles of networking in the industry for game devs worldwide.

"The right community can help you find the **right opportunity** and that community is **Quickscope**

Each Quickscope user's profile acts as a professional industry-specific portfolio that is offered in accordance with the game developer's position within their game dev team. Finally, we provide recruiters with their own unique feature set to sift through the talent on the Quickscope platform and provide them with the greatest ability to find the right talent for any of their open positions.

Quickscope is a place for game devs of all experience levels to come together as a community, and collaborate with each other over their common interests.

Quickscope started off as a passion project for us, a group of second-year university students in Waterloo, Canada. Our co-founders were indulging in video games too frequently during the peak of the pandemic and we thought to ourselves "how can we give back to the industry that brought us so much joy?". Through many conversations with distressed video game developers, we realized that tasks such as making new connections, showcasing your work, and speaking to recruiters can be a hassle on an everyday basis within the industry. This is when we knew that we had a chance to truly make a difference, and simplify everyday processes for video game developers, with Quickscope.

"The more developers we speak to, the more problems we can identify and the more solutions we can create"

The entrepreneurial journey can be difficult for anyone, especially for a young group of 19 year olds so we joined an accelerator program that introduced us to incredible experts in the fields of gaming and business. On top of balancing our time between school and Quickscope, having mentors and advisors dedicate their time to ensure we are on the right track has been an extraordinary experience that we are grateful for.

We have had hundreds of conversations with new and experienced game devs and through these discussions, we have been able to highlight the key features that will be included in our official Quickscope version 1.0 release. The platform will include many more features than previously discussed publicly. We are looking forward to providing video game developers with a platform to truly level up in their careers and help them in any way possible.

quickscope.gg

Quickscope
zack@quickscope.gg
416-417-9371
gg_quickscope 🐦
quickscope_gg 📷
quickscopegg 💬 in

STITCH

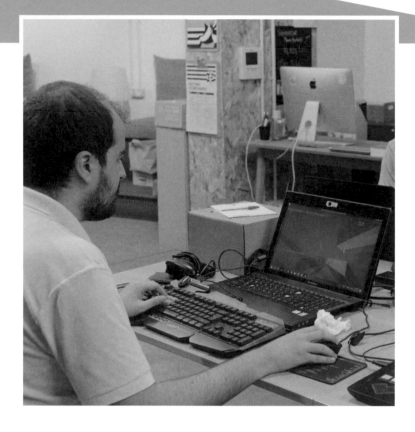

GAME TESTING EVOLVED - CONNECTING GAME DEVELOPERS WITH PLAY-TESTERS.

Indie game developers are the heart and soul of the gaming industry, and without them, we wouldn't have as much innovation as we currently have, and have been enjoying since Pong. With that said, indie game developers are always struggling to create their games because of various reasons, and this is a problem that we need to do our best to help solve.

One of these problems revolve around having financial and resource hurdles in regards to games quality assurance (QA), testing games to find general and critical bugs, gathering player feedback, and attaining market data. These can be obtained by either spending a lot of money, or sign a deal with a publisher where you may lose a lot of your potential revenue, IP rights, deal with creative restrictions and vision interferences, or lastly trying your luck in putting in a lot of labor and spend a decent chunk of money to build your user/fan-base and manage them early on. These are major hurdles that indie game developers would face during their journey of developing and releasing their first or future games, and it's an issue that Stitch is trying to solve.

How is it trying to solve it? By using the power of incentives to obtain higher rates of general and quality feedback and bug submissions, where testers would be rewarded by developers with points for their effort, that they can exchange for premium games like The Witcher 3: Wild Hunt, SUPERHOT, or any other triple-A or indie game that would be available, and they'd be attainable at relatively fast-pace.

There will be other beneficial use-cases for these points in the future, like utilizing them to decrease the price of games or exchanging them for actual money in the form of a cryptocurrency.

There's also a ranking system that would help provide developers with the best testers available, which also act as another incentive for testers to up their testing game to reach a higher rank to obtain various potential perks such as priority access to tests, higher reward amount, decreased game prices, invitation to exclusive tests, better conversion rates for points to crypto, etc.

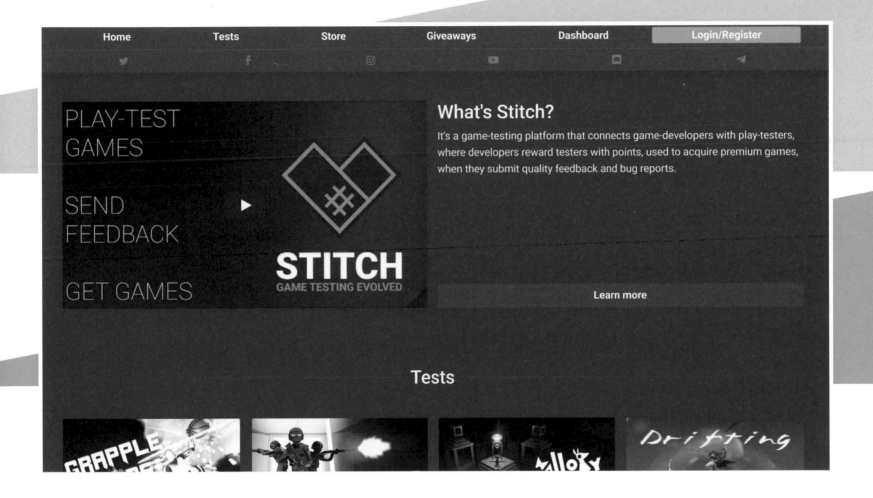

With our love for the indie gaming scene, there were two points we thought of early on when creating Stitch:

1. To create as much value and benefit to indie game developers, as low of a cost as possible.

2. To have a decent business model so we don't go bankrupt and not have everyone lose the value and benefits of the platform. (The power of love for the indie gaming scene isn't enough fuel to keep a business for it up and running, unfortunately)

With this in mind, the main value we provide indie game developers would be to have a large pool of playtesters ready to test their games to provide them with quality feedback and bug reports, at a much lower cost when compared to other available options in the gaming market, if not for free.

The side and future value would be to provide them with tools and services to conduct market research, localization, game validation, increased community engagement, and much more.

The goal with Stitch is to take over the QA and game-testing industry by outsourcing the work to the target audience themselves for indie game developers, with results rivaling the best options that are currently available, if not better, at a much lower cost if not for free. Tilting the gaming industry to focus back on independent game developers.

Stitch
team@stitch.games
StitchGamesQA
StitchNews_

stitch.games

ESTV IS THE FIRST WORLDWIDE 24/7 LIVE LINEAR AND AVOD ESPORTS CHANNEL AVAILABLE EVERYWHERE.

Watch live Esports events, tournaments, interact with your favorite gamer and celebrities, and discover your favorite gamer's lifestyle. ESTV is available on OTT, CTV, OTA and cable including The Roku Live TV Channel, Samsung TV Plus, Dish Sling TV, VIZIO Free Watch, TCL, Hisense, ZEASN, Amazon FireTV, Rakuten TV, RAD TV, PLEX, SelectTV, TikiLIVE, Simul-TV, GlewedTV, KlowdTV, EasyTV, VIVA LiveTV and Samsung Galaxy mobile device.

Partners include over 100 content creators, publishers, and studios such as the NFL Alumni Association, Enthusiast Gaming, Dept. of Defense JBLM, PUBG, Enthusiast Gaming, Simplicity Esports, International Esports Federation, Sony Music, Columbia Records, New England Collegiate Conference (NECC), College Sports Management Group (CSMG), East Coast Athletic Conference (ECAC), East Coast Conference (ECC), Peach Belt Conference, HBCU, MEAC, SIAC, NJCAA, Generation Esports, High School Esports League, Allied Esports, Esports College & Career Pathways (ECCP), ESE Entertainment, K1CK Esports, Cxmmunity, Axis Replay, Gamers.Vote, World Pro Racing, GTR24H, Lionheart IndyCar Racing, Dark Horse IndyCar Racing, Classic IndyCar Racing, E1 Championship, Chess24, Drone Champion League, Preediction, Inside The Game, Skillshot, Boise State, Echelon Cycling Racing, ZMS Live Stream, Ultimate Gaming League, Stargaze, HYPE Sports Innovation, Hearo.Live, Kungarna, We Are Nation, Sector Six Apparel, VRM (Tennis Esports), Turncoin The Xchange, Nodle, Google Tenor and many more.

ESTV's most recent partnership is with Nodle, a citizen-powered decentralized network focused on setting the stage for the next frontier of the Internet of Things (IoT). ESTV will likely scale Nodle's network significantly as ESTV boasts over 29.6 million global viewers, an outreach that will soon be exposed to the Nodle network.

ESTV is set to integrate Noodle's networking library with its upcoming mobile application. In addition, the eSports content streaming provider will promote the Nodle cash app in its 24/7 global broadcasts.

This partnership will expose ESTV users to an additional source of revenue, giving them an option to passively earn Noodle's native token Nodle Cash (NODL) while streaming their favorite sports. They will also be able to redeem their earned rewards for incentives such as the ESTV gear and other offerings by the firm.

Commenting on the partnership, ESTV Founder and CEO Eric Yoon noted that the company is thrilled to integrate Noodle's IoT focused technology,

"We are excited to partner with Nodle to deliver their technology to our upcoming ESTV mobile app ... The more our viewers view content on the

ESTV mobile app, the more Nodle Cash they'll earn. This partnership is truly a win-win-win for ESTV viewers and users, Nodle, and ESTV!"

ESTV is proud to partner with innovative organizations like Nodle, solidifying the spot as the leader and most innovative esports TV and media network in the world.

ESTV
eric.yoon@estv.co
estvesportstv 🖸 🟦 ▶
estv.co 🅵
estv 🛅

estv.co

polycade™

Reimagining arcade gaming for the modern day

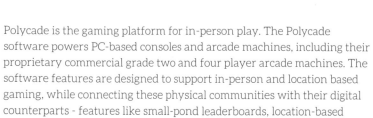

Polycade is the gaming platform for in-person play. The Polycade software powers PC-based consoles and arcade machines, including their proprietary commercial grade two and four player arcade machines. The software features are designed to support in-person and location based gaming, while connecting these physical communities with their digital counterparts - features like small-pond leaderboards, location-based achievements, live streaming, and enabling players to access their game library from any Polycade, commercial included, by simply logging in with the scan of a QR code. Polycade's upcoming meetups and tournaments will take place in bars and universities across the country, helping to build local communities via gaming.

Polycade launched with a Kickstarter campaign, featuring a reimagined, wall-mounted arcade design that challenged the perception of what an arcade machine looks like and where it should be placed. The design came about when Tyler Bushnell, co-founder and creator of the Polycade, mentioned to his wife, a furniture designer, the idea of putting an arcade machine in the living room. She was horrified at the idea of a classic arcade cabinet in the center of the house. Tyler set about to create a design that would feel like a piece of modern furniture in their mid-century style home, and after presenting his wife with a variety of possible designs, settled on the form factor used today. Shortly after fulfilling the Kickstarter orders, Jake Galler joined Polycade as they prepared to build out the software platform and bring high-fives to people across the world!

Polycade Inc.
info@polycade.com
polycade 📷
thepolycade 🐦

polycade.com

GAMERSAFER

SCALING SAFETY AND FAIR PLAY TO MILLIONS OF PLAYERS

SAFETY IS A FUNDAMENTAL PRECONDITION TO CREATING ONLINE SPACES WHERE PLAYERS CAN EXPERIMENT, FORM, MAINTAIN, AND DEEPEN CONNECTIONS. THAT'S WHY WE FOUNDED GAMERSAFER."
— MARIA TAMELLINI
CO-FOUNDER, GAMERSAFER

GamerSafer's mission is to scale safety and fair play experiences to millions of players worldwide. Fraud, crime, and toxicity are present in many online interactions, compromising user experience, lifetime value and engagement.

The co-founders of GamerSafer, a former executive from the gaming industry and a social impact entrepreneur, both gamers and parents of gamers, saw an opportunity to make an impact in this industry.

Bullying, harassment, hate speech, sexism, racism, identity theft, fake or duplicated accounts, bots, scammers, groomers, and predators are common challenges whenever there is dynamic user interaction.

GamerSafer offers to multiplayer games and Esports platforms a digital identity management system to attack the root causes of those challenges. Using computer vision and artificial intelligence technologies, players are verified and authenticated with a face scan in less than one second. To meet different game needs, this process can take place in different stages of players' experiences (pre-game or in-game).

This data enrichment, compliant with all data privacy regulations worldwide, enables a prevention first approach to community management, helps platforms to improve matchmaking systems, and drives user accountability.

With this innovative technology, platforms break the vicious cycle of offenders creating multiple accounts to attack other players or the game itself. The player is still anonymous, but has a protected account with its unique biometric coordinates; preventing abuse, evasion of bans, and perpetration of harms.

GamerSafer technology is cross-platform to support the whole gaming ecosystem and the integration process is simple and customizable. Among the advantages, aside from player verification, there are additional relevant insights like player age estimation,

verifiable parental consent for transactions, in-game preferences to tailor a game's matchmaking, and much more.

In Esports, securing competition integrity is essential from amateur to professional levels. Cheaters are always evolving methods to empty the prize pools, but without a proactive solution like GamerSafer's, even when they are caught and banned nothing prevents them from returning and repeating the aggression.

In multiplayer games, the player's preferences help to create safer environments with improved matchmaking. Game developers can also leverage age-appropriate matching or combine the digital identity insights with moderation solutions to prioritize tickets and optimize operational costs.

Safety is longitudinal, security is paramount, and privacy is a right to all. GamerSafer takes those pillars to create a strong foundation and fight the problem at the source and impact the industry to move towards a more fair and fun future where every player feels empowered to game on.

FIGHTING FRAUD, CRIME, AND TOXICITY; GAMERSAFER TECHNOLOGY HELPS MULTIPLAYER GAMES AND ESPORTS PLATFORMS IMPROVE USER SAFETY, ENGAGEMENT, AND RETENTION AT SCALE.

Gamesafer Inc
maria@gamersafer.com

gamersafer.com

BEΛMABLE

WE FREE THE GLOBAL COMMUNITY OF GAME MAKERS TO FOCUS ON WHAT THEY LOVE MOST: CREATIVITY.

Trapper, Ali and I had lived through building and operating live games like Star Trek Timelines, investing millions to build up the infrastructure to enable it. We didn't think anyone should have to do all of that again. Our team has a unique background that includes not only making games—but making enterprise technology and cloud-based infrastructure—so we felt like solving this problem was a unique calling.

When we look out into the world, we see many trends. Games are becoming more social. Development teams are changing their composition from technologists to artists. Games are shifting from "products" to "economies." Everything you need to create a successful game is only getting more complex. Although 3D engines have brought enormous simplicity to game development, the whole server/cloud side is still a patchwork of bespoke systems. We've created a company to help.

Our mantra is: "We Fight for the Game Maker." The game industry is so hard to succeed in, and we feel that someone needs to be on their side. This is the core of our culture.

One of the things we've discovered is that most teams building live games today tend to get caught up in a lot of artificial bottlenecks around workflow; engineers frequently need to get involved in the most basic processes. Debugging, deployment, updating is a pain (if not impossible). And at the same time, most game developers want to work within the visual design environment (e.g., Unity) or perform live operations tasks from within a web-based interface.

One of our sources of inspiration is Roblox. Like Roblox, we believe there is a great deal of power in top-down frameworks geared towards the creator—as well as a no-code/low-code backend that eliminates the need for DevOps, specialized programming, etc. The approach we are taking with Beamable is to make building a live game as easy as it is in Roblox, but with the freedom to do whatever you want: no living inside a walled garden with big take rates, no creative constraints, and the ability to use a great 3D engine like Unity. The goal is to enable everyone from a small indie studio to a large publisher to scale up to get as big as they need, while bringing joy and simplicity to their day-to-day work.

The product we've invented—the Beamable Live Games platform—has three main areas of functionality:

Fully-managed, cloud-based infrastructure: game developers can build a live, online game without needing to master DevOps, maintain an IT team, or build brittle server code. This enables features to manage content, economy and social systems. It scales automatically, and has a track record of delivering 99.9% uptime to millions of users. Dashboards are built-in so that the people responsible for managing and updating the game can see what's going on with all of their performance metrics—and more importantly—take actions to operate the game, whether that's adding a new item, helping out a player, or scheduling a live event.

No-code workflow: game developers work within their native development environment along with a web-based interface for managing things like item inventories, rules or statistics. Everything is fully integrated, so you can test changes to live game components locally, and then debug, stage and deploy changes as you need.

Extensibility: It's impossible to create every feature that every game developer might need now and into the future, so we created a platform built around a common game programming language (C#) and made it possible for developers to add their own custom modules and microservices.

As we continue to fight for the game maker, we'll help everyone navigate the challenges of the solo-to-social trend, the games-as-economies trend and the shift towards more and more artists on teams. And we'll keep fighting as the industry continues to evolve.

Beamable
BuiltOnBeamable 🐦 f
beamable in 🟦

beamable.com

wethink

Build better humans by empowering individuals with data-driven feedback in regards to how they interact with others through esports and gaming.

The team at weThink spent years working directly with schools, coaches and players to develop programs that focused on social and emotional skill growth backed by research with the Assessment and Achievement institute at Kansas University. Team-based games and esports are the perfect environment for social skills to flourish, and Katrina Salazar's goal is to prove skill growth to all stakeholders from parents to scholastic administrators, and most importantly, to players.

In the summer of 2021, weThink launched the latest version of its skills tracking platform. All skills on the platform fall into five core workforce readiness skills including Teamwork, Character, Problem Solving, Leadership, and Communication. This is the first platform that can accurately measure self-awareness in regards to social skills over time. Through peer and self-evaluations, players can reflect on their skill strengths and map those strengths to specific collegiate programs based on their personal career interests.

For esports coaches and program directors, the platform is a game changer. Team rosters can be evaluated using the platform to understand player-to-player relationships and how they are impacting their performance. A well known fact is that individual talent does not equal team success, and this is especially true when using team-based video games in a competitive setting. Studies show that players

Katrina, Founder, WeThink

with high self-awareness more than double the performance of players with low self-awareness, and finally, coaches have a way to measure this extremely valuable attribute. Aside from the increased performance within teams, weThink skill profiles can be exported and shared with parents, administrators, in college applications, and on resumes to prove growth in the skills that matter most to employers today. LinkedIn's 2019 Global Talent Trends study revealed that 91% of talent professionals agree that soft skills are very important to the future of recruiting and HR. Last, but certainly not least, scholastic esports programs are using the weThink platform to provide "proof of work" for educational institutions. This opens school funding budgets to support esports programs through Career and Technical Education (CTE) and Social-Emotional Learning (SEL). Not only can programs receive more funding, but some have integrated esports into their CTE programs to provide graduation credits for participating students.

While the futures of esports, education, and the workforce are ever-changing, self-awareness will always remain valuable. Not only can students boast about their participation within esports, but they can prove how their experiences increased their performance in the game, at school, and in life.

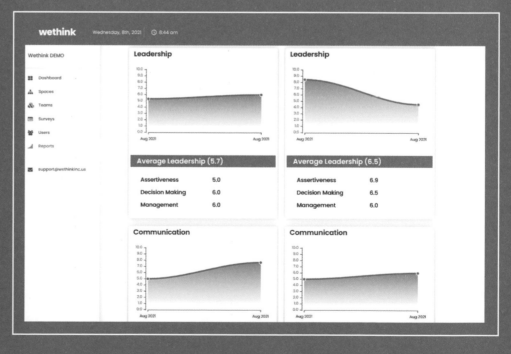

We Think
657-200-1211
wethink_inc
wethinkinc

wethinkinc.us

moz://a builders

DECENTRALIZING GAMING CONTENT AND STORIES FOR CREATIVES LEFT BEHIND.

Have you ever wondered what it takes to create content for games or interactive stories? The overwhelming number of 30+ tools you must juggle? What is the chance for you to succeed amidst the endless pool of published games?

These are the questions driving the team at Cinevva and their game-making tool, VIO. "VIO is for the dreamers, the creatives, the indie developers that are left out of gaming because of the technical barriers" , said Mariana Muntean, CEO & Founder at Cinevva, Inc.

We live in difficult times when one person has to become a little bit of everything – an artist, a programmer, a marketer on top of their daily chores and jobs. And the multitude of tools that we use on a daily basis, instead of helping us being efficient, distract us even more.

This is exactly what a typical video game developer is dealing with as well. Less than 0.1 % indie developers succeed when publishing a project on Steam or on other platforms. Now during Covid, the gap between the elite's game creators and the indies is increasing more than ever, creatives needing tools like VIO to create quality games to promote an idea from early stage to release without frustration and be able to distribute it easily.

The platform's first customers include people like Sofia, an aspiring game developer who wants to make games that teach users the positive impact of money management. VIO is helping Sofia refine her vision and cut down on the number of tools, research, and time she needs to get from idea to playable levels.

The team developing VIO, Oleg Sidorkin, CTO, xIBM Chief AI Architect and Mariana Muntean, CEO, xOrange France B2B CMO met during Founder Institute' Austin events in 2020 and started working on VIO immediately, refining product-market fit during Mozilla Incubator Labs. The product won Mozilla Builders Award in Ocober 2020 and launched VIO 2.0 Open Beta in September 2021.

VIO lives in the world of decentralized peer to peer technology, allowing teams to collaborate in real-time, just like Google docs and mirrors the complex toolchains of professional game engines like Unity. Unity and other game frameworks are heavy frameworks designed 20 + years ago, targeting the experienced game developers and are not adapted for the independent developer stuck at home with flaky at times WIFI. Privacy and freedom of VIO users being in control of their art are also VIO's main distinctive focus - every account is created a unique crypto ID for every creator's account to be able to thrive with powerful monetization options in the new crypto world.

Using simple drag-and-drop actions, creatives layout what they want their game to contain everything from characters to environments to mechanics. Creatives stay focused on their ideas and VIO handles the execution magic behind animations, collaborations, and live editing.

Cinevva and Vioflo are trademarks of Cinevva Inc. in the United States.

Mariana Muntean
312-730-6884
mariana@cinevva.com
CINEVVA 🔗
CINEVVAGames 🐦

app.vioflo.com

REPLAY ESPORTS

IT'S ABOUT THE FAN EXPERIENCE.
NEVER FORGET THAT THE PLAYER IS IN CONTROL.

Clicking out of a pop-up ad? Paying fees to NOT be bombarded with advertising? No one likes ads in their games- not the player and neither do the game developers. It's a terrible experience to be forced to watch ads. Yet game developers have to monetize. Ads are a necessary evil.

Not anymore. Replay Esports is taking the evil out of games. No more pop ads. No more having to pay to play. A matter of fact, Replay wants to pay people to play games, and it's going to change the world of gaming.

Twenty years ago, my first company, Global VR, transformed EA Sports Tiger Woods PGA Tour into an arcade bar kiosk. We awarded $1 Million dollars a year in prizes. It was a huge success. Registration required your social security number. Crazy, huh? Whenever we changed the weather to sunny and 35 mile an hour winds on Pebble Beach, players ran to bars to pay $4 for a chance to win a $10,000 grand prize or qualify for the $100,000 Vegas tournament. Even the bars won, because they sold food and drinks to people who played our games for hours.

EA Sports PGA Tour eSports tournaments were a good fan experience, but how could we make it better? That's the question that spawned Replay Esports. Well, $4 is expensive, and it was video golf. What if it was FREE to play for prizes and we had all your favorite games to play? So the obvious answer is advertisers, but for heaven's sake, no more ads!

INTRODUCING THE FIRST ESPORTS LOYALTY PLATFORM

Replay has built the first ever Esports Loyalty Platform to serve the player first and at the same time benefit the advertiser in a better way.

Replay has no ads. Instead advertisers become brand sponsors to esports tournaments. Replay's esports platform creates an array of different

sponsored tournaments. Every tournament offers different prizes. Are you hungry? Play to win a pizza. Travel? Play for a cruise? New sneakers? Play for Nike sneakers. If the player wins, great!!!!

If the player doesn't win, then they receive points (for real gift cards and merch) and offers from their favorite sponsors. Everyone wins. The player is getting paid to play and the sponsor (or advertiser) is getting a performance based platform that is engaging a hard to reach audience in a powerful and voluntary way.

> "At Replay, we are combining esports and gamification for advertisers (rewards, loyalty points, badges) with video games in a new way to reshape how advertisers connect with audiences. It's an ecosystem where everyone wins."
>
> — Milind Bharvirkar, Founder & President

GROWING THE MARKET EXPONENTIALLY

Statista estimates that brands will spend approximately 1.2 billion U.S. dollars on esports sponsorships and advertising in 2020. Yes! The esports market is growing. Replay believes to grow the esports market we need to change the business model so advertisers can measure a return on investment. So Replay offers two models.

Like Google's pay per click, Replay offers a pay per engagement model for advertisers. Since every engagement ends with a sponsor's offer, the brand can measure their investment in our platform.

Yet, Replay knows that food drives daily engagement, because people eat everyday. Since restaurants like to pay per offer redemption (like Groupon), Replay also offers a pay per redemption model. Restaurants only pay when someone buys an offer from them.

"Coupon sites lack engagement, fun, or rewards. Replay is going to be a massive hit, because it combines games with offers and loyalty. It's cool. It's fun. This will reach the younger generation." said Julien Recoussine, owner of Salesfixx.

SPEED TO MARKET

In today's advertising world, speed and scalability are crucial. Replay has created an esports event campaign system that allows advertisers to create and deploy an esports event in 25 minutes or less! When you combine a measurable return on investment with speed and scalability, Replay is making a revolutionary platform for the multi billion dollar digital ad market.

GEO LOCATION BASED TOURNAMENTS

With one click in our portal, tournaments can be geo location based. What that means is retailers can require that to participate in the event, you have to be at the retail location. Imagine, Taco Bell is giving out concert tickets to your favorite artist. For participating, everyone gets a BOGO burrito. Well, you are at Taco Bell and you are hungry; instant incremental purchases.

> "Our work is creating the foundation for an evolved transactional economy. Shifting the commerce and media models to respond to true user demand is the start of building a major bridge toward gaining control of our data and choices. Gaming is the tip of the spear in getting it right between our physical world and our virtual world."
>
> — Jess Garretson, CMO

Replay Esports
Milind@go4.buzz
Jess@go4.buzz

guardiangamer™

GAMING FROM A DIFFERENT VIEW

"GuardianGamer's mission is to show children how to navigate the online gaming world safely. We provide a pair of eyes and mentorship on behalf of parents/legal guardians. We keep them safe in a number of ways: We monitor their childrens' online interactions, encourage them to develop healthy, self-regulating habits, model behaviors and support their gaming skills, attitudes and behaviors. The goal is to contribute to their development as socially responsible gamers, while providing parents with insightful information about the online sessions."

Heidi Vogel Brockmann - Founder of GuardianGamer

Heidi is an entrepreneur and computer scientist who anticipates the needs of businesses and society as they're transformed by digital technology. She earned her Master's in Computer Science at the University of Twente in the Netherlands.

She is constantly seeking the edge of change and where she finds it, she pushes to capitalize on it to make a breakthrough.

For example, early on she saw that internet video would transform the world of television. So in 2005, she cofounded the interactive media company Avinity Systems in the Netherlands along with her now husband and her college engineering friends Ronald Brockmann , Arnoud Zwemmer, Maarten Hoeben and Andre Blum. The company created technologies that enabled the conversion of television and the Internet. Their work paved the way toward the world of streaming video that we enjoy today through all the popular streaming media services.

ActiveVideo, a US company based in San Jose, acquired Avinity in 2009 and Heidi and Ron then moved to Silicon Valley with their four children in 2013.

Fast forward to today, and it was during the pandemic that Heidi saw how online gaming has become a lifeline for kids who need to maintain social contact with their friends. Gaming enabled them to engage in their natural need for play and interaction beyond just chatting. But she also worried about how little parents knew or understood about what was going on in these online worlds.

Interactive technologies and social media are transforming our kids' worlds. The line between virtual and analog realities is growing blurrier, and parents naturally wonder how their children can navigate safely through these online and offline worlds.

These insights led Heidi to create GuardianGamer. The company offers a platform that is designed for parents with gaming children: It provides children with responsible online mentors and reports to parents about their activities — just like a babysitter would provide a report to parents after a trip to the playground.

Heidi is committed to her mission. She wants to create a safe and positive gaming metaverse for the future.

" *Parents have no control or supervision on what goes on online. Although parents are willing to play games with their kids, they aren't as skilled so they can't really keep up. Some parents don't have time to engage. Parents are worried about online "toxicity" and look for peace of mind and positivity."*

Kids want to play online games but have to deal with their parents' lack of understanding. "They don't understand me." They are influenced beyond their own ability, and unknown sources and need help making the right decisions."

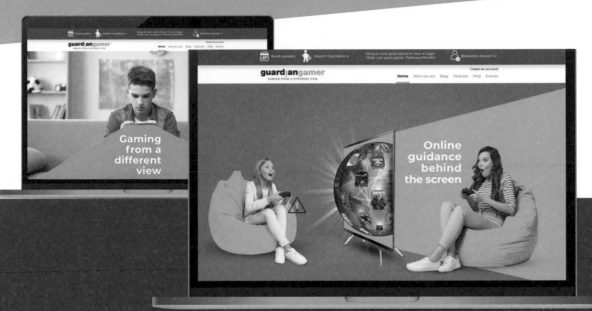

"The goal of the guardian is not to bog down the session or steal the fun from the experience. We are there to enhance and chronicle, to highlight the game session so the parent can look upon the adventure proudly. We also believe in the learning power of independence and want the child to explore gaming on their own, we are simply there when they need help."

CASUAL PLAY

Join one of our trusted Guardiangamers for a freeplay session. Pick a game and start playing!

BUILDING PROJECT HELP

Join one of our trusted Guardiangamers for a freeplay session. Pick a game and start playing!

GAME COACHING

Connect with one of our verified game coaches to take your skills to the next level. Pick a game and start playing!

PROGRAM PACKAGE

Get on track with pre-scheduled gaming sessions designed to help moderate game time.

guardiangamer.com

"Games have so much freedom. you can go anywhere you want."
— JENEVA CHEN

CHAPTER 14

MIXED REALITY

BATTLE RACING: A New Combat Motorsport Built for Drivers, Designed for Gamers...
THE NEXT EVOLUTION OF RACING!

Emotional Ideas, inc. aka EI, is a sports and entertainment technology company revolutionizing known attractions, games, and products for the next generation of entertainment thrill seekers. We are currently taking the popular sport of go-kart racing and combining it with the strategy and skill of Esports gaming to pioneer a new hybrid industry vertical that will lay the foundation of a new combat motorsport called BATTLE RACING. Our "**G**o-kart **M**obile **L**aser-**T**ag" (**GMLT™**) product officially known as the BATTLE CONSOLE is a retrofittable hyper immersive gaming console and controller system for electric go-karts and larger vehicles—transforming the traditional racing experience into a 21st century hyper-immersive, mixed-reality, gaming experience in the physical world. This new motorsport will introduce virtual offensive & defensive weapon items/ powerups to grant players a temporary competitive edge as they dodge landmines along the track and BATTLE RACE for first place. Emotional Ideas seeks to leverage the youth and minority audiences' interest in advanced gaming technology to create a new gamified motorsport that can serve as a future alternative to NASCAR and F1 Racing. Think about it. What if Nintendo's Mario Kart was a pro motorsport played on real electric vehicles (small or large engines) on a real physical track? BATTLE RACING is new combat motorsport; **Built for Drivers but Designed for Gamers!**

Our Founder/ CEO, Joshua Nelson, has always been fascinated with amusement and entertainment attractions. Such passion has often led him to visit new entertainment centers on opening day. So much so, that for his 21st Birthday, he chose to visit one of his favorite childhood pastimes, Chuck E Cheeses! Since 2010, Mr. Nelson has dedicated himself to not only learning the inner workings of the amusement & entertainment industry but also ways on how to further impact its future existence. He recognized that leading organizations within the motorsport industry were struggling to appeal to both the younger and minority audiences. However, the world has seen a spike in interest for gaming and esports. He figured if he could combine new elements of advanced gaming technology with the traditional experience of racing, gamification could be the 21st century redevelopment of motorsports racing.

This epiphany emerged during a casual outing of go-kart racing. He noticed when stuck behind an experienced driver, it was difficult to execute a pass or takeover. He wished he could simply take a page from Nintendo's *Mario Kart* game and use a powerup to shoot the vehicle ahead and speed boost around. After the race, he couldn't stop sharing "what if" scenarios around the potential of gamifying racing, and you know what they say. "If you can't stop talking about something, then maybe you should be the one to do it." In 2014, The Battle Racing technology was just an idea; in 2021, It became a US patented Idea!

Joshua Nelson, Founder/ CEO, Bill McKeel, COO

(GMLT) Battle Console R-Series [1]

Emotional Ideas' business slogan is, "Innovative ideas driven by emotional passion." We know that Battle Racing is an innovative idea, and that it will take a passionate team to bring this to mainstream. Our goal is for Emotional Ideas to be a top innovative leader within the Amusement, Gaming, & Sports tech industries. We are starting with revolutionizing the amusement and pro racing industry. Next, will be other popular attractions and games that need renovating for the upcoming generation.

To date, Emotional Ideas has successfully been granted a US patent, as well as global patent protection, surrounding the battle racing technology. We have developed numerous vendor and strategic partnerships in our effort to create a new global motorsport/ esport hybrid industry vertical. The technology will allow the EI team to change not only the basic racing experience but how fans engage and spectate the sport of racing. Starting with the amusement and entertainment industry, EI will first introduce "Battle Racing" as a fun, new enhancement to the traditional sport of go-karting. As fan engagement and interest increases, so will the push for a competitive recreational league, and eventually, a professional racing league will emerge. In the gaming world, it is a privilege that everyone gets to start on the same level and rely solely on skill and personal talent to get better. As opposed to current motorsports, where money buys the fastest cars and best drivers, "Battle Racing" will offer a competitive racing experience beyond who has the fastest vehicle—expanding into who has both the skill to drive and the talent to play. EI will introduce a new mixed reality of gaming and racing in the physical world that will mirror known combat racing games. Our founder has always dreamt of playing games like Nintendo's *Mario Kart*, Sony's *Crash Team Racing* or *Twisted Metal* in the physical reality, and now, the world has a new hyper immersive way to play & enjoy known combat racing games in real life!

Joshua Nelson, Founder/ CEO

Emotional Ideas Inc
Jnelson@emotionalideasinc.com
+1(901)2770284
emotional-ideas-inc 🔗
emotional_ideas 🐦
Emotional Ideas, Inc. f

Emotionalideasinc.com
BattleRacing.com

Abhishek Kanjilal, Founder & CEO

Anjana Maria, Analyst

Dilip J Thomas, Head Technology

As the forerunners of "Futuretainment", The VirtX is the first of its kind broadcasting & streaming aggregating service in Virtual Reality in the form of shared entertainment (live sports/events/movies/gaming) to the B2C audiences.

The VirtX is a platform which enables networks to broadcast their live content in Virtual Reality to their audience, who can experience the same in a group while keeping it interactive (as in speak to one another directly). Using the same operational algorithm, the VirtX can be leveraged for multiple remote services on the B2B end, bringing down the overhead costs drastically for an organisation.

Breaking out from its niche, its time Virtual Reality stepped into the limelight of the mainstream and we intend to lead the way forward with it. The VirtX was born in 2019, over a drink while talking to my father-in-law (who has had an illustrious career as a naval architect), about remote offshore rig supervision and ship surveys. Back then I was working on a different product and was exploring avenues of integrating VR in it. I have always been fascinated with the AR/VR/MR technology (now XR) from a young age, coupled with sci-fi movies, it was always about,

"what if that were for real?" Being an ardent Liverpool Football Club fan myself, I always wanted to experience real life game in person, with my friends at all venues, which logistically were impossible for me at the time. After interacting with a few industry experts, investors and closed target group audiences, I realized the potential The VirtX held and how it could break out from a niche to being a mass technology changing the market and operational approach across industries. Throughout my career, I have failed a million times and learnt from each to apply to the few successes which mattered productively. End of the day we all need that ONE successful result to make all the difference in life. The road for an entrepreneur is one of the toughest from being a nobody to somebody. My journey has been no less.

When everyone suggested starting with the smaller entities, the years have taught me to go big or go home. Confidence has always been one of my strong points, coupled with metric based market feedback, I reached out to the big players. Everything sounds like clockwork as I pen them down, but I can assure you, it has been anything but clockwork. Sleepless nights, cold leads, deteriorating mental health, financials, family and friends everything collapsed but it was the sheer will and belief in the

THE WORLD'S FIRST BROADCASTING ENABLER/AGGREGATOR PLATFORM IN VIRTUAL REALITY WITH SOCIAL INTERACTION.

Ephrem Carri, Consultant - Maritime

Marcus "Esports, Howard Board Advisor

product which became the main driver in that time. The passion I have towards innovation is what made me what I am today. Ideally I would say, The VirtX is an innovative platform which enables other industry players chalk their path in the world of XR which creates a new avenue for customer engagement as well as operational efficiency. Everyone wants to create a new product and beat the competition.

Our focus is to work with the competition and create something extra ordinary. Even though our operational backend and algorithm are proprietary, I would say the concept of it was brought about by amalgamating existing proven technologies. After all innovation is not only about creating something novel but also seeing things in a different perspective and putting them into effect to maximize the impact.

Within The VirtX, the motivation for the team comes from identifying the market gaps, where our competition has missed and how we can fill in. We are strong believers in breaking the chain. We get excited when our users are excited. Hence innovation is at the heart of our

organization. This year is all about testing and feedback to make the right market fit and ensure a seamless experience. As of now, we are well on track to a formal launch of The VirtX in the spring of 2022 and acquire a market of a million users globally by 2025.

The VirtX Inc.
Abhishek Kanjilal
abhishek@thevirtx.com
(437) 7772387
TheVirtx ⬛
the_VirtX 🟦
TheVirtX Inc ▶

thevirtx.com

VIRTUAL REALITY
A Powerful Tool for Connection and Compassion

Expanding Human Awareness Through the Design and Delivery of Fantastic Experiences.

As a boy, I fell in love with the world of video games. I appreciated the fact that this new hobby of mine had boundaries and rules that could be learned that were always consistent. Soon, I began delving deeper into these boundaries and rules by learning how to code. I spent endless hours exploring Basic on my family's clunky IBM XT. Later on, I was introduced to another chapter in my digital journey: the emerging sector of virtual reality.

I became interested in how this technology could be used to connect and unite people with one another. In corporate settings connection and engagement are often sorely lacking, resulting in employees working far below their maximum potential. My passion for expanding human awareness and personal transformation led me to merge my professional experiences in team building and leadership with my native abilities in technology. Better Than Unicorns is the result of that merger, using virtual reality to foster empathy and connection in the workplace.

Virtual reality is an essential tool for building compassion and expanding awareness about how we relate to failing and learning from those moments. Better Than Unicorns is consistently dedicated to unlocking cooperation and innovation through the power of play. Our virtual reality sessions utilize reflective conversations to uncover how members of a team are best able to cooperate and engage with one another, thus strengthening interpersonal bonds and eventually contributing to the formation of a cohesive corporate culture. With decades of experience in

the virtual reality field, we've attracted partners such as Coca-Cola and GE Aviation, and we are always looking to forge bonds with other cutting-edge organizations. Here at our organization, we consider ourselves to be innovators, especially when it comes to team-building in the workplace.

In fact, innovation in this field is central to this company's mission. In our current collaboration with Elventus, we are using esports and virtual reality esports to enhance player performance in the burgeoning esports industry while maintaining their mental health.

Together Better Than Unicorns and Elventus tap into virtual reality's unique ability to both expedite players' learning yet still emphasize their physical and mental health. Through our focus on the human aspects of high-level competition, we will radiate as a beacon of compassion and balance in this blossoming industry where both are sorely needed. We

Brett A McCall , Futurist, Innovator

facilitate teams to discover more about how they best collaborate by giving them space to face great challenges and discomfort in a safe, supportive environment. The fact that our services are geared around allowing people to wrestle with difficulty, and even failure, is practically revolutionary in a corporate world where only success and results are rewarded and vulnerability is shunned.

Better Than Unicorns
betterthanunicorns
btuvr
betterthanunicorns
dazzle.betterthanunicorns.com

betterthanunicorns.com

Drone Cadets- Is a unique Drone Education Program designed to produce safe and responsible drone pilots of any age

WHAT INSPIRED THE CREATION OF DRONE CADETS?

In 2016 Sgt. Tony Reid, was a corrections officer at Rikers Island, a jail in New York City, working with incarcerated adolescents 16 to 18 years old. For 8 long years, he witnessed first-hand the plight of young men of color who became the casualties of an environment of poverty, crime, and violence. Many bright young men became ensnared in a life cycle of neglect, drugs, and crime; spending their time either on the street or behind bars. Either place could lead to dangerously grave consequences. He began to imagine a way out for these young people and decided he wanted to do something to break the chain.

WHAT ONE MAN CAN DO...

It was in August of the same year that the FAA created the first-ever Remote Pilot Certification* for civilian Unmanned Aerial Systems (UASs). Sgt. Reid received his certification in September of 2016 and his drone career took off. Sgt. Reid founded DroneTECH UAS and the concept of Drone Cadets was born. He began doing workshops, demonstrations, and hands-on drone flight training for kids. It wasn't long before he was invited into local schools and began helping incorporate drones into their STEM curriculums. Whenever kids asked about becoming a drone pilot, he talked to kids about the narrow road that they must follow to stay in school, learn and reach success in life. In 2017 Sgt. Reid partnered with DroneBlocks to expand his curriculum to include coding. He also began his worldwide mission, bringing drones to hurricane disaster-ridden countries like the Bahamas, Puerto Rico, and Curacao. While there he worked to help provide relief, conduct infrastructure inspections, and he brought a needed distraction to children devastated by loss. He taught them to fly!

DRONE CADETS SOARS

In 2018 Sgt. Reid joined forces with Grace Cantwell of Drone Wonders to teach children in underserved communities to fly drones responsibly. Ms. Cantwell's experience as a marketer and professional development trainer, bringing STEM tech tools to schools, taught her that there was no better tool than drones to engage students. It wasn't long before they realized that together, their unique knowledge, insights, and experience could create a richer, more effective Drone Cadets program than ever before. The "Tony & Grace Show" soon helped fuel the demand among students, parents, and administrators for further, more comprehensive drone training. New curriculum, missions, activities, and technology were added, and by the end of 2018 Drone Cadets had launched Level 1 and Level 2 followed by Level 3 in January of 2019. By this time Drone Cadets had taught more than a thousand students to code, fly and repair drones. Our unique method of training has been designed to build character by incorporating ethics, responsibility, safety, and teamwork.

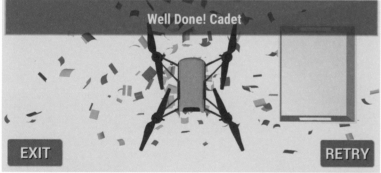

THE REAL SUCCESS STORY

As students grew in age and knowledge, they were encouraged to pursue a career in drones and offered the option of completing their FAA Remote Pilot Certification through our alliance with Drone Lecture. The real success story is about the kids we've helped save. We've witnessed the power of drones to open doors and change lives. We've spoken to grateful moms. We've heard from teachers and counselors. Most importantly, we've seen the reluctant student suddenly drawn to the center of the activity. We've watched the shy student find the courage to lead the class. We've witnessed the angry, detached child calm down, think, focus and become engaged, with a learning mindset. Who knows how many lives could be saved by allowing kids to excel on a path that could lead to a career that provides a living wage, without college? TODAY In early 2020 the new Drone Cadets partnership was launched to bring scalable drone education to schools, after-school programs, and underserved youth. The onset of COVID-19 accelerated our plans to Go Virtual, and DroneCadets. online was born to train students virtually, nationwide and around the world. On March 9 2021, Drone Cadets programs became Accredited by STEM.org the longest continually operating, privately-held STEM education research and credentialing organization in America. In April 2021, after teaching virtually for a year, Drone Cadets began teaching IRL (in real life) again, and it feels so good to be back! We're grateful for the time we had to develop new content, and the student response to our new material has been tremendous.

WHAT'S NEXT?

We've been overwhelmed by requests from people around the US and beyond who see the value in what we do, and want to bring Drone Cadets to their own classrooms. We have begun developing a network of Distributors, who have been trained to use the same content and materials we use in the classroom, in their own communities. As the world of drones becomes more diverse and complex, so will our ability to add new courses, incorporate new technology, and develop better vocational drone training, not just for pilots; but for technicians, coders and data engineers, and flight ops personnel. Demand is on the rise, and Drone Cadets is committed to helping develop a workforce that's in lockstep with the need of employers. The Corps of Drone Cadets will grow right along with the demand. OUR MISSION It is our sincere mission to help break the chains that bind so many, by offering an incentive and an alternative to the high cost of college through drone training. We're dedicated to helping build the ethics and character of our youth while feeding the fertile young minds of our world's future leaders. *FAA's small drone rule under Part 107 was announced June 21, 2016, and went into effect on August 29, 2016. Under this new rule, civilians could become commercial drone pilots by passing an Airman Knowledge Test to receive their FAA Remote Pilot Certification.

ACCREDITED BY STEM.ORG

Drone Cadets
tony@drone-cadets.com
631-384-9817
dronecadets 🔲 🔳 📘
dronetechuas 🔳

drone-cadets.com

drone-cadets.com/drone-cadets-app

CHAPTER 15
VENUES

"True grace is beautiful in its imperfection, honest in its emotion, freed by its own frailty."

— LMORGANA - LEAGUE OF LEGENDS

NERDHUB KENYA'S MISSION IS TO UTILIZE OUR ESPORTS CENTRE TO HELP GIVE YOUNG ASPIRING ESPORT ATHLETES A PLATFORM TO GROW THEIR ESPORTS CAREERS AND COMPETE ON THE WORLD STAGE.

Nerdhub Kenya was started as a platform to give talented Kenyan youth an opportunity to grow. Kenya is an underdeveloped country where youth really struggle to follow their dreams. We are giving the youth the opportunity to be the next pop star, Esports champion, Comic artist, Dancer etc. We are what we wish was around when we were younger.

Nerdhub Kenya was founded by Jameel Sayed and Usama Welton who both are hardcore gamers that would always see Kenyan talent go to waste and would always wonder why the local brands would always overlook the talent.

Nerdhub Kenya's origin story: Usama Welton, Ex Call of duty semi pro, started his Esports career back in 2018 and after seeing no opportunity in Kenya for him he proceeded to join different European teams as a free agent until he was signed by Digital Bandits Esports team and competed for a year climbing the challenger ladders. After gaining lots of experience in the esports scene, he opened the TEx Esports team with the intention of giving local pros the opportunity to earn money through Esports. After a few months he approached several Esports brands that had been around for years and proposed Esports development ideas but was unfortunately ignored or asked "What's in it for us?". Frustrated he proceeded on regardless and kept building the team which ended up having 7 rosters for various titles such as: Valorant, League of Legends, Rainbow 6, Rocket league etc. Recently TEx Esports expanded into the EU competitive scene with a Rocket league and Valorant roster.

In 2021 Jameel Sayed contacted Usama Welton who is a long time friend and began discussing the idea of opening Kenya's first Esports centre that will provide a platform for young talent to prosper especially in the Esports sector. They found that local brands that had been around for years but would only have one off events. After speaking with local athletes the complaint was always the same. "The brands are only interested in profit". Which was a shame. Due to covid-19 the development of the Esports centre was delayed by a 2 months but fortunately were able to build it.

Nerdhub Kenya is redefining what Kenyan Esports is and making history by finally opening doors of opportunity to the youth. The centre works on a membership basis whereby a person a pays a monthly fee of $36 which gives them access to all the facilities, events, tournaments and leagues in any of the categories with no extra payment. Top performers in Esports

events get signed by the organization and will be given salaries and sponsored to compete around the world. Top performers of the arts, dance, music, script writing and comic artists will have their projects funded and we will help them (with help from local publishing companies) to produce their first album, comic, music video which will set them up for a bright future. When it comes to innovation we believe we are making history when it comes to history because the country has trend of one off tournaments for $300 every 2-3 months and the players never progress in their Esport careers. As said before, Nerdhub is changing the trend and will give the members the opportunity to further passions and go full time into what they love. When it comes to innovation, Nerd Hub is leading the pack!

Esports is a global market that is made of major countries like the United States, Sweden, United Kingdom, Korea, etc. Unfortunately, Africa gets overlooked a lot except South Africa which is really developed in the Africa Esports Industry. Nerdhub Kenya wants to put Kenya on the global Esports map.

The first milestone as of 2021 is to send Kenya's first athletes to compete in an international Esports event. We also aim to gain 1000 members by the end of 2021 and be the place where African talent can grow and prosper into something big giving the youth the opportunity, we wish we had!

Why stop there? The NerdHub organization aims to go global, opening branches all over the world to support hidden talent that gets overlooked. As they say, GO BIG OR GO HOME!

Nerd Hub Kenya
Rt. 66, Downtown, Washington, DC
1-800-1234-567
info@example.com

nerdhubkenya.com

ESPORTS BAR GATHERS INDUSTRY LEADERS TO SHAPE THE FUTURE TOGETHER

The world of esports is still young: the community is expanding, business models are fluid, and innovation never stops, as the industry looks to stay fresh and exciting.

Esports BAR is the world's esports business arena, and our mission is **to transform the sport of the digital generation into the future of entertainment.**

We do this by gathering together industry leaders globally to shape the future of esports – a future that is bright.

Esports BAR is part of Reed MIDEM, the world-leading organiser of entertainment content events. Our roots stretch deep into the world of entertainment.

In 2017, **Esports BAR Cannes** launched onto the scene as a three-day event in February, in the same venue as the iconic Cannes Film Festival. Then followed **Esports BAR Miami**, held each September as a four-day event. We like to follow the sun!

The global health crisis threw a curveball. We responded swiftly, taking Esports BAR Miami online in September 2020 to hold our first fully digital, four-day edition: Esports BAR+ Americas. That is, until we can meet again in person.

Esports BAR in numbers

Who attends Esports BAR events?

Anyone who is anyone in the esports universe attends the Esports BAR events, in Cannes or Miami, or both.

You will meet and connect with

- **Industry leaders** and **visionaries** who set the pace.
- Those at the core of esports – **game publishers, streaming platform organisers, professional sports leagues, broadcasters, investors, marketeers.**
- The **brands** – new faces to esports and established players, looking for marketing opportunities to reach a growing global audience.

95%

media, advertising or digital participants are likely to return to get mentoring opportunities to explain esports market growth and how to invest in esports

80%

satisfaction among participants whose main motivation is to meet targeted people to strike business deals with

At Esports BAR, we provide an **immersive experience** – an arena for participants to step into, connect, be inspired and do business, while we are on the field, on the benches, ready to guide you. It's about:

- **Connecting** through 'curated moments' – whether through **organic networking** or pre-scheduled **1-to-1 matchmaking meetings.**

- **Inspiration through insights** – keynotes from high-level speakers, conference & panel sessions and mentoring workshops. We focus our content on **Monetisation, Innovation, Investments & Audiences.**

- **Doing business** like never before – find your future partners and do deals for **sponsorships, franchise partnerships, merchandising and licensing deals, broadcasting rights** and much more.

Esports BAR brings speakers at the height of their game

Our events provide a stage for over 50 speakers – all stars in their fields – to inspire and to share. They range from legendary professional sports players, who've successfully turned their game to esports, to niche market specialists and key figures from the world of business.

We also talk about social inclusion, mental health, and working with young audiences, to help them grow as fans, as people and as community members.

Why not join us at Esports BAR to become the new game changer in the esports universe?

Interested? Find out more about *Esports BAR's website*, and sign up for the *Esports BAR Blog* for the latest esports news from around the world.

Esports BAR
theesportsbar
esports_bar
esportsbar
EsportsBAR

the-esports-bar.com/en
blog.the-esports-bar.com

METRO ESPORTS

METRO IS A BLACK-OWNED GAMING PLATFORM AIMED AT MAKING ESPORTS FOR EVERYBODY

METRO IS A MULTICULTURAL ESPORTS AND ENTERTAINMENT PRODUCTION AGENCY, CREATING AND PRODUCING DIGITAL, SOCIAL, MOBILE AND LIVE EVENTS DESIGNED TO ATTRACT, ENGAGE AND UPLIFT A BROAD AND DIVERSE AUDIENCE OF GAMING AND TECHNOLOGY ENTHUSIASTS.

Shaon Berry, CEO & Founder, Metro Esports

A college football player, I don't come from the world of esports as I only understood competition from an athletic perspective. In 2009 I launched a company called JuniorRank Sports in an effort to create showcase opportunities for student athletes to display their natural skills to college programs looking to offer scholarships. That platform grew almost 400% over the next 2 years, as I went from creating local events in the Chicago area attracting less than 50 athletes at a time, to the year 2011 where I was producing high-profile / high-volume events in every major market. Title sponsored by the United States Marine Corps, our Semper Fidelis football program went from a concept designed in my living room to an annual bowl game that ran on the NFL, CBS Sports and ESPN television networks until 2016. Over the course of those years, I was able to help more than 1,500 young athletes get partial or full athletic scholarships. Additionally, I was able to scout and identify high school talent such as Jared Goff, Todd Gurley, Deforest Buckner and many more NFL 1ST round draft picks and Super Bowl Competitors.

In the year 2017, I was approached by a very large national organization who wanted to know if I was still producing esports events because I would purchase XBOX's and PlayStation consoles for my weekend events, in an effort to keep the young guys busy at the host hotels and not too eager to go out. This practice somehow created a reputation for me as an esports event creator and after some industry due diligence I was hooked. The transition from traditional sports to esports for me was all about the industry laws of probability. It's much easier for me to identify or develop a potential game programmer, game developer, game designer or event caster than for me to find a guy that 6'5 inches tall and weighs 400lbs. Esports offers so many tech-focused professions, I thought it was the socially responsible thing to do in offering more practical and realistic career opportunities than the NFL or NBA.

The Metro Organization is an innovator in that we are constantly looking for new ways to organically add culture to an equation that has been

left out since the start of the industry more than 40 years ago. Looking for creative and authentic ways to attract and engage a black & brown audience has reshaped how we look at everything we do from teams, to events, to production. Our tech-education program is focused on offering alternative pathways, particularly for young people from communities or institutions that lack resources, equipment or access. We are doing our best to be agents of positive change.

Metro is a Philly based 7,000 square foot gaming and technology education center. Our local partnerships with the YMCA, American Cancer Society and Drexel University here in Philadelphia, allows us access to a diverse pool of quality interns and strategic partnership initiatives supporting targeted and specific areas of the city.

We greatly look forward to:
- *The launch of The Philly Metro-Squad - The world's 1st multicultural/coed Pro Valorant team in the fall*
- *Our 2021 cultural partnership with ESL/Dreamhack giving us the opportunity to create unique events and activities focused on engaging an untapped market of gaming & tech. enthusiasts of color.*
- *The launch of the next (2) Metro Esports Gaming & Technology Center locations in the US*

Metro Esports
sberry@metrosport.us
630-639-6317
metroesportsus 🇫 🐦 📷 in ▶ 💬

metroesports.gg

"Esposure is connecting esports and education to create opportunities. We are committed to doing our part in building the esports talent pipeline through our Education to Entertainment ecosystem." Danny R. Martin is the Co-Founder and CEO of Esposure, Inc., a global esports technology company with an Education to Entertainment (E2E) ecosystem focused on developing the next generation of esports professionals and competitive gamers. The STEM.org accredited curriculum and cutting-edge technology

is designed by gamers and created to educate, entertain, engage, and empower the esports community.

Danny started his journey in the esports industry at the University of Texas at San Antonio (UTSA). He was a student athlete with limited time, but he made extra money repairing gaming equipment for classmates. Majoring in small business management and entrepreneurship, it wasn't

THE GOAL FOR ALL OF OUR PROGRAMS IS TO EDUCATE, ENTERTAIN, ENGAGE AND EMPOWER.

and self-funded his own esports organization by turning his 2,000-square-foot Downtown Dallas loft into a gaming esports arena. After a few years, he expanded and opened two arenas with over 40,000 sq. feet. Fast forward to 2020 when shelter-in-place orders were in effect, he recognized the need to pivot his company from its origins as a proprietary platform for hosting gaming tournaments to instead focus on growing their efforts to support the esports community with online educational resources and production services. In 2020, Danny and his leadership team reimagined and transformed Esposure into an esports technology company with innovative programs and a high-quality production team.

While many live esports events were cancelled and arenas went underutilized, Esposure was developing the next generation of talented videographers, content creators, graphic designers, and a best-in-class production team. Danny laid the framework for a new and enhanced Learning Management System (LMS) and built a STEM.org Accredited curriculum. His vision and leadership to execute the transition provided access to quality esports education for students across the globe and a pipeline of talent to sustain the industry growth. Perseverance, resilience, and courage were just a few of the many attributes that contributed to the transformation of the business.

Danny credits his ability to persevere to his days running track in his hometown of Lancaster, Texas throughout high school and at UTSA. "Building a business is like a marathon. There are constant ups and downs, but you must understand goal setting, pace, and milestones. You have to have the energy to keep pushing forward – enough energy to be better than your competitors." As a business owner and CEO in one of the most competitive markets for esports, Danny Martin has already made his mark on the industry as a trailblazer. But he has his eyes set on something even greater: together with Esposure, Danny is on a steadfast pursuit to educate, entertain, engage, and empower 20,000 students and young adults with STEM esports programs and career exploration by 2025.

Additionally, Danny is passionate about increasing diverse representation within STEM and esports, both areas that significantly lack diversity. Danny is breaking the mold of the esports industry and empowering others to do the same by paving a pathway to professional careers in esports for diverse individuals across the globe. He is overcoming the misperception that there is no future for kids who like to game beyond becoming a professional player. Esposure's mission is to increase access to one of the fastest growing industries in the world, while providing a comprehensive pathway for aspiring professionals within the esports industry. To further support his mission, Danny and his team helped develop the company's charitable foundation, Esposure4All, which seeks to eliminate barriers that would normally keep underrepresented populations from learning about opportunities and benefits in the emerging world of esports. Esposure4All has committed to developing esports labs and enabling youth to continue exploring opportunities within esports.

long before he recognized the financial opportunity available in organizing large-scale esports tournaments. While in college, Danny saw the vision and began building a network of gamers comprised of friends and contacts on campus.

From that database of gamers, Danny started hosting tournaments, and his first esports business, Geekletes, was born. After leaving UTSA, Danny's career and interest in esports continued to grow. By 2015, he co-founded

Esposure
903-776-7873
admin@esposure.gg
esposure 🐦
esposure.gg 📷 📘

esposure.gg

THERE'S A NERD IN EVERYONE

Nerd Street Gamers is a national esports infrastructure that puts accessibility, integrity and opportunity at the forefront of everything they do. As gaming communities slowly began to gain traction on a small scale, the CEO of Nerd Street and Localhost, John Fazio, knew that individuals nationwide would soon realize the passion and talent that gamers bring to the esports industry, hence Nerd Street and Localhost were born. Nerd Street was founded with the purpose to lower the barrier of entry for competitive gamers and its sister company, Localhost, serves as the premier location for esports competitions, training sessions, and more. Together, both companies provide a point of entry for competitive gamers, casual gamers, and anyone with a spark of interest in gaming and esports.

At its core, Nerd Street main goal is to increase accessibility within the esports industry and its gaming communities, through innovation. The emergence of The Block is a direct reflection of its core. The Block,

(approximately 40,000 square feet in size) will be the world's first esports industry campus, equipped with global broadcast studios, dedicated training centers for professional teams and schools, plus an educational space for community partners. Furthermore, a 20,000 square foot Localhost facility capable of hosting community, scholastic, amateur, and pro-level events will be available publicly to the gaming community. The Block will also serve as the new headquarters for the national esports network, Nerd Street. The Susquehanna Soniqs, will be the first professional esports organization to take advantage of its amenities through a five-year partnership. Other partners that will take advantage of this facility include Comcast NBCUniversal LIFT Labs, Team Altemus, Aim Lab and TechGirlz. Located in the heart of Philadelphia, The Block will increase networking within the esports industry and gaming community, as a culture of inclusivity and accessibility will emanate from the facility's staff and atmosphere.

Nerd Street Gamers is a national network of esports facilities and events, dedicated to providing every level of gamer with competitive opportunities to hone their skills, network, and become a part of an ever growing community. Their devotion to make esports accessible, digestible, and inclusive to everyone not only deals with competitive gaming opportunities, but education advancements, opportunities to work towards real jobs in the industry and connecting communities who have never experienced esports before. Every resource provided by Nerd Street Gamers has the common goal of lowering the barrier of entry into the esports industry. To effectively achieve this goal, collaboration is a key element for success. This is why Nerd Street Gamers has experienced exponential growth and accumulated partners such as 5 Below, Comcast Spectator, Mavix, Mike and Ike, SeventySix Capital and Founders Fund. With the unannounced pandemic in 2020, Nerd Street Gamers was able to pivot and contribute to unprecedented events that made esports history, as they dominated the online scene. One of those events, the FTW Summer Showdown, showcased the first and largest all women tournament of its time. In collaboration with Comcast Spector and Riot Games, the FTW Summer Showdown shined a light on strong, confident, and talented females behind and in front of the camera. The rippling effect of this event supported the continual mission of building a positive environment to showcase incredible female talent. Through further collaboration with companies such as the NFL, NBA, Special Olympics, Dignitas, and Twitch, Nerd Street Gamers will continue to provide opportunities for all levels of gamers despite race, religion, culture, and gender.

Localhost is a network of gaming and esports centers located across North America. It was created to lower the barrier of entry to esports by providing high quality gaming equipment for affordable pay-as-you-go pricing. They provide a homebase for gamers of all skill levels to compete, build community, and improve their skills. Even during the pandemic, as Nerd Street Gamers was able to pivot its efforts and effectively conduct business online, Localhost expansion was well under way. The pandemic was not able to stop either company from reaching out their hand and opening the door to esports for many individuals across the nation. One way Localhost was able to open the door was through a partnership launched during the pandemic with Parks and Recreation departments around the country. These partnerships were first launched in Philadelphia, PA and Brentwood, MO with the goal of bringing competitive esports experiences through camps and programs, both online and in person at Localhost. With a focus on child development, these after school programs encourage gamers to socialize with others and develop critical thinking skills, all within the environment of esports.

Nerd Street Gamers
Nerd Street 🐦 📷 📘 📺

nerdstreet.com

CHAPTER 16

NONPROFITS & ADVOCACY

"Strength lies in knowing oneself."

— PLANESCAPE: TORMENT

JUST ESPORTS

Just Esports is an organization that is dedicated to working on justice initiatives in the esports and gaming space. Much of their work focuses on educational programs aimed at empowering others to promote justice in their respective groups and providing individuals with the best tools to build out esports communities that serve all people.

Just Esports began as some conversations between Jack Blahnik and Russ Hamer, who had worked together when both were at Illinois State University, Jack as a student and Russ as a philosophy professor. As Jack entered grad school and the conversations continued, both saw an increasing need for the esports ecosystem to improve in terms of diversity, equity, inclusion, and access. So, they decided to start their own org so that they could be a part of the solution. With Jack's focus on esports programs and community development and Russ' background in ethics and justice, the duo work to build better esports communities and invite more people into those communities.

Jack and Russ both recognized a number of problems that are facing the esports industry today. Esports is male dominated despite studies showing close to gender parity when it comes to video game demographics. This is the case not only in terms of pro players but also in terms of individuals working behind the scenes for various esports orgs, for collegiate programs and their teams, and in the high school scene. Esports also struggles with questions of access. In order to regularly compete you need a good internet connection and usually a PC that you don't have to share with family members. Such a requirement limits esports participation to those in society with extra disposable income. Additionally, historically marginalized individuals are often unwelcome in esports and gaming communities. Esports communities in the US prioritize PC games and those games have audiences that trend white. Thus gamers of color are often left out of the conversation or considered not "real" gamers due to their platforms of choice. Given all of these issues, and hoping to make even the smallest of impact, Jack and Russ started working together to do what they could to improve the esports scene.

In line with their goals, their first project was a collegiate esports DEI handbook. They built a team that included Verta Maloney, John Cash, Kyra Wills-Umdenstock, and Julian Fitzgerald and together the group created a document that helps collegiate esports programs breed excellence and success by embracing DEI. They made this handbook free to download

Jack Blahnik - Co-Founder

from their website (www.justesports.org) so that access wouldn't be a problem for anyone. The handbook covers a wide variety of topics such facility design, student behavior policies, student leadership and training, game and platform selection, and a variety of other topics that are all pertinent to a collegiate esports program. Just Esports also worked to make sure that this document was applicable to a wide variety of individuals and so they made different policy suggestions to student leaders, program directors, and upper administrators like Deans or VPs. There are lots of good resources that work to convince people that diversity, equity, and

JUST ESPORTS – BUILDING A BETTER WORLD FOR EACH AND EVERY GAMER

Dr. Russ Hamer - Co-Founder

Having completed their Collegiate Esports DEI Handbook in June of 2021, Just Esports has now turned their focus towards new horizons. While the handbook will be something that they continually update, they're now focused on exciting new projects. One of their projects aims to build connections and pathways for young people to enter into the esports scene at the professional level by providing a platform for students to present research, original ideas, and business pitches with corporate partners and academic leaders providing mentorship. They hope to provide youth with access to professional development opportunities to help grow our next generation of esports leaders without having to rely on paying dues to professional organizations or having the free time to go to networking events.

Just Esports exists so esports can be infused with justice and thus be something that benefits all of us and not just those who it currently privileges.

inclusion are important but unfortunately there aren't many that are directed towards esports and the unique challenges that it faces. Just Esports worked to bridge that gap with a specific focus on the collegiate scene, as it's the area that Jack and Russ are most familiar with. The handbook doesn't merely convince its audience that DEI matter, it also provides concrete policy recommendations so that a well-intentioned but otherwise uninformed individual can improve their program immediately by adopting new policies that promote the interests of their historically marginalized students.

contact@justesports.org
just_esports_ 🐦

justesports.org

WE BELIEVE THAT EVERY PERSON, REGARDLESS OF AGE OR SOCIOECONOMIC STATUS, CAN LEARN ADVANCED COMPUTER SCIENCE AND DIGITAL MEDIA SKILLS.

Brass City Gamers Tournament's mission is to educate our local community in STEM learning including digital media, gaming, coding, and information technology, our aim is to foster strong computer competency skills to prepare for the developing new-collar jobs of the 21st Century.

We are a 501c3 nonprofit organization located in Waterbury, CT. We provide our local community esports tournaments for charity and fundraising purposes to raise awareness on social issues. Additionally, we collaborate with our local library to provide after STEM related after school programs to our local students and parents. We hosted numerous tournaments with the students of the Waterbury UConn Campus and students from Naugatuck Valley Community College (NVCC).

My name is Hector Navarro, and I am 36 years old. I was born into poverty in Puerto Rico. When I was eight years old, my mother moved to Massachusetts with me and my 3 younger siblings.

Two years later we moved to Waterbury, CT where I attended the public school system. When I turned 17, I wanted to become a game developer. However, the school I wanted to attend indicated that my mother made

too much money for me to receive financial aid. They never took into consideration that my mother was a single mother with multiple jobs taking care of 4 boys.

I was convinced to join the Marine Corps to pay for college, I deployed to Iraq from 04-05 during Operation Iraqi Freedom II. I got out of the Marines in 2011 and returned to Waterbury. With the help of family and friends, we incorporated Brass City Gamers as a nonprofit in 2017.

From 2016 to 2018 I attended NVCC and obtained my associates degree in cyber security. Currently, I work in IT service delivery as a senior technical analyst and VoIP subject matter expert.

I believe that our organization is an innovative organization that enables innovation to our consumers through our services. Our tournaments provide our local gamers and community members the opportunity to further enhance their skills and compete in a local level. This increases comradery and morale in our community. Our classes provide students the creative outlet to create their own websites, code their own mini games, develop their own social media strategy, and create a streaming platform

as an additional source of income. We also are in the process of developing robotics, esports, and blockchain curriculums.

The city of Waterbury promotes, advocates, and prepares students for manufacturing. However, teachers are receiving minimal training and resources to prepare our students for the 21st century jobs. Our services serve as a support system for the community that provide students an educational resource which allows them to practice and improve their technical proficiency. We offer a unique opportunity to server our residents by collaborating with our local library to provide necessary technical resources. We offer an engaging and fun experience through our classes which improve students overall academic performance. Additionally, through our tournaments we engage both parents and children simultaneously in a fun and competitive environment.

Our goal has always been to integrate our curriculums and classes into the public school system. We are excited that later this year, through a partnership with local nonprofit Bridge to Success, we are working with one of the elementary schools to provide an afterschool coding program for the students. This is the first step of many that will allow us to introduce more STEM related programs and classes to public school students focused around esports, computer science, cyber security, coding, digital media, crypto currency, and blockchain technology.

Hector Navarro, Chief Executive Officer at Brass City Gamers Tournament

Brass City Gamers Tournament, Inc
hnavarro@brasscitygamers.com
203-805-7684
26 Aron Ave
Waterbury 06708
United States

brasscitygamers 🐦 📷
BrassCityGamers 📘
Hector Navarro 💼
Brass City Gamers Tournament ▶

brasscitygamers.com

CODE COVEN

Our team is currently comprised of 7 bewitching all-stars, Tara Mustapha, Francesca Carletto-Leon, Karla Reyes, Nata Gedevanishvili, Kinsey Erickson, Myleah Lofland, and Lauren Moses.

BEWITCHINGLY DARING TO DEFY THE ODDS IN GAMING AND BEYOND

The gaming community has always been full of diverse people and communities. However, the developers of games have not always reflected the same diversity. Marginalized people have not been offered many of the same opportunities as their counterparts.

There is a need for a solution to remedy this problem. That's where Code Coven comes in. Code Coven aims to be intrepidly daring, providing the next generation of developers and leaders with the skills and confidence needed to thrive in the games industry. And that's the kind of solution required for this long-running problem. Tara Mustapha, the founder of Code Coven, says that there wasn't just one tipping point for creating Code Coven. Instead, it was a culmination of observations made over her 16-year career in the games industry. "I analyzed my experiences and those of my colleagues and used my design thinking to try to design how to make those experiences better. I am inspired by the work of Mary Beard, Mary Portas, Caroline Criado-Perez and Chimamanda Ngozi Adichie, powerful women who challenge the inherent systems that define our world today." People of marginalized genders are familiar with constantly having their abilities questioned.

Without knowing anything about them, they are assumed to be lesser based on someone's else's perception of their gender. Tara experienced it firsthand in the workplace. "I've borne witness to non-cis men having to prove their 'gamer credentials' to be in the room, being passed over for jobs and promotions even though they are more qualified than their cis male counterparts, being paid less than them too, being tokenized at gaming events, and not given the investment in their self-development or their own companies. So what drives me is simple - what would this look like if it were easy?" Code Coven is built upon three pillars. The academy, accelerators, and the studio. Each aspect of this "triforce" is an integral part of Code Coven's model. We consider ourselves innovators of inclusivity. How does Code Coven enable innovation? The work our alumni creates speaks volumes about their innovation. Due to their background, they're able to craft stories that may have otherwise never been explored— narratives of gender, sexuality, race, social status, religion, and more.

Through Code Coven, we create formalized educational spaces that embrace curiosity and welcome everyone, no matter what their existing relationship with technology might be. So, for example, our Intro To Game Making course has zero expectations of prior knowledge or games literacy. Instead, we build our curriculum to adapt to the interests and needs of each cohort.

Francesca Carletto-Leon is the Head of Curriculum and is an Instructor for the Code Coven academy courses. Her approach is to teach and innovate with an open mind to bring aspiring game developers closer to their dreams. "When someone hasn't heard of a certain game or lacks insight into the game development process, we don't say "I can't believe you don't know that" and instead say "I can't wait to help you learn and understand this thing that I love." Learning is a method of self-empowerment and by removing the fear of failure, Code Coven is supporting marginalized developers as they reach towards their futures," says Carletto-Leon. And Code Coven has the numbers to show their impact. In 2020 alone, Code Coven directly supported 100+ underrepresented game developers from 15+ countries, built a 150+ strong mentor network, paid out $110,000+ USD in stipends to fund diverse creators, and granted $25,000+ USD in scholarships. Furthermore, their Discord community has grown to 600+ members. Head of Business Development & Instructor Karla Reyes says that these numbers highlight the influence Code Coven has had on the games industry. But it's not just numbers that Code Coven has to prove their influence.

Their community flourishes under the kindness and support that those in it share. "Everyone in our community is kind, supportive, and focused on empowering and uplifting each other. As a result, we've had alumni continue to collaborate after graduating from our programs and go on to self-publish games or secure deals with publishers. Furthermore, we have supported our partner studios with directly hiring talent from our community," says Reyes. Code Coven was also awarded the 2020 Women in Games Global Advocacy Award and Gender Diversity Initiative of the Year.

It's time to move across the country, and the only person with a car is your ex-partner. Suck up your pride and play through your trip and relationship's bumps, obstacles, and detours. Mismatched Games and Code Coven published Detours on Steam and itch.io within a year of Summer Program 2020 completing.

The Introduction to Game Making and Professional Development course is an 8-week course that introduces students to game development using the Unity engine. It also prepares students to evolve the games industry, giving them the tools to ensure a better future for themselves and their peers. We provide scholarships to BAME/BIPOC creators for these courses.

The Safe Spaces Now Game Jam was a 7-day event hosted in partnership with UN Women. During this event, 70+ game developers, creators, and diversity advocates banded together to explore ways to cultivate safe spaces, both physical and virtual, and prevent and mitigate abuse rooted in misogyny.

Summer Program with Facebook Gaming: We collaborated with Facebook Gaming to empower early-stage game developers with structured guidance, mentorship, and financial support through our 11-week game development incubator.

The best way for others in the industry to make a difference is to simply hold a mirror to their own studios, employees, and teams. Mustapha says that it starts with auditing your own studios and practices. "Showing self-awareness is the first step towards being able to make an intentional change. They don't have to be sweeping changes, but just enough to see the day to day growth. They need to hold themselves accountable to seeing improvement in diversity in all places." Our innovation doesn't simply stop with our narratives. We innovate the industry's systems too. Code Coven ran an accelerator in support of the IGDA-F & Grant for the Web to support marginalized game developers. These game developers were provided with the power, resources, and guidance to design games and integrate new methods as alternatives to traditional web monetization. We also teamed up with Facebook Games for their Summer Program, an accelerator that allows teams to earn a stipend, learn from industry experts, and get mentorship.

As a global organization, Code Coven can extend our reach to places around the world that may not already have an established game development community. We foster developers in those regions to promote their growth and expand the definition and perception of who can be a "game developer." Going forward, our goal is to continue fostering a coven and community that will support, educate, and uplift one another while spreading kindness through their medium - no matter where they go. If you're interested in sponsoring Code Coven, you can find information on our site. "With enough strong allies, we've been able to focus on redesigning these invisible systems to be able to work towards parity and a kinder, inclusive environment for all." CEO & Founder, Tara Mustapha.

To keep up with the organization and our programs, you can follow Code Coven on social media & join our Discord.

code_coven 🐦
codecoven.co 📷
codecoven ♪

codecoven.co

YOU CAN DONATE NOW TO SUPPORT OUR MISSION.

WHO WE ARE

The Varsity Esports Foundation is a global non-profit organization established to offer financial assistance to schools and to provide a pipeline for students to reach their potential through esports. We strive to increase literacy around the esports industry's positive impact on healthy lifestyles, mental health, community, and STEM.

WHY SCHOLASTIC ESPORTS?

97% of US students ages 12-17 play video games according to the PEW Research Center. 50% of students in the US fall in the category of high-poverty or mid-high poverty. These students in low-income areas lack access to programs that foster STEM learning. STEM accredited esports curriculum with esports clubs in High Schools have shown to increase a student's GPA by 1.7, and their attendance by 10%. Esports clubs are for the kids who do not typically participate in any extracurricular activities.

VIDEO GAMES ARE FOR KIDS AND MAKE YOU LAZY

The average age of a gamer in the US is 31 years old, out of the 227 million players across all ages, with 45% identifying as female. Groundbreaking studies show that time spent playing video games can be good for your wellbeing. Video games improve memory, sensory-motor skills, gray matter volume, executive function, job-related skills, and show no association with depression.

ALMOST 28 BILLION HOURS OF FREE ONLINE STREAMING WERE VIEWED IN 2020 ON TWITCH, FACEBOOK, AND YOUTUBE.

When your teenager is entertained by watching a famous streamer or "Youtuber" play a video game, they may also be learning how to get better at a game, building community, connecting with others, learning tips about streaming and branding building, or even how to make money themselves by playing. Most parents are watching TV alone of live sports that they may never play or have played before.

5,500+ MIDDLE SCHOOLS AND HIGH SCHOOLS HAVE BEEN A PART OF AN SCHOLASTIC ESPORTS PROGRAM OVER THE LAST 9 YEARS.

The two largest scholastic esports organizations in the world: NASEF (North American Scholastic Esports Federation) which is on a mission to provide opportunities for ALL students and HSEL (High School Esports League) which is the largest and longest-operating competitive gaming organization for high school are both serving students and educators. These organizations are leading the scholastic esports community forward.

OVER $20 MILLION IN SCHOLARSHIPS AVAILABLE

There are hundreds of colleges with esports programs and over $20 million in scholarship money, based on data from NJCAA, ECAC, UEA, NACE, and other collegiate esports organizations. Sadly about $4 - $5 million

> " The Varsity Esports Foundation has helped our team out so much by providing financial support to students in need that may not have normally been able to compete. It has also reduced the stress for me as a coach and allowed our team size to increase significantly and gain more traction within our school.
>
> -Dana Lique, Coach at
> Flagler Palm Coast High School

www.VarsityEsportsFoundation.org

> " The Varsity Esports Foundation financial assistance support accelerated our 1st-year esports team to an elite, district-leading team. Thank you for making this a possibility for our school.
>
> -Kyle Schoenhofer, Coach at
> Wichita High School Southeast

www. VarsityEsportsFoundation.org

Largest scholastic esports league in North America
COMMUNITY OF 5,500+ SCHOOLS & 150,000+ STUDENTS WHO TRUST HSEL / NASEF TO ALWAYS PUT STUDENTS FIRST

Middle School Esports League

High School Esports League

NASEF
NORTH AMERICA SCHOLASTIC ESPORTS FEDERATION

GENERATIONESPORTS

Bubba Gaeddert, Executive Director

of those dollars go unused because there are not enough students in the pipeline to recruit. Find opportunities to earn scholarships for your students. With almost all teenagers in the US playing video games, why not get them involved?

SCHOLASTIC ESPORTS GIVE STUDENTS CAREER OPPORTUNITIES

The young women and men who comprise the esports world are more than the gamers. There are a number of different pathways and roles that must be filled for esports to continue to thrive! Use esports and gaming curriculum to support scholastic esports programs to provide a pathway to college and career opportunities.

WHY SHOULD YOU SUPPORT THE VARSITY ESPORTS FOUNDATION?

Reach out to our executive director Bubba Gaeddert with any questions and how you can support students and schools across the globe by giving them access to scholastic esports. You can donate now to support our mission.

816-920-3016
contact@varsityesportsfoundation.org
908 Baltimore, 2nd Floor
Kansas City, MO, 64105
VEsportsFDN
varsityesportsfoundation
Varsity Esports Foundation

varsityesportsfoundation.org

Coalition of Parents in Esports

REVOLUTIONIZING ESPORTS TOGETHER

Cofounder Chris Spikoski and his son Sceptic

Coalition of Parents in Esports is a 501c3 nonprofit founded by parents of pro esports players and content creators who recognized a need of engaging parents in the growing esports industry so more kids are able to pursue their passions with the support they need. How our children engage with online video games has changed their behaviors in profound ways that can be scary to older generations. Mainstream media spends countless fear mongering hours instructing parents how to limit or stop this implied destructive behavior, when in actuality, we should be embracing it and working with our children so they get the most out of what modern technology has to offer for how they learn and grow.

Social media and gaming has fundamentally changed the way they connect with their peers, consume entertainment, learn about the world around them and even how they choose to compete and spectate sport. Parents who grew up before personal screens were ubiquitous, have more fear about online social interaction and more concern about the physical and mental effects of all that screen time. As parents who were thrown into this brave new world by our own childrens' competitive and creative esports pursuits, we became unsuspecting pioneers of new ideas about parenting children who experience much of their world online. We were all just as skeptical as any parent, but we soon each realized there were some amazing benefits that far outweighed the negatives, and those challenges could be managed with parental guidance. That guidance required knowledge, and we soon learned there was little information available to help parents who wanted to support their child's gaming ambitions. Coalition of Parents of Esports was founded to change that dynamic and ensure parents everywhere could find the information and resources necessary to be their child's support and cheering squad, just like any other organized sporting activity or creative endeavor.

Gaming has taken on the role as the next counterculture after the likes of rock'n'roll and extreme sports before it. Gaming is equated with rebellion, bad behavior and deterring children from worthwhile pursuits like education and physical sports. Through our own children, we realized none of that is accurate. As we were being vilified in the press and by our friends for letting our kids game, we were watching our teenagers master amazing business skills like networking and communication in a digitally connected world. We have also watched gaming and streaming inspire interest in technical careers, video production and entertainment. Some of our kids pursued other competitive sports before esports, but many of them were shy kids who were not involved in organized activities. 80% of kids currently involved in esports programs through their schools would have not participated in any other extracurricular activity. Think about that fact. The benefits of participation in school sports are well-known for the mental and physical development of our youth. Esports is reaching the kids previously excluded from these important developmental experiences.

So what do we plan to do about it? COPE is committed to revolutionizing esports by engaging parents, changing the dialogue and removing the negative stigmas that inhibit success. COPE seeks to build community and raise awareness on the benefits of esports for the personal, educational and career development of our youth by providing resources to make esports more accessible to all, more rewarding to current pros and content creators and more universally recognized and respected by those yet to know the value and joy of esports.

When CoFounders Chris Spikoski and Shae Williams (parents of esports pros Sceptic and Duster respectively) were first introduced to the esports industry, they focused on helping their own children navigate this exploding new entertainment and sporting genre. As they connected with other parents of esports influencers, they realized they all had similar stories of success and frustration. They also realized they were all being asked for similar guidance from aspiring gamers and their parents. It was apparent that it was time for organization. It was time to assist other parents through COPE by providing community and support for families in esports.

COPE's greatest achievement is establishing the COPE Community Fund to recognize and reward exceptional talent and drive through scholarships for education, equipment, and family travel to tournaments and conferences. Equipment, training and travel can be expensive, but COPE seeks to level that playing field for deserving students.

So, as a parent, aunt, uncle or grandparent, what can you do? That is one of our most frequent questions and the easiest to answer. Get involved. Take the opportunity to let your kids teach you about their favorite games, their favorite platforms and their favorite pros and streamers. Yes, we know they might try to gate keep you. When did that ever stop you? It shouldn't here either. Get to know their online friends just like you would their school friends. Learn their favorite game and how to cheer them in their next tournament. We guarantee you will be pulled in to the competitive excitement.

Like any extracurricular activity, kids need to earn their practice time by prioritizing school and chores appropriately. Communication is key. Plan practice times and know their tournament schedule. Ensure your child learns that peak physical and mental health is key to success and protection against injury. All that time sitting and doing repetitive motions can take a toll. Strength training can counteract the effects and aerobic training can build the physical stamina needed for long matches. Mediation, yoga and other mindfulness exercises will build the mental strength needed in stressful endgame competitions. It is a sport. Training is important. Don't even get us started about inside voices vs outside voices! Competition inspires passion. Anger will be expressed at a mouse just like a bat. Teach them that controlling those emotions makes them better competitors, and respecting their equipment will come with maturity. Don't dismiss their emotions. You would be right there with them if it were a bad call on the field. Teach them coping mechanisms and give them space to process frustrations, just like any sport.

Esports today really is more than just playing video games in your parent's basement. Our kids are embracing the technology of their generation and learning how to make it work for them for fun, sport and connection. Instead of trying to squash it, COPE strives to help parents embrace it and work with their children to ensure they get the most out of their experiences. Just like any social group or activity, there is always the possibility of negative interactions, but with parent involvement, children will be equipped to face those challenges and will be confident to ask you, their parents, for help and guidance. COPE feels that when parents learn how much their children can benefit from healthy, fun and interactive gaming, esports will truly become the next big thing. Your kids are already there. Join them and enjoy it together! Join the Coalition of Parents in Esports and let us help you.

Cofounder Shae Williams and her son Duster

Coalition Of Parents In Esports
cspikoski@gmail.com
COpe.gg
copegg
cope_gg

cope.gg

We are Giiks Game City (GGC), a non-profit organization with the primary goal of organizing gaming events, TV content, creating and re- modify existing local and contemporary games, for a wider audience.

Video gaming, a subculture of E-Sports (Electronic Sports) is seeing rapid growth in Ghana. The ubiquity of PC games, playstation and Xbox and mobile games in Ghanaian homes are evidence of the high proliferation of electronic games have attained in Ghana.

In spite of the evident growth, the industry still faces some bottlenecks including the lack of financial backing, poor reach, Inadequate logistics and the absence of collaboration amongst key players in the community.

Live streams, discussions, co-operative and competitive games. What are you waiting for?

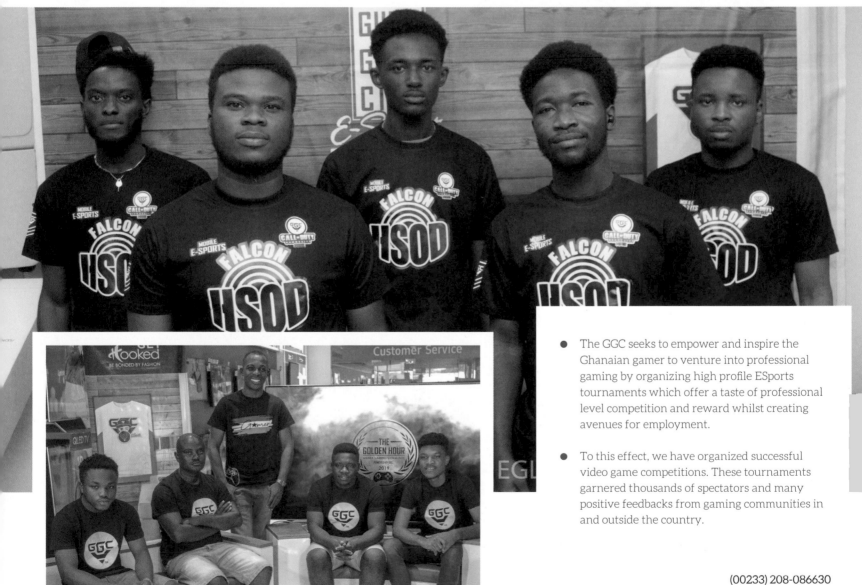

- The GGC seeks to empower and inspire the Ghanaian gamer to venture into professional gaming by organizing high profile ESports tournaments which offer a taste of professional level competition and reward whilst creating avenues for employment.

- To this effect, we have organized successful video game competitions. These tournaments garnered thousands of spectators and many positive feedbacks from gaming communities in and outside the country.

(00233) 208-086630
NIVEA MEN SOCCERMANIA
ggcchannel

CHAPTER 17
LIFESTYLE BRANDS

*"We all make choices,
but in the end...
our choices make us."*
— ANDREW RYAN - BIOSHOCK

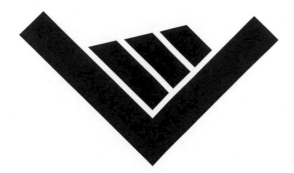

VIDEO GAME FASHION DONE RIGHT.
BY GAMERS. FOR GAMERS.

Austin Keller, Founder & CEO

NOTES: Sniper catches glint of another snipers scope. It's over.

Tribe Label is a lifestyle brand with a focus around gaming but with community at its' core. We're creating a brand that you can connect with and be proud to wear. When you're searching through your closet for something to wear and you see a Tribe Label piece, we want you to go for it. Every. Single. Time.

Our Founder & CEO, Austin Keller, has been playing video games for as long as he can remember, but he's also been interested in what he wore since his early teenage years. The only problem with that? Well, there wasn't a brand that puts gaming/fashion together, or at least there wasn't one that he thought did it well. All of the "gamer" apparel has been the standard picture/quote of [insert famous video game character/franchise here]. That's not to say there is anything wrong with that, but Austin wanted to wear a brand that had more substance; a brand that made custom designs on comfortable & fashionable clothes that said: "I play games".

The birth of Tribe Label wasn't an immediate one, but Austin knew he wanted to create a brand that was all about gaming & community. Not knowing exactly where to start, he picked a company name and logo. "Tribe". A group of people who are of the same kind or have the same interest. "Shaka". Used to convey the "Aloha Spirit", a concept of friendship, understanding, compassion, and solidarity. Afterward, Austin had the logo created but sat on the idea for a while. Doubt! It can happen to the best of us. Eventually, a close friend of his saw the logo on his phone's wallpaper, asked about it, and confirmed his suspicions that Tribe is a great idea. Shortly after, Tribe Label was born!

It's clear that gaming & eSports are here to stay, and all of these fans should have a brand that they can get behind. We know & recognize that some eSports organizations are getting into apparel as well, but no one has created a brand without a team/org affiliation. That's what Austin has set out to do. The process has been long and, at times, hard; from the initial idea, to the creation of the product, and then getting that item to the customer's front door is very involved, and it can be even harder when everyone on the team is maintaining full-time jobs! But, we're excited to keep putting out new designs and learning from our community. We want to know what everyone likes, dislikes, and why. We'll continue to improve, and one day you'll see the shaka and immediately think of Tribe.

Tribe Label
contact@tribelabel.gg
tribelabel
jointribelabel

www.tribelabel.gg

NOTES: Battlefield reference. RPG another plane after ejecting.

RITUAL MOTION IS THE LEADING WELLNESS MEDIA BRAND SERVING AN AUDIENCE OF MILLIONS IN THE GAMING AND ESPORTS COMMUNITIES.

The products and services we offer are all aligned with our strategic mission: creating products and content for the good of gamers.

Dana Paul, the co-founder and CEO of Ritual Motion, realized there was a gap in the gaming and esports industry around health, wellness, diversity and true human connectivity after watching his five kids and their friends play video games.

He set out to support this massive community of 2.7 billion gamers worldwide with products, and quickly pivoted to providing expert content and eventually the creation of an exclusive community platform featuring live video streaming and peer-to-peer networking.

Since its inception in 2018, Ritual Motion has evolved in the way that many startups do: rapidly adapting to the feedback and response of its audience. Our start as a consumer product company positioned Ritual

Motion as an innovator who developed custom products created to treat the physical ailments gamers largely suffer.

Gaming Skins, our most popular product, are handmade fingerless gloves that provide flexibility, protection, and stabilization for the hands and wrists of gamers all over the world. Our Skins can be customized and come in a selection of unique colors, sizes, and patterns.

We also offer additional wellness products for gamers, including blue light glasses and healthy superfood Snack packs, each with a specific formula for energy, focus, supporting healthy sleep, and boosting concentration.

In addition to e-commerce, Ritual Motion produces an array of rich multimedia content surrounding important (but underrepresented) topics in gaming like inclusivity and diversity; health and wellness; and education. We strive to provide a unique, safe, and inclusive space for gamers to congregate.

and enthusiasts all over the world to produce informative and interactive user-generated content based around the positive values of wellness, diversity, and inclusion.

Ritual Motion's GUILD features live streaming sessions and interactive community networking. Members create content, collaborate with peers, and share their knowledge and experiences with the gaming and esports communities. These sessions are also made available for on-demand viewing.

The gaming and esports communities thrive on collaboration. As we move forward into the next phase of Ritual Motion's GUILD, many gaming and esports organizations are using the platform to showcase their informative content, host company events, and network with the gaming and esports communities at large.

The socialization of gaming will drive the next major wave of adopters, and this is the primary avenue where Ritual Motion is focused. Our latest service, Ritual Motion's GUILD, is a first-of-its-kind live video resource built by gamers, for gamers.

Ritual Motion's GUILD: Gamers United in Live Discussion launched in May 2021. It calls upon our unique and robust community of gamers, streamers,

Ritual Motion
support@ritualmotion.com
8GuchEDNX 💬
ritual_motion 📷 🐦 📺
RitualMotion 📘

ritualmotion.com

#TheFutureIsFemme

Our mission is simple: to shake the foundations of the gaming industry, one empowered woman at a time by providing a safe space for female gamers to play and showcase their talents.

While we're not the first to recognize the stigma of women in video games, we're one of the first to take the initiative to challenge the status quo and move the needle to "warp speed ahead". We are being the change we want to see in this space. Ours is a movement, not just a mission- that will change and rewrite the code on the gaming experience forever. The Femme Gaming community provides an inclusive environment for female gamers to showcase their talent, make connections in a safe, like-minded community and simultaneously build each other up. We believe when women support each other they are unstoppable. Femme Gaming is the amplification tool for women around the world to connect, grow and share their passion for esports & gaming. This shouldn't seem innovative at all but we know first-hand there is a gap to fill in this space. This gap has been attributed to and characterized by social conditioning for boys and girls, societal constraints, access to resources and innovations within the gaming space itself. Frankly, putting up with the "boys will be boys" narrative, a simple phrase albeit, has excused and excluded all kinds of different people in society in general.

Innovative programs through STEM are attempting to close the gender participation gap at the primary and elementary school levels. Femme Gaming's goal is to do the same for the adult female community likewise. We do so knowing the average age of all female gamers is 20's through late 30's. Femme Gaming is able to accomplish this tactically through our community, our social media platforms and our supportive engagements. We are led by our ever-present shared value of the education and elevation of our community #FemmeArmy. Our goal is to close the gap in skills development through curating and showcasing our talented, female community with tournaments,, We augment this strategy with live twitch streaming, training, development and partnership collabs. We encourage and enable an innovative space as an example to others by balancing the current trends of engagement i.e. TikTok with traditional mediums of shareable content that walks the talk for a diverse, female community of gamers.

We continue to utilize our platform as emerging leadership in this space to innovate and narrate what we want to see in the esports and gaming world for all women. Let's face it, the fiercest and bad-ass game characters are often female, subtle validation that #thefutureisfemme. Started in 2020, Femme Gaming now boasts over 10,000 community members across social media platforms and looming collaborations with recognizable brands that share our values, understanding this is just the beginning.

In our eyes, innovation means taking the failures of modernity and turning them into thought-starter, conversational topics paired with "actionables" that will change the face of the gaming industry. Simply put, we want female empowerment and representation to be a way to measure the industry's success, as much as capital gain or trendy marketing innovations. We want to marry and evaluate qualitative data with quantitative data through our community architecture and engagement. We want to amplify and leverage those findings to disrupt the current misconceptions and make way for an inclusive, gender equitable economic landscape and gaming culture. We know data informs behavioral shifts, so it's about to get loud. We want to change the games space forever - innovate forward!

Our reimagined gaming industry is free of discrimination and harassment against women. Recognizing the underrepresentation of women in the gaming space and addressing it are only two baby steps to drastically change the climate. While we know we are on the right track, we need everyone to be an ally. We are proactively pursuing co-conspirators in

and grow your network, show support and engage in community. This is an "out there in the open secret". Engage in the spaces you'd like to be; encourage those in that community and they will do the same for you in turn. You'll find this to be a remarkable confidence builder. Finally, build your community with the same passion as you would your brand. Recognize trends in omni-channel marketing and implement them into your business strategy. Keep your standards high, and don't bend to external pressures. Your brand is your promise and make sure every single touch-point lives up to it. Finally, find your unique space. There is more to gaming than playing the game. Learn what other opportunities are available in the space you're pursuing. That is where real change lives and the possibilities are endless.

Toronto is one of the most diverse cities in the world and a breeding ground for success stories in all kinds of industries. We are proud to be based in this city. It is a melting pot of trend-setters, innovative thought leaders and inclusive communities. Recently, Toronto Stock Exchange added Enthusiast Gaming and OverActive Media to their trade listings and we expect to see exposure on other gaming/esports names in the near future. Toronto boasts an exciting environment for creative, innovative business ideas:. It offers a superior quality of life, ever-growing talent pool and an enthusiastic sports fan climate base. There are also a wide range of resources available to budding entrepreneurs such as accelerators and incubators, job boards, investor pools and shared work spaces purpose built to support entrepreneurs on their paths to success. Ready player one? Yep, she's ready.

support of the movement. Organizations, brands, executive leadership and all of the game developers are needed to embrace and activate this culture shift. It starts from the top of the organizations down and from the inside out. The effort has to be intentional and there needs to be an economic strategy behind it to support sustainable change. Marketing strategies for video games have only recently been specifically targeted to women, and some attempts have received unnecessary "anti-simp" backlash. All players in the game must be part of the movement to drive any long term impact. We believe that the amplification of hard data will create the industry shift we are looking for. Likewise innovations such as tournaments featuring co-ed players and promotions (much like those featured in the Olympics and traditional sport) will literally display the progression of esports ecosystem as a game-changer in sport optimization. We likewise need culture carriers of #thefutureisfemme in order to gain sustainable traction. Even when that is done, there will always still be a need for the Femme Army. There will always be a requirement for a sheltered community to empower, encourage, and cultivate the female gamer from grass roots to pro, from behind the scenes to the front of the screen.

All success stories start with an idea and a whole lot of "learnings" formally called "mistakes.Don't kill it before it's been realized. Think "you owe it to yourself and your supporters to at least try." Entrepreneurs and new businesses live and die by the setting of goals and recommitting to those each day. Set goals and remember that failure is a learning lesson every time. Failure and success are marital partners-'til death do they part. You optimize at the same time. It's a good thing. It is important to utilize

Femme Gaming
info@femmegaming.gg
femmegaming 📷
FemmeGamingGG 🐦
femmegamingg 📺
femmegaming 📘

femmegaming.gg

DELL Technologies

Defying Boundaries with Dell Technologies and Alienware

Dell Technologies and Alienware actively encourage students and educators to defy boundaries utilizing gaming and esports. We believe that gaming and esports can provide both entertainment and opportunities for students to thrive in their educational environments. Not only can esports encourage improved mental and physical acuity, but it can also strengthen students' global and professional competencies; students can gain many skills such as clear communication when making game calls in the heat of the moment, teamwork towards a common goal, and collaboration and organization to pull together an entire stream or live event. We at Dell want to support educational institutions around the world in this innovative method of learning and creating communities for their students. We strive to support educators' esports efforts with resources around inclusion and diversity, academic research, networking for collaboration, and career pathways.

Girls Who Game (GWG) is an extra-curricular program created by Dell in partnership with Microsoft that provides an opportunity for young girls and underserved students across North America to learn more about gaming and the use of Minecraft as a learning tool, while developing their global competencies, such as communication, collaboration, critical thinking, and creativity. The club provides a personalized, safe and supportive community of practice with coaches, mentors, and role models to engage the players and build their self-efficacy and confidence. By the end of the club term, the players have a greater self-awareness of their improved knowledge, skills, and dispositions, and are empowered to become leaders in Science, Technology, Engineering, and Mathematics (STEM fields) and the growing esports movement across the education landscape. GWG also aims to build capacity with female educators on how to effectively integrate game-based learning into their core content curriculum.

Our Esports Research Collaborative meets monthly and was formed organically from a desire to connect globally with other researchers. This is a group of passionate and dedicated coaches, directors, researchers and medical doctors who not only believe in the power of esports but are also devoting their invaluable research efforts to improve the health, sustainability, and processes associated with esports.

Dell has also created resources such as our K-12 Esports Curriculum for club programs, a Getting Started Checklist for educators in both K-12 and Higher Education, and case studies and customer story videos from many of our educational customers who have seen the benefits of esports programs in

their schools. We also host a free summer esports conference, gathering dozens of speakers from around the world talking on subjects such as convincing administration of the benefits of esports programs, diving into research around global college and university esports courses, certificates and degrees, how to ensure that student health and wellness is at the forefront, and how to encourage inclusion and diversity. Dell Technologies also hosts an Esports for Educators Discord server, facilitating a network that both K-12 and Higher Education can utilize to ask questions, share challenges and successes, and even organize games together. Finally, we also have a team of Education Strategists with experience from pre-K to PhD who are well-versed in helping educational institutions achieve their esports aspirations.

Another important aspect of our investment in esports is our more than decade-long partnership with professional esports organization Team Liquid. We've partnered with them for both of their Liquid Hacks events, where hundreds of young adults have competed over a weekend to build prototypes for particular challenges (such as the PrideMakers Liquid Hack event honoring Pride Month in June) focusing on health and wellness and innovation in gaming and esports. Team Liquid and Alienware have also launched the Good in Gaming platform with programs for fans and students to grow, learn, and compete. The driver behind this platform is that everyone should have the opportunity to pursue a career within gaming and we are committed to helping students explore, experience mentorship, and find a path into the industry.

Dell Technologies and Alienware are proud to support gamers and educators in trying to create a world of gaming where they can be themselves, learn, collaborate, and turn their passions into fulfilling career pathways.

Dell Technologies
danielle.rourke@dell.com
HiEdDanielle 🐦
daniellerourke 🔗

Esports in Education webpage:
www.delltechnologies.com/en-us/ industry/education/esports.htm

Girls Who Game program:
girlswhogame.com

Good in Gaming program:
teamliquid.com/alienware

CHAPTER 18
MARKET RESEARCH

*"If our lives are already written,
it would take a courageous man to
change the script."*

— ALAN WAKE

niko°

COMPANIES NEED TO UNDERSTAND THE MARKETS IN WHICH THEY COMPETE.

When consumers and students think of the video game industry and esports, they think of the excitement and entertainment of it all – but rarely about the data that guides the strategy of a business and of the game development plan. A market research firm provides the data that helps companies make smarter decisions about the direction of their business, games, tournaments, marketing and more. Without an agnostic market research provider, each company would need to "figure out" what gamers would like their games, and what the rules are in different geographical markets, and what a consumer might be doing along with playing a game. Each game company can see the data analytics of their own gameplay and usage, but this is only about the games that they put out. It is not about the global market for gaming or other entertainment.

If you were to recall reading an article that says, "The video game industry grew by 58% this year compared to last year, based on the revenue generated by games," that article will have been based on data that takes a lot of time and effort to produce. Typically, such data is produced by a market research firm. One segment of market research is to help companies understand foreign markets, because to succeed outside of one's home market you must understand the markets where you are going.

The founder of Niko Partners, Lisa Cosmas Hanson, has a personal motto of "peace through intercultural understanding." Niko Partners takes action on that motto every day, by bringing information, insights, data and strategic analysis to clients regarding many global video game markets.

Niko Partners is a market research firm covering games, esports, and streaming in Asia. We are local experts with a global perspective, leaning on local analysts and global insights for our overall strategic analysis that we provide to clients all over the world.

We provide qualitative and quantitative data collection and analysis, market models, forecasts, and strategic advisory services regarding market intelligence, insights and strategic advice that our clients need to truly understand the gaming markets and gamers in 11 markets in Asia as of mid-2021, and adding more as we speak.

We also provide a very wide range of custom research, including, but not limited to focus groups, gamer surveys, IPO and market opportunity analysis, market entry strategy, partner selection, transaction advisory services, and investor due diligence.

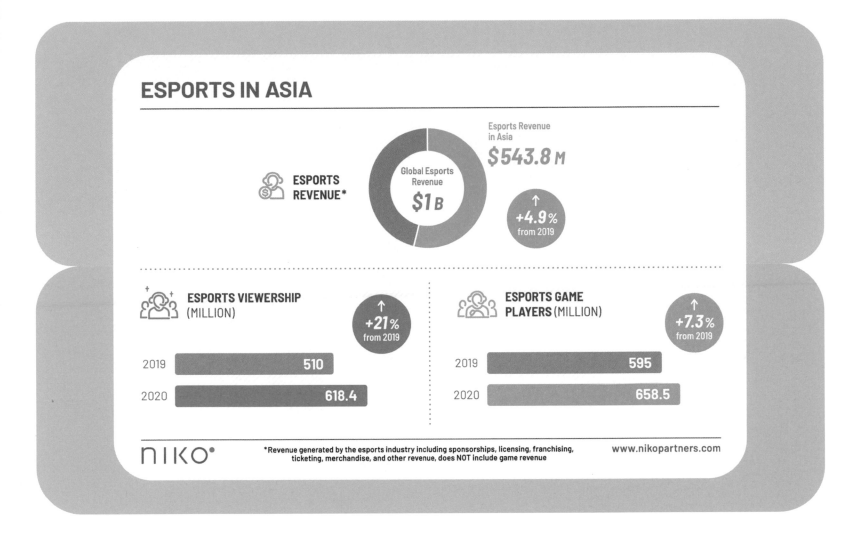

ESPORTS IN ASIA

ESPORTS REVENUE*

Global Esports Revenue
$1B

Esports Revenue in Asia
$543.8M

↑ +4.9% from 2019

ESPORTS VIEWERSHIP (MILLION)

↑ +21% from 2019

2019 — 510
2020 — 618.4

ESPORTS GAME PLAYERS (MILLION)

↑ +7.3% from 2019

2019 — 595
2020 — 658.5

niko°

*Revenue generated by the esports industry including sponsorships, licensing, franchising, ticketing, merchandise, and other revenue, does NOT include game revenue

www.nikopartners.com

We've helped game publishers, platforms, hardware makers, esports, consumer brands, investors, payments providers, hedge funds, and consulting firms understand and succeed in the world's largest and fastest growing games markets, which are in Asia.

Niko Partners launched in 2002 by building the first baseline study on the China video games market. Since then, we have been exclusively researching and analyzing the video games markets and consumers in Asia, starting with China and adding Greater Southeast Asia to our coverage in 2010, again the first company to do so. As of 2017 we began coverage of Japan, Korea, and India, and in 2021 we are adding the Middle East game markets (which actually is Western Asia) to our research coverage.

Niko has a complex methodology for producing data, insights and analysis – the methodology shifts for each type of assignment we take on. In general, for our market model, we combine data collected from primary and secondary sources and layer on our own assumptions to build a model. The key to our research is that we talk to people - executives at games and hardware companies, esports companies, hardware companies, financial institutions, media organizations, and more, as well as local government officials, and most importantly the local consumers. We've built our business on the belief that demand-based market intelligence is more important for a company to understand than supply-based market sizing.

We have a global team of analysts who are native speakers in the countries we cover conduct all of our primary research. They are out there fielding surveys, running focus groups, talking to gamers, visiting events and venues, and regularly meeting with games industry and government sources. We collect and aggregate data and news in the Asian countries we cover - on a daily basis We follow all of it, in every country, in every language. Our analysts are more than just analysts, they are core gamers who are active in their local gaming and esports scenes. This lets us understand what truly makes each of these diverse and totally unique markets tick. There are things you just cannot understand unless you are on the ground and part of the local scene. When something happens or a trend emerges, we don't just follow and analyze news releases or reported stories. We reach out and talk to gamers in the local market and find out what's going on.

Hence, Niko Partners acts as the on-the-ground resource for objective data, analysis and insights for clients of all types who depend on the video game industry globally for their own success. For more information, visit nikopartners.com

Niko Partners
niko-partners **in**
nikochina **🐦**

nikopartners.com

TWO CHILDHOOD FRIENDS WITH ONE BIG IDEA — THAT'S THE GIST OF NEWZOO'S BEGINNINGS.

Full Version | 2021

Global Esports & Live Streaming Market Report

Market Sizing | Forecasts | Activating in Esports and Streaming
COVID-19 Impact | Live Streaming in China | Trends

Peter Warman, CEO and Thijs Hagoort, CFO

Newzoo started out as a company that connected people in the games industry with people who, each for their own reason, had an interest in this thriving business. But while talking to big consumer brands, investors, and game companies, Peter and Thijs quickly noticed something curious: there was little to no actionable market data on games. They set out to solve this issue first. Long story short, Newzoo officially started researching, modeling, and reporting on the games market in 2008.

The first edition of the iPhone also launched in the summer of 2007. This impacted Newzoo's success, as this disruptive device changed the way the world thought about the digital landscape and the commercial significance of mobile gaming. Unlike market intelligence companies that were estimating boxed product revenues at the time, Thijs and Peter envisaged a bright future for mobile gaming and tracked this emerging space from day one.

But Newzoo wasn't its founder's (Peter Warman and Thijs Hagoort) first venture into the world of business. Far from it. After becoming friends playing basketball in high school, the industrious duo sold custom-designed t-shirts. Those early days taught them a valuable lesson: custom production based on manuals does not scale very well. To build a high-growth business, you need a different approach. They soon flooded the basketball club with a line of fresh but standardized shirts.

Since then, the pace of change has been sky-high, as have Newzoo's growth and desire to be ahead of the curve. The company focused completely on market intelligence and analytics, anticipating major shifts in technology and consumer behavior with an impact across many industries. This, of course, included esports.

The Global Growth of Esports
Trends, revenues and audience towards 2017

© 2015 NEWZOO
V 1.0 | JANUARY 2015

© IMAGE COURTESY OF ESL

Modelling the Esports Market

Newzoo first began talking about esports in a free report it released in 2013 called Power to the People. Following this, the team began to extensively track and model the esports market from both an industry and a consumer perspective. In January 2015, it released the landmark Global Growth of eSports: Trends, Revenues and Audience Towards 2017, becoming the first market research company to size and forecast the esports market. The report provided a much-needed overview of the esports economy and a realistic estimate of its future potential in terms of viewers, participants, and revenue streams. Since then, Newzoo has released six more annual global reports and has become the world's go-to destination for esports data and insights. In 2021, the company expanded its report to recognize the significant role that live streaming plays in the gaming and esports ecosystems.

Newzoo's revenue forecasts are widely quoted in the industry. These are based on its predictive eSports market model, incorporating data from many sources: macroeconomic and census data, primary consumer research, data provided by its industry data partners, public event data for viewership and attendees, media reports, and third-party research. These include revenue actuals from leading teams and companies in the industry. In August 2021, this included 26 partners across the globe, located in North America, Europe, Australia, China, South Korea, and Latin America.

Aside from esports market sizing and forecasts, Newzoo's subscribers also have access to in-depth game streaming data, esports team and competition viewership metrics, an esports sponsorships database, and consumer insights of esports fans. All accessible via the Newzoo Platform.

Newzoo
questions@newzoo.com
+31 (0) 20 66 35 816
Newzoo

newzoo.com

comscore

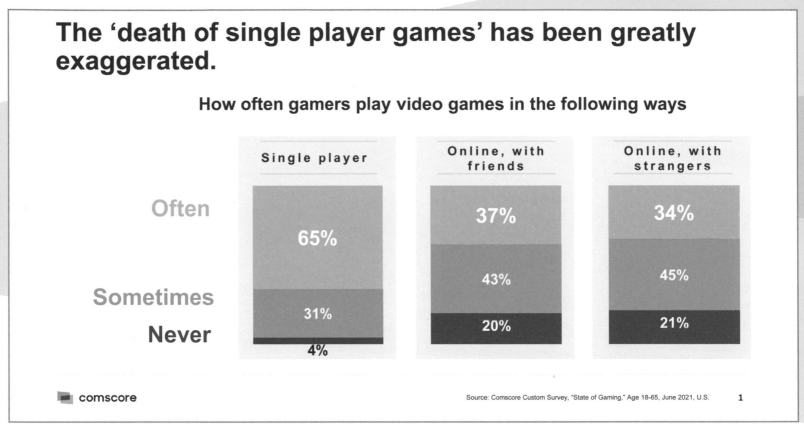

The 'death of single player games' has been greatly exaggerated.

How often gamers play video games in the following ways

Single player	Online, with friends	Online, with strangers
Often 65%	37%	34%
Sometimes 31%	43%	45%
Never 4%	20%	21%

comscore

Source: Comscore Custom Survey, "State of Gaming," Age 18-65, June 2021, U.S.   1

Comscore is a trusted partner for planning, transacting, and evaluating media across platforms. Game publishers, platforms, brands and their agencies use Comscore audience measurement, marketing impact and survey solutions to find opportunities within the evolving gaming landscape.

For more than 20 years, marketers, agencies, and media sellers have relied on Comscore's industry-leading viewership data and consumer intelligence to make business decisions with confidence. With a data footprint that combines digital, linear TV, over-the-top, and theatrical viewership, Comscore has unmatched expertise in quantifying multiscreen behavior of audiences and provide reliable and comprehensive cross-platform measurement.

With most gamers (77%) playing games across not just one but multiple platforms, and with the pandemic affecting attitudes toward esports and live streaming, it is now more important than ever for advertisers, sponsors and their agencies to fully understand this growing category. The gaming landscape can no longer be called a niche market—it has grown to reach a majority of American households and has consumed a sizeable portion of time spent online. For example, in June 2021, 38 million U.S. households were active on a gaming console.* Specifically on mobile, the gaming category makes up 74% of the total mobile app audience and accounts for 182 billion minutes spent on mobile.

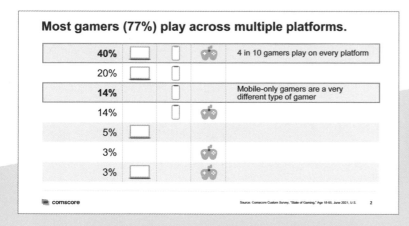

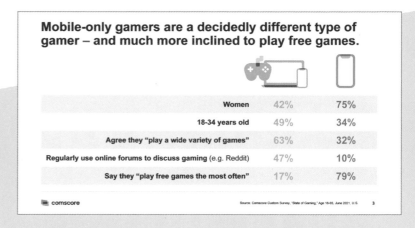

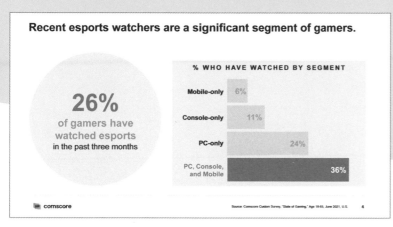

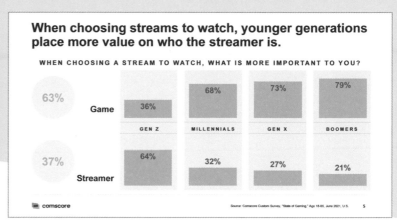

Comscore offers a variety of solutions to help you get a pulse on the gaming landscape and evaluate in-game advertising impact and audiences.

Measuring gaming audiences on PC, mobile, and console

- Comscore Brand Lift Surveys and Branded Content insights help marketers and publishers better evaluate the impact of intrinsic in-game advertising on key branding measures, such as awareness, favorability, recall and purchase intent.
- Comscore's PC and console gaming trackers reveal monthly demographic and behavioral measurement to drive understanding of game players at the platform and title level. Everything from what games they play, how often, and more.
- Comscore's syndicated digital planning tools provide a complete, unduplicated view of how audiences consume gaming content, video across devices, mobile gaming visitation, duration, and audience insights at the app and browser level.

Understanding esports and livestreaming audiences

Comscore gaming solutions provide an in-depth view of how online audiences engage with esports and livestreaming-related video across desktops, smartphones, tablets and over-the-top (OTT) devices. We measure branding effectiveness in esports events and sponsorships providing a comprehensive view of branding impact over cross-platform campaigns as well as lift by platforms, network, publisher, placement and creative. As esports television programming expands, Comscore TV products enable precise, massive-scale measurement of esports television audience viewership, viewers' Advanced Audience profiles, and cross-viewing habits with other telecasts.

Annual State of Gaming Report

Comscore is proud to present a special gaming insight report every year, leveraging custom survey insights for deeper understanding of gaming audiences. The report examines the behavior, sentiment, attitudes, and preferences of today's desktop, mobile, and console gaming audiences. Utilizing both passively collected data from Comscore's massive datasets and a robust custom survey, this report contains over 80 pages of insights and provides additional customization options.

Comscore's ability to recruit and survey gamers around the globe can provide both broad reach and granular insights to help understand the gaming audience. Whether focused on platform-level insights or key trends including esports, cloud gaming, or virtual reality, Custom Surveys can capture direct feedback from key audience segments.

The online and mobile gaming industry has seen impressive growth over the past several years, and it has earned its spot as a dominant category in online and mobile media consumption. As gaming industry continues its upward trajectory, a complete and comprehensive view of gaming, esports, and live streaming audiences are a necessity to create meaningful engagements with these valuable audiences.

Comscore
Comscore
comscore.com/Insights/communication-preference-center

comscore.com

CHAPTER 19

ESPORTS VIEWER DEEP DIVE

"The future growth of esports audiences is less about 'esports' and more about 'entertainment'."

— KAROL SEVERIN

EXPERTS IN ENTERTAINMENT INTELLIGENCE

THE MIDIA STORY

MIDiA is an entertainment intelligence company. It was founded in 2013 by long-term media and technology analyst, Mark Mulligan, and his fellow co-founders, Tim Mulligan and Karol Severin. MIDiA's founding vision was to provide the definitive take on strategy, consumer, and market insight where entertainment and tech meet – with emphasis on a holistic approach across traditionally siloed industries. Additionally, the founders wanted to ensure democratisation of cutting-edge insight for organisations and interested individuals of all sizes, addressing the information gap faced by students and early-stage start-ups.

By building a cross-industry view of the digital entertainment world, with world-class data and ideas, MIDiA quickly established itself as a global leader in music, and growth across games, video and sports followed shortly after. Seven years since its inception, MIDiA is proud to support many of the world's largest players in entertainment and tech, from iconic record labels, Hollywood networks and studios, and games publishers, right up to the tech majors and their life-encompassing ecosystems. Yet, all this success never clouded MIDiA's ongoing commitment to 'pay it forward'. From the get-go, it has provided higher education institutions with heavily discounted (non-profit) rates to make its cutting-edge insight accessible to students and start-ups when it matters the most. Today, MIDiA provides students at academic institutions, such as NYU, Berklee and the University of Kentucky, with access to research and strategy insight that will help prepare them for their professional career journeys.

Karol Severin - Lead games analyst, Co-founder

Mark Mulligan - Lead music analyst, Founder

Tim Mulligan - Lead video analyst, Co-founder

MIDIA IN GAMES

MIDiA was the first entertainment intelligence company to predict the peak of the attention economy. Simply put, there were no longer any new 'free hours' for consumers to allocate to new forms of entertainment. The MIDiA team was quick to identify that growth was going to become increasingly binary, coming at the expense of others. Because our analysis and data are built around the interconnected nature of digital entertainment, MIDiA has proven to be uniquely well placed to help companies navigate the post-peak attention economy.

Following the stellar rise of gaming and its establishment as a cultural denominator, alongside music, sports and video, MIDiA's games coverage focuses on spotting market and consumer cross-entertainment opportunities early enough for companies to get ahead of the pack. MIDiA is able to provide its clients with this sort of insight because we focus on the gamer as an entertainment consumer in a holistic sense, and identify where game(r)s fit within that broader view, rather than simply looking through the lens of games.

Here are just a few examples of where this distinct approach enabled MIDiA to make 'ahead of the game' calls:

- The growth and profitability issues of the esports sector early on, and informed clients that solutions lie in bringing wider entertainment aspects to the proposition. The esports viewer dossier (inserted in this book) is just one example of a data resource we publish for clients
- The games subscription revolution along with the effects it was going to have on the traditional games industry landscape
- The opportunities stemming from building symbiotic, rather than transactional, relationships between entertainment sectors
- The pitfalls of competing in a siloed entertainment sector manner, rather than with a holistic approach to entertainment (MIDiA identified Netflix's opportunity to move into games as early as 2017)

MIDiA's games coverage presents monthly reports and data on business-critical consumer trends, in addition to market and strategy trends.

Alongside cross-entertainment opportunities, we support games clients with insights on marketing, product inception and business strategy. In turn, our games coverage also helps non-gaming entertainment clients understand and navigate making the most of opportunities in the games sector, while keeping the nuanced dynamics of clients' own sectors in mind.

To get a further gist of how we think and what we cover, subscribe to our free weekly newsletter at www.midiaresearch.com

MIDiA RESEARCH
info@midiaresearch.com
midiaresearch
midia-research

midiaresearch.com

SOUTH KOREA AND BRAZIL LEAD THE CHARGE IN TERMS OF ESPORTS VIEWER PENETRATION
Esports viewer consumer penetration, Q1 2021

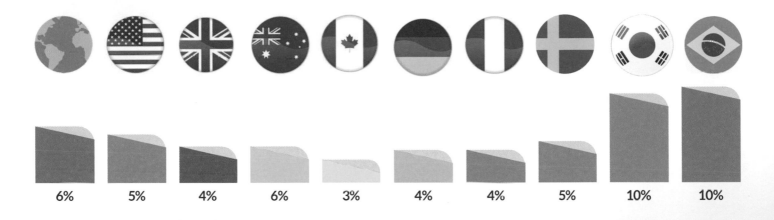

% of segment

6%	5%	4%	6%	3%	4%	4%	5%	10%	10%

ESPORTS VIEWERS

Esports fans watch a lot more sports and news than the average person, but their preference for drama, reality and comedy is less than that of most consumers.

TV GENRE FANDOM OF ESPORTS VIEWERS VERSUS CONSUMER AVERAGE, Q1 2021

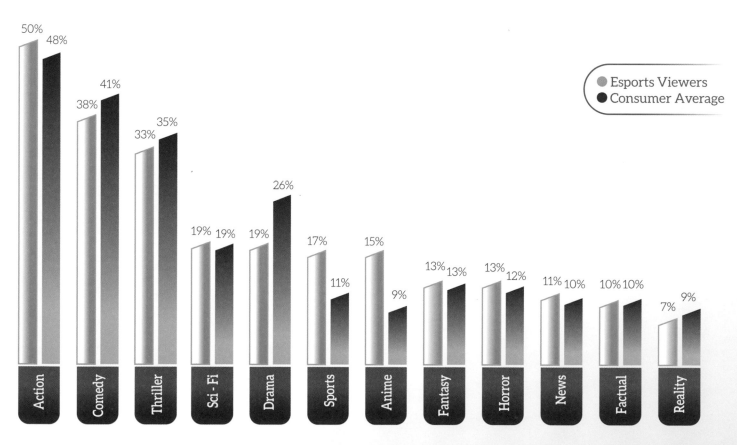

● Esports Viewers
● Consumer Average

Genre	Esports Viewers	Consumer Average
Action	50%	48%
Comedy	38%	41%
Thriller	33%	35%
Sci-Fi	19%	19%
Drama	19%	26%
Sports	17%	11%
Anime	15%	9%
Fantasy	13%	13%
Horror	13%	12%
News	11%	10%
Factual	10%	10%
Reality	7%	9%

Source: MIDiA Research Consumer Survey 03/21 n = 9,000 (US,UK, Australia, Canada, Germany, France, Sweden, South Korea, Brazil)

Not all esports viewers are gamers - 50% of esports viewers spend less than 5 hours a week playing games and 15% of esports viewers don't play games at all.

ESPORTS VIEWERS ARE HIGHLY ENGAGED CONSUMERS ACROSS ENTERTAINMENT
Weekly time spent by esports viewers across digital entertainment, Q1 2021

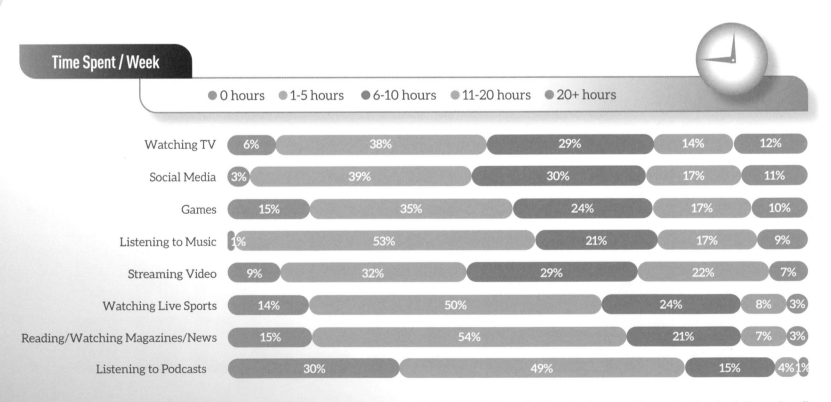

Time Spent / Week

● 0 hours　● 1-5 hours　● 6-10 hours　● 11-20 hours　● 20+ hours

	0 hours	1-5 hours	6-10 hours	11-20 hours	20+ hours
Watching TV	6%	38%	29%	14%	12%
Social Media	3%	39%	30%	17%	11%
Games	15%	35%	24%	17%	10%
Listening to Music	1%	53%	21%	17%	9%
Streaming Video	9%	32%	29%	22%	7%
Watching Live Sports	14%	50%	24%	8%	3%
Reading/Watching Magazines/News	15%	54%	21%	7%	3%
Listening to Podcasts	30%	49%	15%	4%	1%

Source: MIDiA Research Consumer Survey 03/21 n = 9,000 (US,UK, Australia, Canada, Germany, France, Sweden, South Korea, Brazil)

SPENDING ACROSS ENTERTAINMENT IS MAINSTREAM FOR ESPORTS VIEWERS
Monthly money spent by esports viewers across digital entertainment, Q1 2021

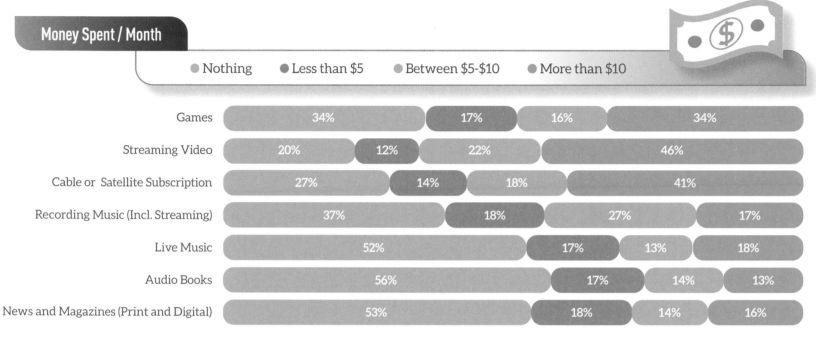

Money Spent / Month

● Nothing   ● Less than $5   ● Between $5-$10   ● More than $10

	Nothing	Less than $5	Between $5-$10	More than $10
Games	34%	17%	16%	34%
Streaming Video	20%	12%	22%	46%
Cable or Satellite Subscription	27%	14%	18%	41%
Recording Music (Incl. Streaming)	37%	18%	27%	17%
Live Music	52%	17%	13%	18%
Audio Books	56%	17%	14%	13%
News and Magazines (Print and Digital)	53%	18%	14%	16%

Source: MIDiA Research Consumer Survey 03/21 n = 9,000 (US,UK, Australia, Canada, Germany, France, Sweden, South Korea, Brazil)

ESPORTS VIEWERS ARE TWICE AS LIKELY TO USE YOUTUBE PREMIUM AND DISNEY+ THAN AVERAGE CONSUMERS AND THREE TIMES AS LIKELY TO USE APPLE TV+

Weekly active user penetration of SVOD services, esports viewers versus consumer average, Q1 2021

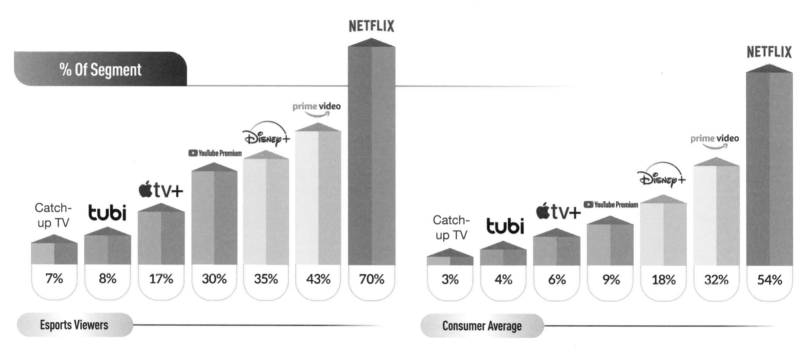

% Of Segment

Esports Viewers

Catch-up TV	tubi	Apple tv+	YouTube Premium	Disney+	prime video	NETFLIX
7%	8%	17%	30%	35%	43%	70%

Consumer Average

Catch-up TV	tubi	Apple tv+	YouTube Premium	Disney+	prime video	NETFLIX
3%	4%	6%	9%	18%	32%	54%

Source: MIDiA Research Consumer Survey 03/21 n = 9,000 (US,UK, Australia, Canada, Germany, France, Sweden, South Korea, Brazil)

Esports viewers are significantly more active on social media than the average consumer, with their favorite social media platform being Instagram, followed closely by Facebook and Whatsapp, with Discord coming in last of the big 9.

Weekly active social media/messaging app penetration of esports users versus consumer average, Q1 2021

● Discord ● Snapchat ● Pinterest ● TikTok ● Twitter ● Facebook Messanger ● WhatsApp ● Facebook ● Instagram

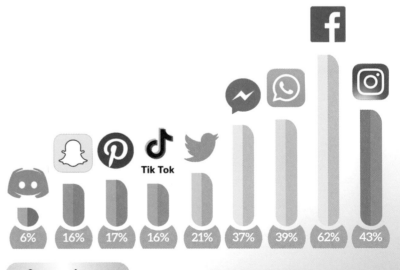

% Of Segment

Esports Viewers: 22% 28% 29% 34% 43% 46% 52% 64% 65%

Consumer Average: 6% 16% 17% 16% 21% 37% 39% 62% 43%

Source: MIDiA Research Consumer Survey 03/21 n = 9,000 (US,UK, Australia, Canada, Germany, France, Sweden, South Korea, Brazil)

ESPORTS VIEWERS ARE NEARLY FIVE TIMES MORE LIKELY TO PAY-PER-VIEW FOR SPORTS THAN AVERAGE CONSUMERS

Sports behaviour of esports viewers versus consumer average, Q1 2021

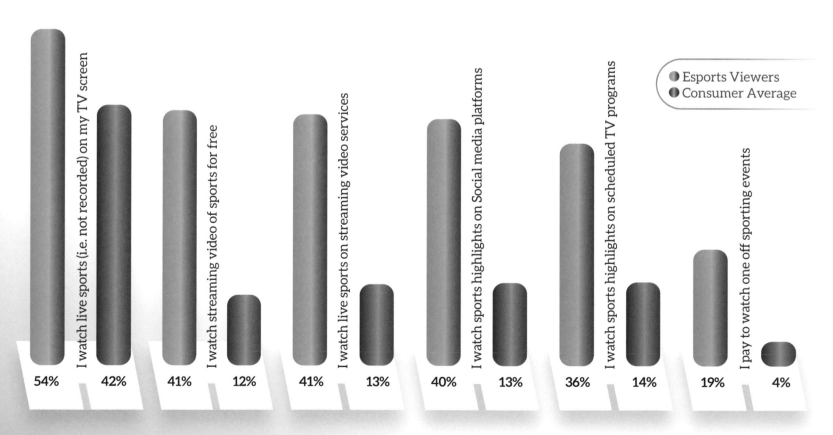

Esports Viewers
Consumer Average

I watch live sports (i.e. not recorded) on my TV screen — 54% / 42%

I watch streaming video of sports for free — 41% / 12%

I watch live sports on streaming video services — 41% / 13%

I watch sports highlights on Social media platforms — 40% / 13%

I watch sports highlights on scheduled TV programs — 36% / 14%

I pay to watch one off sporting events — 19% / 4%

Source: MIDiA Research Consumer Survey 03/21 n = 9,000 (US,UK, Australia, Canada, Germany, France, Sweden, South Korea, Brazil)

ESPORTS VIEWERS ARE FOUR TIMES MORE LIKELY TO DECREASE REGULAR LIVE SPORTS ATTENDANCE POST-COVID

Sports behaviour of esports viewers versus consumer average, Q1 2021

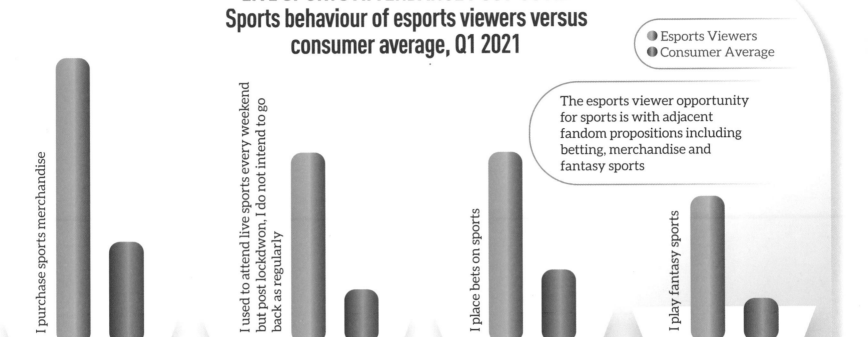

● Esports Viewers
● Consumer Average

The esports viewer opportunity for sports is with adjacent fandom propositions including betting, merchandise and fantasy sports

I purchase sports merchandise — 29% / 10%

I used to attend live sports every weekend but post lockdwon, I do not intend to go back as regularly — 20% / 5%

I place bets on sports — 20% / 7%

I play fantasy sports — 15% / 4%

Source: MIDiA Research Consumer Survey 03/21 n = 9,000 (US,UK, Australia, Canada, Germany, France, Sweden, South Korea, Brazil)

CHAPTER 20

BEYOND GAMING

"Gaming has enabled us to embrace and rediscover, time and again, the wonder of what makes us uniquely human."

— MITCH REED

WE PLAY FOR THE WORLD

Terrell Bennett, Diversity and Inclusion Officer

A 501(c)3 nonprofit charity dedicated to communities, leaders, and organizations by offering innovative consultant services.

In 2018, UKnightedXP, Inc. (UKXP) was like all ventures in the beginning – an idea and a dream.

Devastated by Hurricane Michael, the Panhandle of Florida was reeling from one of the most devastating Category 5 hurricanes in the history of the United States.

The founder and CEO of UKXP, Mitchel Reed, planned a relief effort with a focus on bringing 'gamers' and like-minded people together through social media. The idea was to help a devastated local community by connecting passionate gamers with a unifying cause.

At the time, Mitchel was on active military duty and took personal leave. He immediately set about coordinating with local nonprofit organizations that were accepting donations and had active work orders that needed to be filled. In the absence of infrastructure, the best approach was to assist and scale existing mission-aligned efforts. This allowed UKXP's volunteer team to maximize efforts and participation.

The event proved to be an enormous success for the community. UKXP's efforts resulted in thousands of dollars in donations, many thousands of work orders completed, and dozens of families received aid from volunteer 'gamers' - and raised a whopping support valuation of nearly $225,000.00 USD in just five days. The strategic vision and impact of those efforts that week forever changed many lives, as well as the direction for UKXP.

Mitchel put together a team of volunteers and talented, successful professionals to begin the process of building a charity. Its focus was to help organizations develop programs leveraging gaming and gaming culture to further their charitable missions.

Mitchel Reed, Founder & CEO

Ashton Cooksey, COO

Nathan Holt, Board Member, SEO

The organization adapted its mission and abilities to meet the varying needs of its clients and communities in the Southeastern United States. UKXP formally registered as a nonprofit charity with the mission of 'advancing the world through gaming, education, and charity.'

Through innovative thinking and adaptation, UKXP has been able to successfully help leaders garner a meaningful appreciation and knowledge for utilization of gaming and gaming culture to support their communities' needs. This is achieved through strategic consulting, coaching, and mentoring.

UKXP also believes in having fun. The future the organization envisions maximizes productivity through ingenuity. The aim is to establish cohesive teams through reliable sourcing across the gaming industry to plug in its partners to continue building momentum for the future.

Growth is inevitable in industry and this same growth can lead to efforts that see an evolution in problem-solving. Municipalities can have programs that seek to unify their communities over a common bond. Families can implement systems to teach and raise children through a confidence-building support system. Companies can use big data as a means to help fundraising efforts or boost their community impact from the desires of customers. These resources are available; it's what communities do with them that counts.

UKXP constantly seeks opportunities to identify mission-aligned leaders, communities, and organizations to work with.

UKXPs' innovation lies in its mastery of the basics - and their vision for the strategic. This nonprofit's model as a charitable consultancy allows it to serve as enablers of innovation: helping to address global humanitarian, bipartisan issues such as helping to bridge the informational divide or the accessibility and affordability of the Internet.

Connecting with people and spaces at the right time and right place is a timeless formula for success. UKXP has identified an important component of their consulting formula. It is embracing their ability to efficiently and effectively help their clients navigate the chaos of the information age. Leaders and organizations must collaborate, leverage technology, and scale.

Although much about the future is uncertain, UKXP is committed to helping leaders and organizations navigate the chaos.

UKXP is often asked: "How do we steward the future of the information age?" Their answer is a resounding "together!"

CROWDSOURCING

Crowdfunding grabs headlines for social impact and community advancement, but crowdsourcing is the real strategic victory for the digital age.

The gaming community is artfully adept at harnessing the benefits of crowdsourcing. The power of crowdsourcing is nearly limitless. From the most complex digital environments, gaming communities with the assistance of UKXP have recently proven the ability to bring about real-world, grassroots-level community action.

To illustrate crowdsourcing's influence, Mitchel tells us the origin story of UKXP. UKXP advocates building a better world through gaming, education, and charity.

"In 2018, hurricane Michael wreaked havoc on Florida. My initial response was: how can I help? Of course, picking up a chainsaw to help people is a natural instinct. But I thought there must be a way to do this through gaming. With gaming community members based in Florida, we looked at

ways in which we could get connected. By leveraging social platforms and the games I played on, I could connect with people on Discord and World of Warcraft, on voice servers, and some of my PlayStation Network group, and we connected our gaming network into an ecosystem. From this ecosystem, we could crowdsource enough intelligence to put together the concept of UKXP. The objective of UKXP was to support others in doing their missions better by bridging those organizations and empowering gamers and gaming culture. We helped crowdsource not only money for relief aid, but volunteers for projects and resources for non-profit organizations. In a week of doing that, we crowdsourced about $250,000 of work orders and all the logistical information and analysis needed to accomplish that end state. We weren't a charity and had no credibility, but we had a group, called it a thing, and we did what we could."

Crowdsourcing models also benefit from business practices such as AGILE. Most notably, AGILE is commonly known to reduce the probability of failure. The ability to leverage highly scalable mediums to collect and/

or extrapolate data, and channel efforts for the benefit of the greater community – offer potential solutions and capabilities for people that may not have been otherwise possible. It inspires and empowers people to act and generate a real-life impact.

In the gaming sphere, crowdsourcing is an enabler of innovation and a force multiplier. People come together on their digital dashboards, combine their digital tools, and create innovative methods of communication to share their stories or narratives. Players are known to utilize crowdsourcing to defeat complex in-game encounters, rallying dozens, sometimes hundreds or even thousands together. Crowdsourcing for gaming is deeply and richly embedded in its DNA: it collects human intelligence. Ironically or not, the gaming industry has passively adopted and actively practices the Japanese 'Kaizen' philosophy of continuous improvement.

Crowdsourcing allows game developers, storytellers, and players to take their ideas from paper to pixels and invest it right back into their communities – often with very limited or even no budget. Reducing operational costs means creating opportunities with less: less equipment, fewer people, and less capital.

"Gaming provides a creative medium to accomplish greatness," explains UKXP's Reed. "It also encourages innovation and provides an unprecedented medium for progress in the Information Age. When you present a medium that encourages and facilitates people's entrepreneurial spirit, it facilitates innovation. If you allow people's unbridled ingenuity, free to create, it's incredible what people can achieve. That's what gaming does so well. When

you combine creative freedom and outlet with a concept like crowdsourcing, the sky is the limit. The biggest limitations in our world right now are the leaders who don't see that and accept it for what it is."

Circling back to community advancement through gaming, crowdsourcing potentially has answers to global issues. Crowdsourcing helps people address limitations of dated methodologies and processes for missions and projects limited by things such as geography, finances, manpower, technology, etc. The scope and scalability of crowdsourcing mean people can accomplish more with less, and more effectively.

The best part? Gaming is fun – and the gaming community does crowdsourcing arguably better than anyone. As an industry, UKXP stands behind the assertion that we should collaborate to invest in and continue the path to articulating the tangible, measurable future of gaming – and at UKXP, we plan to find the right folks to help humanity do just that.

Influencers such as MrBeast and their #TeamSeas initiative – our team loves what they're doing with crowdsourcing. In time, we hope to work with them and others to take all of these initiatives to the next echelon.

That's the real vision – and those guys are our modern heroes for the upcoming generation. The bigger they are, the more who follow, the greater the impact. There is no limit to crowdsourcing in the digital era and the positive social impacts it can have on our world.

CYBERSECURITY AND SAFETY

The internet metaverse is the epicenter of today's global commerce. Unfortunately, it is also the most contested space in the world - Cybersecurity and safety protocols are more important today than ever. It just so happens that the gaming ecosystem can help unlock not only the potential of people but the ensured success of our 'connected' future.

The cyber environment is no doubt complex. Vulnerability, trust, physical and emotional wellbeing, and data protection are traded every day without thought or consequence in digital spaces. As advocates for advancing the world through gaming, education, and charity, UKXP is well placed to carry the torch for this fight.

No matter what level of interest or profession you may find yourself involved with, solutions are urgently needed to better keep Cyberspace safe. UKXP is a 501(c)3 charity working to help inspire others to combat threats within the digital metaverse.

Cybersecurity and safety is a convoluted subject. UKXP approaches this matter from a safety-first standpoint; and then cybersecurity, the technical aspect, follows. The vulnerability of people accessing digital mediums – be it gaming forums, online play, voice servers or other elements – is of paramount consequence demanding higher levels of attention and prioritization from leaders and influencers in the gaming space.

A prevalent issue polluting gaming culture is a myriad of destructive social behaviors. Sometimes they manifest in the form of bullying or harassment, but less noticeable and more subtle adverse behaviors can compromise the physical and emotional safety within the digital and gaming space. UKXP understands the difficulties in facing the complexities of online gaming and, through their consultant services, can help leaders and organizations address many major issues, including Cybersafety and Security.

It's not all doom and gloom, thinks UKXP. "Younger generations are gaining street smarts across online gaming," says Mitchel. "The threats they face daily have led to the emergence of a very complex set of cyber street smarts."

Education needs to be a strategic priority for the gaming – and digital – landscape of today. UKXP believes through education, the gaming community can actively engage on this topic and advocate for change.

Cybersecurity should be prioritized throughout the digital space. Threats are growing at an alarming pace. In today's contested cyber environment, we are now faced with 5th and 6th generation threats. These threats possess the real potential to jeopardize the future of the digital metaverse. The list of cybersecurity dangers grows, but today they include third-party software, ransomware, DDoS-based threats, and even cloud-based threats – to name a few. Digital mediums have become weaponized, sometimes even chaotic and dangerous, and the threats are outpacing those who can police it.

This is why education is an imperative means to effectively combat such threats. UKXP's approach is to remain aligned with the scholastic system at every echelon, thus empowering leaders and teachers across the spectrum to provide awareness and education to the current and future generation of gamers.

The gaming industry has many of the most user-friendly application interfaces in the world. From an industry perspective, UKXP believes that the adoption and gamification of wider digital spaces will help to enforce stricter cybersecurity barriers and protections. This is best illustrated in one of UKXP's projects with the Center for Cyber Safety and Education. UKXP developed a training program focused on Cybersafety in gaming for parents.

This incredible program from the Center for Cyber Safety and Education (and to find out more, please support and visit them at https://www.safeandsecureonline.org/s/gaming), is being shared by their team throughout over 20 countries and 20 languages to their 170,000 members. Together, we are equipping parents with cybersecurity and safety information, along with the tools they can turn to in better protecting their families.

LEADERSHIP & LEADERSHIP ENGAGEMENT

The significance of reach and influence in the gaming landscape cannot be underestimated. Mitchel Reed and Ashton Cooksey currently lead UKXP. Their unique military backgrounds, leadership experience, and passion to help others have taken the grassroots and strategic advancements in the gaming space to the next level.

Within gaming communities, understanding the capacity of a leader's reach and influence is critical. Neither should operate in a vacuum or as a standalone. Reaching people without generating an influence will lead to failure in brand or mission awareness. Whether you're a company president, senator, a city mayor, or an esports team captain, both criteria need to be analyzed for optimal involvement.

"We need to convey an emphasis on the changing tide of information dissemination and how to best draw on positive connections through influencers," Ashton believes. "Leaders have an unprecedented means of reach and influence, providing narratives to carry further and faster across engagement spectrums. These platforms have grown to new levels that allow for immediate impact while inspiring people of varying backgrounds to accomplish shared goals across our communities."

This influence can bring both positives and negatives. This is why there is an importance to assist leaders in the power of their influence. Leadership engagement is instantaneous, it's mobile, adaptive, and it's accessible. Mitchel explains: "It is important for leaders to engage their followers' understanding of societal influence from an anthropological standpoint. The next generation of influencers is being molded today. What is intriguing is the number of people holding high levels of influence today are not in formal leadership positions but are promoted through informal channels."

Informal leaders are small to medium content creators in our gaming communities: they have a nested influence over their audience and succeed or fail by the health of their community. These informal leaders depend on that relationship. For the gaming industry, wielding influence in a positive way is important to continue seeking when considering the social impact of gaming on education, entertainment, connectivity and accessibility of communities and people across the world.

Informal leaders can interact through various mediums. Leaders with a strong audience have stronger control of a promoted narrative around - this can hold both positive and negative consequences. "Unintended consequences among social influences are more commonplace," cautions Ashton Cooksey. "There are informal leaders who do not realize the impact of their messages, while others do so with the intent of controversy to draw greater captivation. No one has taught or shown them that there are secondary or tertiary effects they can be significantly impacting. Instilling this understanding will carry incredible weight for the future direction of leader and influencer engagements."

Businesses, brands, governments and many others can utilise the gaming community to better leverage a unifying influence through message development and industry coaching assistance with those in leadership.

UKXP advocates for this through their work in the gaming industry. Says Mitchel: "Many leaders and brands struggle to inspire their employees while operating in a remote environment. Before the COVID-19 pandemic, workplace leaders were seldom required to achieve buy-in within a remote work environment. Leaders are having to find creative ways to motivate teams and accomplish complex objectives from a distance – something the gaming community has done successfully for decades."

Gaming can teach sustainable business and life concepts that people and communities can draw on for community achievements. One of the most important keys to gaming is that it teaches people to work and play together in a unifying manner that brings together forward-leaning accomplishments. That's the power of leadership and leadership engagement – through gaming.

UKnightedXP, Inc.

uknightedxp

uknightedxp.org

THE ECONOMICS OF GAMING

Every day around the world, gaming culture displays examples where play and community transcend geographic limitations and cultural differences. The gaming world provides mediums for others to set aside differences in exchange for accessibility and acceptance. These are two traits businesses strive to achieve but seldom attain that are readily commonplace in the gaming world. The accessibility and scalability of gaming present opportunities that benefit global models for economies at scale; particularly vulnerable and underserved populations.

Cultural influences from developers are reflected in the games themselves. It is an opportunity to inclusively draw people together. Gaming combines creativity and innovation to better reflect our own humanity via dreams in the gaming space. It is how the gaming world has influenced cultures and communities across the planet and will continue to do so.

Esports (for the moment) lacks some aspects of the diversity and inclusion often found in other gaming communities. Esports predominantly feeds off urban culture - and not gaming culture. Currently, gaming communities exist alongside esports with very little overlap.

Adding to this, esports is an emergent, competitive, and rapidly growing segment of the gaming space. Currently, the landscape is largely defined by competition for market share – and teams vying for spotlight,

influence, fame and money. Due to the quickly evolving landscape of esports and the nature of its ecosystem, it has been largely defined by urban culture over gaming culture. It is a deeply niche area of the gaming culture with few sustainable financial models in practice – but it has a distinctly strong and significant presence on social media and mainstream marketing.

Ashton Cooksey, Vice President and co-founder, wants to draw focus to the aspects underrepresented in online gaming: "Esports as an industry can hold an opportunity for someone to cultivate a set of skills through communication, teamwork, or problem-solving. By building these skills, we can inspire a person's confidence to have a sense of belonging and give the motivation to strive for personal success."

UKXP is one of the organizations searching for solutions to integrate and leverage esports to create scholastic, economic, and social benefits at scale. "Over time and if successfully implemented at scale, this will create a drastic change in the gaming landscape as well as our professional workforce, in what the gaming community will look like," says Mitchel. "Once esports has matured and is more inclusionary of communities at the municipal level with established training pipelines, social impact programs, and scholastic opportunities, esports will ultimately stabilize.

We assess that the future of esports will provide an avenue for reliable income and commerce with superior marketing platforms and capabilities for businesses worldwide with higher ROI 'Net Zero' capabilities, and unprecedented social impact. The secret to success is mass collaboration in order to surpass current limitations of market share and stimulate needed growth... a natural component of novel advancements."

Scholastic development and programs play a critical role in UKXP's strategic priorities. They currently work and support numerous organizations and clients with their efforts focused on positive, global social impact. The organization collaborates with school systems, districts, states, regions, and senior leaders with a top-down approach to integrating gaming in this manner. By identifying relevant leaders and organizations, UKXP's consultant model provides the highest ROI possible for the time and effort spent on their strategic priorities. Their clients can utilize their influence to build relationships and connect with communities through the representation of gaming culture.

Says Reed: "We found that by interacting and directly supporting district superintendents or regional directors to launch programs, we have greater buy-in and appreciation. Earlier in 2021, we presented to a board of directors and mayors that encompassed 16 counties and 64 municipalities in Northwest Florida. The audience was attentive and curious to learn – and these are difficult conversations they have never had before about these topics. It is pivotal these discussions continue to happen with senior leaders to draw a path forward relating to inclusivity, accessibility, and education through gaming. We're building communities at the grassroots level to see that gaming and gaming culture is being leveraged for social good – and ultimately providing economic opportunities."

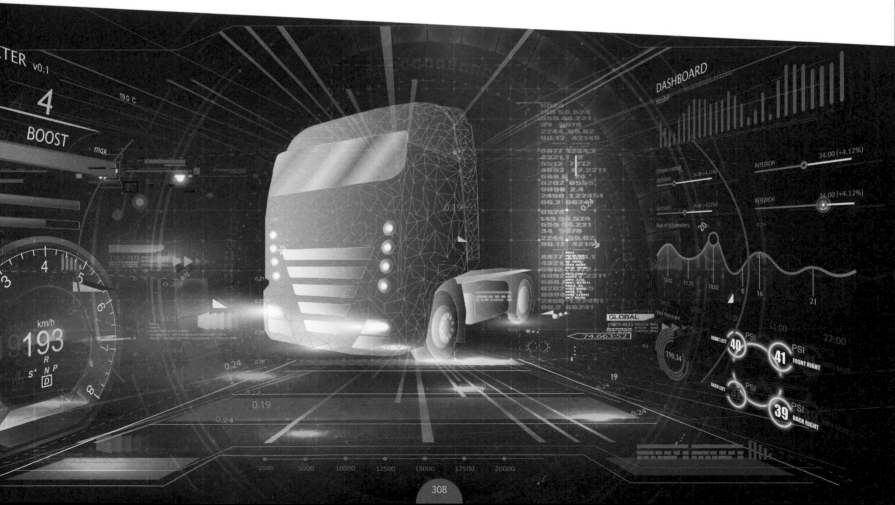

THE SOCIAL IMPACT OF GAMING

How can gaming be better utilized for positive global impact? This question is central to the philosophy of UKnightedXP, Inc. (UKXP). Mitchel's deep understanding of the gaming industry and gamer culture place UKXP as a bridge between mainstream society and the gaming world.

The gaming industry today encompasses over 2 billion gamers worldwide, with deeply rooted communities. The gaming industry encompasses both digital and physical games, from trading card games and tabletops to consoles and personal computers. Gaming continues to have a fundamental impact on society through its accessibility and connectivity. It is becoming easier to get plugged in and there are more options than ever for players to achieve a desired level of engagement. Because of this, among other factors, there are now many charitable nonprofits in the industry striving for advancement in a myriad of high social impact causes worldwide.

"The gaming culture has grown around connectivity and the Internet, allowing us to immediately talk to people worldwide," says Mitchel. "That's created instant commerce on easily accessible, readily available global platforms. Gaming takes all of this and elevates it to the next level. It presents global opportunities within what is arguably the fastest-growing, farthest-reaching, and most diverse people-centric ecosystem on the planet."

Ashton Cooksey, Vice President and co-founder, views accessibility as an opportunity to align through new spectrums. "We are seeing businesses promote charitable initiatives with platforms that would have never been discussed 5 to 10 years ago. The various ways in which gaming can take shape have allowed for a revolutionary market structure where virtual and real communities are equally important to drive social influence."

The gaming culture has endured a stigma for decades. As with all aspects of life, there are always negatives. For UKXP, these adversities present learning opportunities.

Stereotypes of gamers and gaming have long played a role in shaping much of today's gaming ecosystem. However, advancements in information dissemination and education have helped to propel gaming onto the scene of mainstream media and popularity. With a generation committed to diversity and the COVID-19 pandemic, gaming has seen tremendous success and momentum as people rallied to unite in remote, digital environments. Ultimately, gaming has helped serve as a bridge to build and develop communities.

Says Mitchel: "In the history of all things, stigmas have typically existed around things that were novel. Many scientists, including Greek philosophers, spoke out that the earth wasn't flat and were often ridiculed for their assertions. Those men and women were outliers combating stigma and persecution."

UKXP's team asserts that resistance to the gaming culture is largely the result of rapid societal advancements in quick succession. These changes exasperated the divide between generations, which has grown at an accelerated rate. In order to bridge the gaps left in the wake of rapid advancements, an extraordinary amount of education and cultural adaptation are needed to embrace the pace of technological change.

Modern gaming, whether digital or physical, is an intrinsic method of play for people in most countries throughout the world. It continues to provide an accessible medium that transcends geographic limitations and cultural differences.

What is the extent of the social impact of gaming? The ability to share an adventure, creativity, innovation, thoughts, feelings and hope leave UKXP's team no doubt that gaming and play build powerful, emotional bonds with irreplaceably unique experiences. The gaming community embraces and thrives by uniting people in their similarities, not dividing them for their differences. Games, gamers, and gaming communities exist through some of the most incredible, diverse, and influential people our world has ever known.

What will tomorrow hold for social impact and gaming? UKnightedXP believes that answer is simple, and their mission says it all. 'Advancing the world through gaming, education, and charity.' *#WePlayForTheWorld*

Creating opportunities for connecting societies and communities should be a priority for all leaders. UKXP has identified scholastic education as being one of the single greatest strategic focal points to influence social impact and help bridge the generational divide.

UKnightedXP, Inc.
uknightedxp

uknightedxp.org

GAME

PLAY

YES

OVER

GAIN?

NO

INDEX

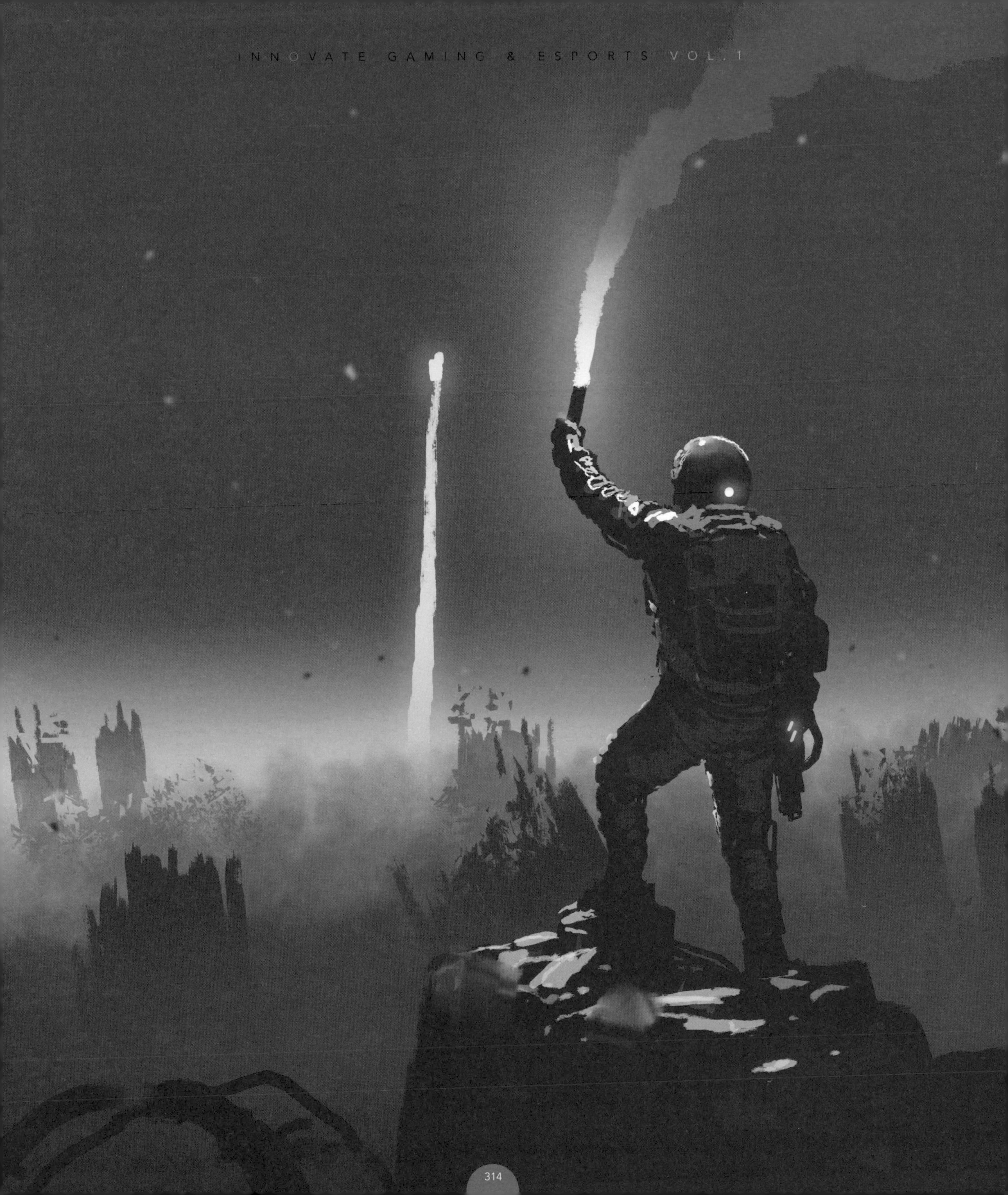

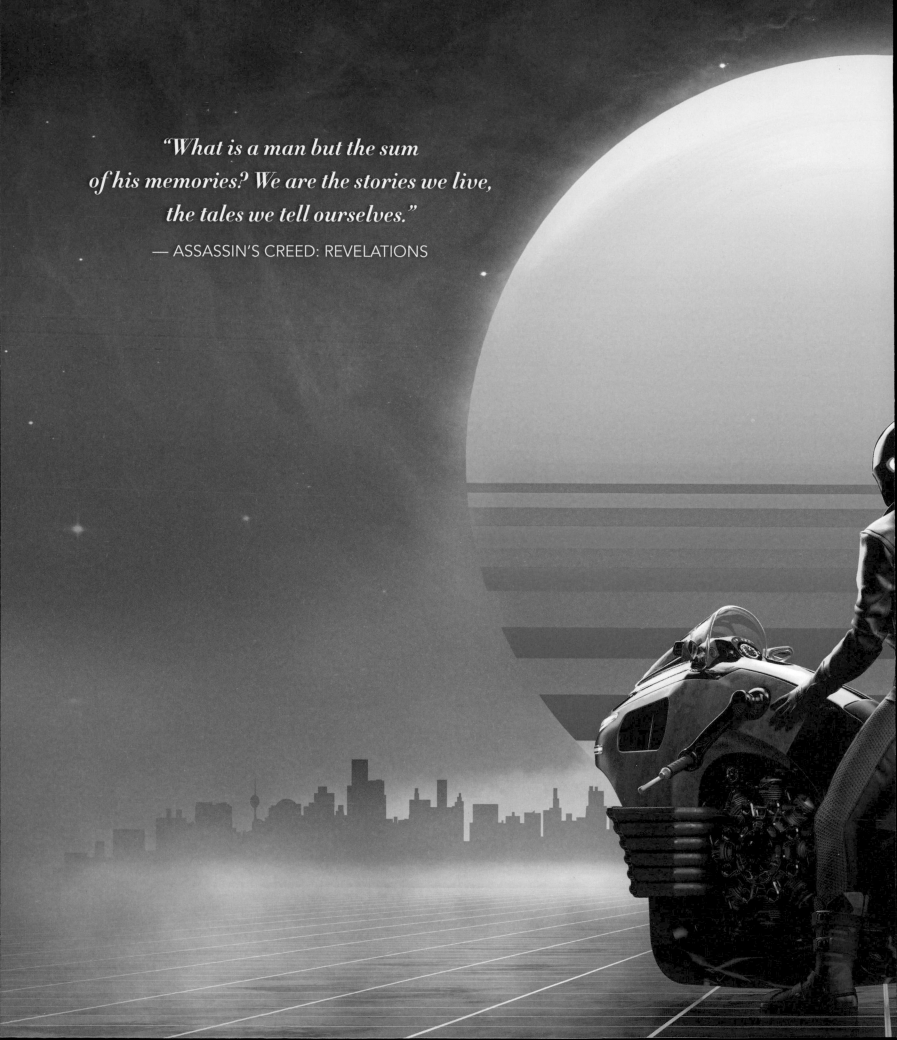

"*What is a man but the sum of his memories? We are the stories we live, the tales we tell ourselves.*"

— ASSASSIN'S CREED: REVELATIONS